THE TUC AND THE WORKING-TIME QUESTION

THE TUC AND THE WORKING-TIME QUESTION

Policy, Action and Outcomes in Twentieth-Century Britain

Alice Russell

The Book Guild Ltd
Sussex, England

First published in Great Britain in 2000 by
The Book Guild Ltd
25 High Street
Lewes, East Sussex
BN7 2LU

Typesetting in Times by
Acorn Bookwork, Salisbury, Wiltshire

Printed in Great Britain by
Antony Rowe Ltd, Chippenham, Wiltshire

A catalogue record for this book is available from
The British Library.

ISBN 1 85776 575 3

To the memory of my parents
Ellen and Joseph Wilkinson

CONTENTS

LIST OF TABLES

FOREWORD

Introduction

The working week in Britain is longer on average than in any other European country;[1] and the historical evidence suggests that, more often than not, both working hours and earnings in Britain have compared unfavourably with the standards obtaining in most other countries at a similar stage of economic development.

Working time is a profoundly important issue in the modern world, with its globalized economy and cybernetic systems of communication and control, for new information technology, microelectronics and telecommunications networks are leading to widespread displacement of labour; and without a drastic reduction of hours worked, unemployment will be a permanent condition of life for large numbers of people worldwide.[2] A legally imposed maximum on weekly working hours has been the focus of contention between the UK and the rest of the EU; and the controversy will no doubt continue to recur in the future. As long ago as 1983 the European Parliament adopted a resolution for measures which would in the short term effect a significant reduction in daily, weekly and yearly working hours in all member states in order to ameliorate unemployment.[3] Proposals initiated in 1989, and much amended by 1992, sought to impose a maximum of 48 actual working hours per week, averaged over an agreed reference period. It was not until the British Government in 1996 had secured a loophole which robbed the measure of its obligatory character, that the British Government was prepared to endorse the EU's Draft Directive on hours of work.

Few people who are capable of working for a living today escape the need to do so. Faced with the alternatives of a job that pays a decent wage on the one hand and, on the other, unemployment and dependence upon state insurance schemes in years when the governments of many countries are intent on pruning back their state welfare systems,[4] the preference of the vast majority of people is only too obvious. Amelioration of unemployment is a important reason for shortening working time, but there are other cogent reasons.

It is axiomatic that the measurable means to meet the quantifiable cost of living, and the amount of time, calculated daily, weekly or annually, expended in fulfilling that material objective can be reckoned as 'sold time' — that is, time sold to an employer who buys it at the labour market price. The remainder is 'free time' or 'leisure time' which the worker may use in whatever ways or for whatever purposes are regarded as desirable or necessary. For workpeople, the relationship between working time and free time has been a contentious issue from the beginning of industrialization.

In addition to the quantifiable aspects of work, measured in terms of the amount earned during the time spent in the performance of work tasks, there are the qualitative aspects of paid employment: a feeling of satisfaction or of alienation, a consciousness of achievement or of frustration, a sense of status and purpose or of inconsequence, the experience of absorbing interest and creativity or of mind-numbing boredom and apathy. But if paid work is necessary for the vast majority of people for much of their lives, so also is free time, for even the most absorbing, satisfying, creative and well remunerated toil must regularly cease that it may continue.

Work, it is commonly argued, allows us to appreciate free time and, conversely, free time gives meaning and purpose to work. The trade unions have invariably had higher earnings as a bargaining priority, but they have been equally aware of the relationship between working hours and leisure time, and concerned to increase the latter to give work people 'time to spare' for the many activities and responsibilities, pleasures and obligations that are as important to life as earning a living. There is a world of difference between 'job satisfaction', as conventionally defined, and 'satisfaction with the job', which may be defined as contentment with mundane work that provides sufficient income and leisure time to enjoy life outside the workplace.

The British trade unions have always been deeply concerned about hours of work in the British economy, in Europe, and in the rest of the developed and developing world. The inexorable advance of science and technology has brought with it both threat and promise: the threat of shrinking employment and the promise of more leisure. The future alternatives, it is argued, are greater competition from more job seekers for fewer job vacancies, or a more equitable distribution of the available work by shortening working time and increasing leisure time. The arguments of today are not new; but although they were pressed by former generations, they are claimed to be more urgent today than ever before.

About half a century ago Marcuse asserted that automation, properly controlled, offered the possibility of a reversal of the relationship between working time and leisure time, with proportionally less of the former and more of the latter. In Britain, observers were soon hailing the dawn of the 'age of leisure', in which everyone would have more free time at their disposal to expend in ways other than earning a living.[5] The leisure age, however, did not subsequently materialize in the 1980s in the anticipated form. More recently, 'technological utopians' have argued that the microelectronics revolution, effectively harnessed, will eventually offer release from the constraints of 'formal work' and increase personal freedom. Masuda, for example, claims that in a future computopia 'free time' will replace 'material accumulation' as society's overriding goal:

> Time value is on a higher plane in human life than material values as the basic value of economic activity. This is because time value corresponds to the satisfaction

of human and intellectual wants, whereas material values correspond to the satisfaction of physiological and material wants.[6]

Attractive though Masuda's idea is, it rests on an apparent presupposition of satisfied material needs for the physiological plane of existence. From a more down-to-earth point of view, the trade unions have often asked whether we live to work or work to live; and in deciding, without much difficulty, that the objective of work is to enable us to live, have argued that life involves far more than a mere physical and material existence. The worker desires not only a sufficient material standard of living corresponding to rising expectations of what constitutes sufficiency, but also a better quality of life; work, the amount of pay received for it and the amount of time spent at work, daily, weekly and annually, should be such as to leave enough residual time to enable the worker and his or her family to lead enjoyable and fulfilling lives.

Earlier stages of industrialization, the first based on steam technology and the second on electricity and oil, both produced prolonged struggles between employers and their workforces over the productivity and hours issue.[7] The productivity gains of the steam age offered the possibility of shorter working time which might take the form of either fewer jobs and more unemployment or fewer hours per worker and less unemployment. Workforces made the latter choice, reflecting their leisure preference at the prevailing level of earnings and their fear of unemployment in the future.[8] The rising productivity permitted by steam-powered machinery was followed by a reduction of weekly working hours in the nineteenth century from 80 to 60, and then to 54 in the most advanced sectors. Likewise, the marked increase of productive efficiency in the age of oil and electricity led to further reductions to a basic week of 40 hours in the third quarter of the twentieth century. The microelectronics revolution has given us the third stage of industrialization, and it is now claimed to be possible to reap the productivity gains of the computer and the new information and telecommunications technologies.

Rifkin and a growing number of other observers are urging the inevitability of reducing working hours once again, now to 30 or even 20 per week, to bring labour requirements in line with the new productive capacity of capital.[9]

The relationship between productivity improvements and hours reductions in the past, however, was not so simple and straightforward as the foregoing argument suggests. In the twentieth century, as in the nineteenth, the shortening of working time was not the only reward sought by the unions from rising productive efficiency, but one item in a package of rewards, which came in the course of time to include not only weekly hours and the pay rate, but a range of benefits such as sick pay, paid holidays, retirement pensions, redundancy compensation, and pay supplements of various kinds, such as shift premia, special allowances for unsocial hours attendance, dirty or hazardous work, and, most importantly, overtime rates that made a clear distinction between the basic and the actual working week and which had originally been intended to discourage employers from requiring much of it by making it more costly. The unions' bargaining priorities have not remained constant but have changed according to the needs of the moment. At the same time, negotiations with employers have been conducted within an evolving structure of economic, social and political institutions, against the backdrop of changing economic and labour market circumstances, and subject to the vagaries of government policy and legislation. All of this suggests that, at times, some claims would be pressed harder than others, and that concessions would be won more readily in some situations than in others.

The unions were perfectly well aware that in seeking the shortening of working time, they would also have to protect earnings, and that they would need to support their claims for reductions of working hours with cogent arguments and good reasons backed up by strong evidence. The British TUC drew a sharp distinction between the desirable and undesirable kinds of free time. The first would provide leisure to be enjoyed at the end of the working day and working week, at regular intervals during the working year, and at the end of working life; the measurable economic dimension of material standard of living would thus be linked with the socio-cultural dimension of quality of life. The second and unwanted kind of free time took the forms of involuntary unemployment and of short-time working where full-time employment had been assumed. Leisure such as this was something to be endured rather than enjoyed; and it served not to raise quality of life but to undermine material living standard.

There has been a tendency, which is still in evidence today, to vilify the trade unions for acting against the public interest, to accuse union leaders of irresponsibility, and to blame the unions in general for most of the country's economic ills. Lower productivity in Britain than in other countries at a comparable stage of economic development has been attributed to the 'lazy British worker'; strike-proneness was known in Europe as 'the British disease'. The failure of British industry to compete more effectively in world markets used to be explained as largely the result of unions' insistence on restrictive practices and observance of skill and trade demarcations. Overmanning, caused by the unions' ability to maintain job rights and trade boundaries, was identified by Clegg[10] in 1964 as 'one of the major scandals of the British economy'. A similar retrospective view was taken in a Government White Paper in 1991, which referred to the general acknowledgment of Britain's poor industrial relations as 'a fundamental cause of the weakening of the British economy'.[11] Journalistic histories of the union movement highlight headline-hitting incidents which testify to its extremism, and show the unions in the worst of all possible lights. In contrast, the ultra-left school of thought has reproached the unions for being too moderate and failing to act more decisively to propel society into the socialist utopia.

To dwell on the melodramatic and the sensational, however, is to distort and misrepresent the role played by the TUC in the twentieth century to improve workpeople's standard of living and quality of life. The effort has been persistent, for the most part patient and painstaking, sometimes punctuated by outbursts of indignation from the experience of frustration and wilful misunderstanding from sceptics, and largely the kind of effort that does not create any stir of interest from the press and the media as a whole. That effort, however, has produced some noteworthy results; its history is far more important in the longer term than the sporadic excesses which produced the banner headlines that increased newspaper sales. While such excesses have occurred intermittently and have usually affected only part of the union movement, the TUC's welfare initiative has been determinedly persistent, ongoing, and sustained year in year out; and it has involved the whole union movement.

THE PURPOSES OF THE BOOK

The aim of the book is to give an analytical account of working-time changes in twentieth-century Britain. First it will be instructive to identify the TUC's objectives in this sphere, to ascertain what the targets were and how they changed in the course of the century. The second aspect of the working-time question is concerned with the reasons which were given in support of claims for the shortening of working hours: what lines of argument did the unions press and what evidence did they adduce to back their demands? Third, there is the matter of strategy: what means and methods did the unions consider and actually use in pursuit of their working-time goals, and did the means to the ends change as the century progressed? Fourth, it will be illuminating to discover when general or widespread hours reductions occurred, and whether the changes are to be explained mono-causally or multi-causally. Another pertinent question to be addressed is the extent to which the unions achieved their targets, and how long the process took.

There were, of course, agencies, in addition to the unions, which had an important influence upon hours of work. The most significant of these are the Government and the employers. An understanding of the working-time trend may be assisted by consideration of the interplay between the policies of the unions, the Government and the employers during the course of the twentieth century, and the effect of employers' intervention in the arrangement of working time. Lastly, it will remain to ask what light the historical evidence sheds on present-day working-time patterns, and what future trends are indicated. Should we embark upon the twenty-first century optimistically?

NOTES

1. Among numerous others are articles in *The Western Mail*, 19 October 1996 and *The Independent*, 17 October 1996.
2. Rifkin, J. (1995), *The End of Work: The Decline of the Global Labor Force and the Dawn of the Post-Market Era*, New York, Putnam, chs 11 and 12.
3. Evans, A. and Palmer, S. (1985), *Negotiating Shorter Working Hours*, Basingstoke, Macmillan, p.11.
4. Seldon, A. (ed) (1996), *Re-Privatizing Welfare: After the Lost Century*, London, Institute of Economic Affairs.
5. Parker, S. (1971), *The Future of Work and Leisure*, London, MacGibbon & Kee, and (1976), *The Sociology of Leisure*, London, Allen & Unwin; Roberts, K. (1970), *Leisure*, London, Allen & Unwin; Jenkins, C. and Sherman, B. (1979), *The Collapse of Work*, London, Eyre Methuen; Veal, A.J. (1987), *Leisure and the Future*, London, Allen & Unwin.
6. Masuda, Y. (1981), *The Information Society as Post-Industrial Society*, Washington DC, World Future Society, p.74.
7. Rifkin, J., *op. cit.* p.222.
8. Bienefeld, M.A. (1972), *Working Hours in British Industry: An Economic History*, London, Weidenfeld & Nicolson.
9. Rifkin, J., *op. cit.*
10. Clegg, H.A. (1964), *Socialist Commentary*.
11. Government White Paper (1991), *Industrial Relations in the 1990s* Cm.1602, p.8.

PART 1
1900–39

1

TUC Policy and Action to Shorten the Working Week, 1900–39

Introduction

The trade unions' aim of reducing the working week pre-dates the formation of the TUC in 1868. Industrialization and the spread of machine-regulated production processes had effected a widespread displacement of the informal work rhythms of the past by standardized machine-paced working patterns and a marked lengthening of the 'customary' 10-hour day to one of 12 hours or more.[1] Workpeople's protest, in the form of strikes, damage to labour-saving machinery, a rudimentary style of collective bargaining, and petitions for statutory measures from the Government to restrict hours of work, is well documented. Much has been written about the legislation, enacted on compassionate grounds in the nineteenth century, to protect juveniles by controlling hours of work in employing enterprises classed as factories, but workers were agitating for shorter factory hours long before middle-class moralists took up the cause of reform and the need for legislation to curb the excessively long hours worked daily in the factory-based sector of the cotton industry.

The 10-hour movement was spearheaded in the 1830s by the more effectively organized branches of the building and engineering trades, whose demands included, apparently for the first time, claims for 'premium rates of pay' for 'overtime' hours.[2] The movement for the 9-hour day and 54-hour week began to take shape in the 1840s and 1850s before the 10-hour day had become general, although it was not until the beginning of the 1870s that any notable progress occurred. Initially, union-negotiated agreements on basic working hours, with additional hours paid at higher rates, were intended to discourage employers from requiring overtime working too readily or too frequently; but overtime proved attractive to workpeople as a means to increase their earnings, and it could sometimes be contrived. The practice of 'systematic overtime working', the Webbs have suggested, began with the adoption of the 9-hour day and 54-hour week.[3]

The 8-hour day and 48-hour week had existed as an ideal for many decades,[4] but it was not until the later 1880s and 1890s that the aim became the focus of agitation as being within the realms of practical possibility.[5] At the dawn of the twentieth century, therefore, the TUC's working-time target was already set. Policy and action to achieve it developed against the backdrop of fluctuations in the state of the economy, technological advance which affected employers' labour requirements, the chastening experience of world wars and one of the worst recessions in recorded history, structural change in the economy, the amount of bargaining clout the unions could exert in prevailing labour market circumstances, and a total union membership which, from 1900 to 1939, swung between the extremes of 1,994,000 and 8,340,000.[6]

The unions' working-time strategy was to formulate a general policy at TUC level, to set targets, to identify ways and means of achieving them, to pinpoint the reasons for their claims, and to work out cogent lines of argument to persuade employers and government ministers to respond favourably. It was envisaged that progress could come through a combination of negotiation and legislation. Voluntary collective bargaining with a single employer or groups of them produced local or district agreements covering the few; but following the Whitley Committee's recommendations of 1917 for the creation of joint industrial councils[7] and the extension of the trade board system where organization was weak, the unions were able to use industry-wide negotiations and national agreements as the most effective means to greater gains for larger numbers. The system of joint industrial councils did not provide the unions with a simple solution to the working time problem, however, for many of the councils fell into decay during the interwar recession and were not resurrected for some years.

Another possibility presented itself after the First World War, with the creation in 1919 of the International Labour Organization whose functions included the improvement of workpeople's welfare in all member states, by the setting of international standards in a series of Resolutions, Recommendations and Conventions. But, as the unions discovered, this particular way forward was not an easy one to follow.

The What, Why, How and When of the TUC's Demands

The shortening of working time in the nineteenth century had been the outcome of voluntary negotiation and sectional legislation applying to 'vulnerable groups' and specific trades. The unions' efforts to secure general legislation, which would affect the many rather than the few, had been unsuccessful. Even the narrower path forward by sectional legislation was not straightforward, for the Miners' Eight-Hour Bill, strongly supported by the unions, was defeated in the House of Commons in 1900.[8]

A resolution, moved by J.R. Clynes[9] and carried by a large majority at the 1905 Congress, called for the 8-hour day, a 48-hour week, and the abolition of systematic overtime working in all trades, in order to provide employment for workers seasonally laid off and for those now being displaced by labour-saving machinery. It was the state's responsibility, he declared, to regulate working time so as to distribute it more equitably; for while many people were currently unemployed or under-employed, many others were vastly over-worked. A shorter working week was justified also on health and safety grounds, for it would 'tend to the diminution of the enormous number of injuries sustained by workmen and the growing number of accidents caused by the fatigue of long hours of labour and the faster pace of work.'

There was strong support for the motion, but some anxiety about the likely repercussions was voiced by the Lancashire Cotton Spinners' delegate. Four-fifths of the cotton industry's products had to find markets overseas, and British employers were already facing keen competition from rival producers in the USA where textile workers' hours ranged from 58 to 72 per week. If shorter working hours were to raise the production cost and selling price of British cotton goods, export markets would be lost and the result would be higher, not lower, unemployment in textile Lancashire. The point was taken, but the majority view at Congress was in favour of a general shortening of working time. The means to reducing the hours of labour without injury to export industries would be a contentious issue at many future Congresses.

Similar resolutions supported by similar arguments were carried in the following years, and copies dispatched to the Prime Minister. New machinery, more efficient production methods and higher labour productivity, it was asserted, should have led to the shortening of the working week and the easing of physical strain on manual labour. Yet progress through collective bargaining was slow; overtime working persisted, and the fault did not lie entirely with employers: 'For the sake of grabbing the overtime, some of the men ... spoil the good work that the unions do.'[10] Delegates were reminded in 1912, a year when well over 40 million working days were lost through strike action, of the 'urgent necessity of limiting or abolishing overtime working' which was 'detrimental to the health and well-being of workpeople.' Neither the rallies and demonstrations held in London and the provinces in 1911 and 1912,[11] nor the TUC Parliamentary Committee's overtures to government ministers, had any effect in persuading the Government of the need for general legislation for the 8-hour day. James Hill of the Boilermakers, an advocate of direct action, was scathing in his contempt for union officers who were failing to effect even slight improvements in working hours. The '8-hour resolution', which

Congress had carried, year in year out, since 1877, had become 'something of a hardy annual' and the subject of 'pious empty rhetoric'. An intensification of the unions' efforts was needed as a matter of urgency, for reports from regional union officers disclosed that some employers were seeking to increase the hours of labour.

Employers could perfectly well afford to concede the unions' claims, Mr Hill continued, for 'there never was a time before when we experienced so great a boom in trade, and when wealth was being more quickly made by the employing classes...' General legislation was advocated as the most effective means of shortening the working week; but, again, reservations were voiced, this time by the Tramway Workers' delegate. A statutory measure, he warned, would need to contain safeguards for drivers and conductors in tramway services to prevent an employer from splitting up the 8 hours into two or more periods spread over a day of 12, 14 or even 16 hours. With split-shift working, an 8-hour day would provide no real increase in the leisure time at the worker's disposal.

When Congress met in 1913, Bills had been introduced into the House of Commons, at the instigation of the TUC Parliamentary Committee, including the Eight-Hour Bill, the Agricultural Labour (Wages and Hours) Bill, and the Miners' (Eight-Hours) Bill, and delegates were informed that a few trades had now gained the 8-hour day by negotiation with employers. In discussing the shorter hours question that year, Congress identified two main lines of argument in support of their claims: the 'economic' and the 'moral'.[12]

The already well rehearsed economic line of argument, resting on the current prosperity of trade, rising profits and dividends, higher labour productivity, and the fatiguing intensification of the work pace, had now been elaborated to include the longer journey to work and the illogicality of the manual/non-manual differential in working hours. With urban development, affecting the location of business premises and residential sites, many workers now lived some distance from their place of employment, so that their leisure hours were curtailed by the time spent travelling to and from work. At the same time, delegates could see no economic justification for the manual/non-manual hours differential; professional and white-collar grades had both a shorter basic working day and longer holidays than manual workers; yet the latter's work was physically more arduous and exhausting. The distinction between the two was irrational.

The reasons that the unions labelled 'moral' are perhaps more suitably described as 'socio-cultural'. They were explained in the strongly class-conscious language of the underdog who feels justifiably aggrieved about his or her narrowly constrained life chances and humble status, and who longs for something better. Work, it was argued, was not 'the be all and end all of existence'. Aspirations were rising, and the 'workman of today' was no longer 'content to occupy that lowly status' in which his role was 'to make fortunes for other people to spend and enjoy.'[13] The 'better things' in life ought not to be beyond workpeople's reach:

> What is the good of giving us a great empire, a great history, splendid traditions, great poets, arts, great dramas – what is the worth of all this to men and women who have no means whatever to enjoy them? You cannot expect men to walk into libraries and art galleries unless you give them the necessary time and facilities for cultivating their reading and thinking faculties.[14]

It would be difficult to find a more impassioned plea for workpeople to have the time more fully to appreciate and enjoy their own country's rich cultural heritage which was clearly a source of great pride to them.

An over-cautious stance on the working-time question, with which some unions had been reproached by the more thrusting trades, was explained perfectly reasonably by a delegate from textile Lancashire. Many workpeople feared that the shortening of hours, whether by legislation or by voluntary agreement, would lead to a corresponding reduction in their earnings or to action by employers to offset the time lost by a further intensification of the work pace. There would be far more enthusiasm among rank and file union memberships if there was some guarantee that shorter hours would not result in a smaller pay packet: 'The hours question is essentially a wages question.'

During the First World War the unions, by and large, countenanced the very long hours worked, but the TUC never lost sight of its longer-term objectives. Several resolutions on working hours in different trades were carried by large majorities in 1915. The campaign for the 8-hour day had ceased for the time being, the Boilermakers' delegate stated, because there were more urgent issues concerning national security in time of war; but, when the peace was declared, the need would be for a united effort by all the trade unions for *general* legislation rather than the *sectional* legislation mentioned in several resolutions at present before Congress: 'I cannot understand why this trade and that trade should be seeking ... [legislation] for themselves. If we are ever to bring this thing about, we must concentrate on one united effort.'[15]

Several trades, even so, while subscribing to the principle of general legislation, continued to press their own sectional interests in the not unreasonable belief that special pleading of their own case might make faster headway than the far more radical proposal for enactment of an all-embracing measure, against the resolute opposition of the Government and the employers. The wait could be a long one, and past experience demonstrated the much stronger possibility of advance trade by trade.

There was no mention yet of the practical difficulties of framing legislation that would be equally effective in reducing working hours in firms great and small, in industries serving the home market and those heavily dependent on exports, in both day work and continuous shift working, and in sectors where employment was regular and in others where it was characteristically discontinuous, seasonal or casual. This would be one of the problems to bedevil the interwar efforts of the International Labour Organization to produce workable Conventions on the hours of labour.

Resolutions carried by Congress in 1917 and 1918 called for an Act of Parliament to impose a 'maximum 48-hour week without reduction in standard weekly wages.' Some delegates, foreseeing a rise of unemployment following demobilization, urged industrial action as the most immediately effective means to the shortening of working hours and creation of jobs. The recent escalation of strike action had aroused public indignation, accusations of irresponsible unionism, and disquiet about the power of shop stewards in some trades. Such reactions, and the 'bully boy' image of the unions presented in the press, may explain why the Transport Workers' delegate counselled that 'the better way' was 'by legislative enactment and enlightened public opinion'. The present state of industrial relations, he admitted, seemed conducive to winning the 8-hour day by direct action, but he warned that concessions thus forced from hostile and resentful employers could be short-lived; the capitalists' turn would come again in times of depressed trade and the unions' working-time gains would be lost. The best way to win and retain a general hours reduction was by an Act of Parliament, which would fix lower basic hours, place legal limits on overtime, and protect the weekly rate of wages. He believed that there was every chance of success, 'with the extended franchise, a larger number of Labour candidates in general elections, and the prospect of a stronger Labour Party in the House of Commons.'[16]

There had evidently been some very recent moves down to and even below a working week of 48 hours, for James Hill sought to amend the work-time resolution for 48 hours to one for 44 hours. In the building, engineering and shipbuilding industries, district agreements had been concluded for basic weeks of 45 and 47 hours, and the likelihood was that, with legislation for 48 hours, employers would renege on these agreements and increase working time. This 'preposterous' suggestion was greeted by a clamorous outburst of angry protest and a war of words, until Will Thorne of the General Workers intervened to prevent a full-scale brawl. He persuaded Congress to endorse the 44-hour target – but for reasons other than those given by James Hill. Thorne's warning of the prospective rise of unemployment on the return of four to five million men from the fighting front, and the jobs that would be lost with the closure of munitions factories and cancellation of government contracts in the private sector, evidently carried some weight. A general reduction to a 48-hour week would be insufficient to effect the absorption of such large numbers into employment.

In 1919, 1920 and 1921, when turbulent industrial relations caused losses in working days amounting to some 35 million, 26½ million and nearly 86 million respectively,[17] the unions notched up some remarkable successes in both shortening the basic working week and raising rates of pay. The time was evidently opportune to advance by collective bargaining backed by industrial action, James Hill observed, but Congress must not lose sight of the need for legislation to *secure* the concessions won.

The rate of progress in reducing the basic working week slowed down and came to a halt as the brief postwar boom subsided. With the inexorable rise of unemployment and short-time working, the unions found themselves in a weak bargaining position, and employers who had conceded hours cuts were now reportedly seeking to claw them back. With their recently won gains in danger of melting away, it was time for the unions to try a new strategy. The International Labour Organization seemed to offer a way forward.

The ILO and the Washington Hours Convention

The International Labour Organization had been set up after the First World War, following the creation of the League of Nations under the Treaty of Versailles. Its general meetings were attended by representatives of governments, employers' organizations and workpeople from each member state, who participated in the proceedings by voice and by vote. An important part of the ILO's work was to formulate 'Recommendations' and 'Conventions' setting standards of social welfare and the treatment of labour, and to monitor the extent to which member states were honouring the formal pledges they had made in these spheres. The object was to devise a programme of international labour legislation, and Conventions ratified by governments were expected to have the binding force of international treaties.

The preamble to the Treaty of Versailles acknowledged the injustice, hardship and privation suffered by large numbers worldwide, and urged the need to improve conditions 'as, for example, by the regulation of hours of work ... the prevention of unemployment, the provision of an adequate living wage...'

The first IL Conference, held in Washington in the USA in 1919, adopted a Convention embodying the principle of the basic 48-hour week in industry, with the intention of improving the lot of the manual wage-worker. The Convention was strongly supported by representatives of the TUC, who took a leading part in its origination. The British Government's representative, having first requested and received instructions from home, voted for it. Subsequently, however, the British Government refused to ratify it.

The TUC had sent delegates to ILO general meetings, now held in Geneva, each year, but it was not until 1924 that Congress began to exert pressure on the British Government to ratify the Washington Hours Convention. This would be its main strategy to the end of the interwar period, supplemented by whatever could be accomplished by affiliated unions through collective negotiation with employers. The ominous rise in unemployment, which would get very much worse, and the unions' steadily weakening bargaining position, spurred the TUC to make the most strenuous of efforts to bring international pressure on the British Government to ratify the 1919 Convention.

With a Labour Government, albeit a minority one and one that would prove to be short-lived, circumstances seemed promising in 1924. That year, the TUC mounted a major campaign for general legislation to limit working hours, in what the General Council regarded as the most auspicious political climate to date. A statement, prepared by the General Council on behalf of the TUC late in 1923, was submitted to the Minister of Labour in February the following year. Its opening paragraph stated:

> On behalf of the British Trades Union Congress, we have to make representation to you in relation to our proposal that immediate steps be taken by the Government to give effect to the numerous decisions placed on record in the Peace Treaty of Versailles, in the findings of the National Industrial Conference convened by the British Government in 1919, the Draft Convention of the International Labour Conference at Washington during October 1919, the pledges of Ministers which have been placed on record from time to time, and numerous Trades Union Congress resolutions in relation to a legal maximum week for wage-earners.[18]

Between 1885 and 1923, the statement continued, the TUC had passed no less than 66 resolutions endorsing the principle of the 8-hour day or 48-hour week. The reasons for general legislation to limit working hours had been outlined on countless occasions, and there was widespread support from wage-workers and enlightened public opinion for a statutory measure.

The British Government, it was pointed out, had convened a National Conference in 1919, which had been attended by representatives of government departments, employers' associations, and the trade unions. Speeches had been delivered by Ministers, declaring the Government's intention to take legislative action to regulate the hours of labour. The Conference had appointed a Special Committee, with a view to drafting a 48-hour Bill, but, although there had been general agreement between the employers' and workers' representatives at that time, the Government subsequently had a change of heart and nothing was done.

The 1919 Washington Conference, the statement noted, had adopted a Convention to establish a maximum 48-hour week in all ILO member states, but the British Government, although under a moral obligation to give effect to that Convention, had persistently refused to ratify it. Its attitude had already had repercussions in other countries whose governments were now having second thoughts about implementing its provisions. Britain, it was alleged, was setting a bad example, when, as the principal industrial nation in Europe, she ought to be leading the way in improving labour standards.

One of the strongest of the TUC's arguments, and one most likely to win over the Government and find favour with employers, was that ratification of the Washington Convention by all ILO member states, encouraged by Britain's leading example, would promote 'fair international trading standards'. Britain, it was asserted, was disadvantaged at present. Statistics collected by the TUC General Council showed, perhaps to its surprise in view of recent fears voiced at Congress, that of a total trade union membership of 4,688,609, as many as 3,524,714 (roughly 75 per cent) currently had a basic working week of 48 hours or less on the basis of collective agreements; and there were others, not covered by formal agreements, who had similar hours. Although there was no explicit statement to that effect, the implication was that ratification of the 1919 Convention by the British Government would not inconvenience those employers who had already reduced working time, and would ensure emulation by the rest. If Britain did not take steps to ensure that her trading rivals adopted the 48-hour week, she would be at a disadvantage in overseas markets. In other words, Britain had nothing to lose and everything to gain by supporting the ILO's initiative to establish a common working-time standard throughout the developed and still developing world.

The Minister of Labour, in his reply to the TUC, expressed his intention to recommend ratification of the Convention and to introduce a Bill to impose an upper limit of 48 hours on the working week. All the signs were promising. A resolution carried by Congress in 1924 emphasized the importance of 'an Act legalizing a maximum 48-hour week,' but it also exhorted individual unions to negotiation of even shorter hours: '...that having regard to the unemployment existing among many thousands of workers and the subsequent poverty and loss of morale, an ordinary working week of 44 hours ... [should] be instituted.' There was no certainty that an Act would be safely passed, however; as one spokesman put it: 'We have failed up to now ... I do trust that our Labour Government will not compromise on this matter.'

Fears were voiced at the 1924 Congress that an Act which merely legalized the provisions of the 1919 Convention would jeopardize the position of those manual workers who were already working basic hours of less than 48. Another problem with legislation that merely embodied the regulations written into the Washington Convention was that the Convention, and therefore also the anticipated legislation, applied only to industrial workers; it did not apply to employees in distribution and commerce. Legislation ought not to discriminate in favour of one group; there ought to be no distinction between manual workers, shop assistants, white-collar grades and professional classes in the matter of working-time.

Congress continued to carry resolutions on working-time and to discuss the matter at great length year by year, but there was little further progress to report. The Labour Government had been hastened out of office without fulfilling its intentions. Ben Tillett confessed to feeling 'ashamed of my own side'. The electorate, he felt, had a lot to answer for, for 'if the Labour Government had been a real government, with power and authority, I feel sure we should have got this thing through'. Evidently, there had been a recent hardening of attitudes at ILO general meetings, for most governments were now siding with employers in opposition to labour's representatives; and the argument that working hours had implications for the health, happiness and efficiency of workpeople seemed to be falling on deaf ears.

There was some sign that matters were progressing, even so, for in 1926 Britain's Minister of Labour convened a conference in London with the Labour Ministers of France, Belgium, Italy and Germany to discuss the working-time question. It was felt that the Washington Convention lent itself to widely differing interpretations, and that there was much that needed to be clarified and more precisely defined if the main provisions were to be practicable for all industrial workers in all the European member states. In the meantime, the TUC General Council had been in regular consultation with the Minister of Labour to discuss such points as definitions of hours of work, the working week and overtime, and also matters such as Sunday working, shift systems, work in continuous process industries, intermittent work, exceptional pressure of work, and the position of the railways.

The outcome of the conference of ministers was the 1926 London Agreement. The General Council urged the British Government to take the necessary steps to expedite its implementation by the five governments which were party to it – but all in vain.

That year, Ernest Bevin moved a resolution:

> That having regard to the fact that the five great powers have agreed the interpretation to be placed upon the Washington Convention (Hours of Industrial Employment) this Congress is of the opinion that there is now no valid reason why complete ratification should any longer be delayed.
>
> This Congress therefore calls upon His Majesty's Government to ratify the Convention forthwith.

The Government, Mr Bevin stated, had first objected to the Convention because it was too rigid; then they had insisted that they could not ratify it because the interpretation of it by other governments was not rigid enough. As the problems of interpretation, administration and regulation had all now been resolved by the London Agreement, the Government's persisting disinclination to introduce a Bill was a matter of great mystification to the TUC.

Somewhat ominously, although not altogether surprisingly, the British employers had issued a manifesto at the 1927 IL Conference, expressing their opposition to the 8-hour day and to any form of legislation to regulate working time. That same year, after receiving several deputations from the TUC, the Minister of Labour alleged that difficulties still existed, despite the London Agreement, and that ratification was not yet possible. Letters were exchanged between the TUC and the National Confederation of Employers' Organizations, but little progress was made. The Government and employers believed that the 'Convention pure and simple', without amendment or modification, was impracticable. They wanted the Convention revised; the TUC wanted it ratified in its original form.

With a Labour Government in 1929, the TUC was again distinctly optimistic: 'The British workers, by their votes ... have opened the way for ratification of the Convention.' The Labour Party and the TUC had issued a joint manifesto in the run-up to the general election, stating that:

> The Washington Hours Convention would have been ratified in 1924 had not the Labour Government been overthrown by a combination of Conservatives and Liberals. The Labour Party is pledged to the ratification of the Convention, as well as to the repeal of the Act which lengthened the miners' working day...[19]

The Government's intention was to introduce a Bill which would take account of both the Washington Convention and the London Agreement. [20]

The employers immediately declared that they had no intention of abating their opposition; in their view, the Convention, with or without the London Agreement, was 'not an instrument calculated to bring about any appreciable measure of uniformity in the working hours of the various countries.' Evidently the employers had no confidence in international measures of this kind, and were unconvinced of the efficacy of an international 48-hour week as the basis of fair trade. They were not unanimously opposed to the 48-hour week in principle, for a number of them had agreements with the unions for a working week of even less than 48 hours. They had more trust in their British employer colleagues and in the British tradition of negotiating with the trade unions than in foreign governments' pledges scrupulously to observe both the letter and the spirit of the Convention in question. It may be that, with longer experience than the trade unions of dealing with foreign countries, the Employers' Federation had become more cynical and more wary of committing themselves to a framework of regulations which others might observe only in the breach.

The TUC, apparently convinced that the Labour Government would pass the long-awaited legislation without let or hindrance, was already demanding better. The Washington Convention applied only to manual workers in industrial undertakings and specified a 48-hour week. Pressure for hours limitation for other classes of employees and for less than 48 hours was already being exerted in the ILO by the International Federation of Trade Unions, the International Federation of Commercial, Clerical and Technical Employees, and other bodies representing the salaried. The IL Office began to collect information on existing laws, regulations and practices on working hours for these groups. In Britain, Ben Tillett and Mr Poulton sought the advice of the various unions with white-collar memberships.

The possibility was foreseen that there would be some difficulty in agreeing on a definition of 'non-manual' and in deciding which groups should be covered by the envisaged Convention. British workers' representatives at the ILO, in collaboration with trade unionists from other countries, urged that the classes to be covered should be as wide as possible. Employers' representatives expressed the opinion, voiced by them ten years earlier, that the subject was 'not yet ripe for treatment'.

Britain's Labour Government introduced a Bill into the House of Commons, seeking to limit the basic working hours of industrial workers to 8 in any one day and 48 in any one week, with strict controls on overtime. However, TUC policy on working time had already moved to one which was more ambitious than the 1919 Convention, the London Agreement, and the Government's Hours of Industrial Employment Bill. In 1930, in the context of worldwide recession and soaring unemployment which showed every sign of worsening, the International Federation of Trade Unions carried a long and detailed resolution on working time at its Stockholm conference.

The IFTU's resolution noted that most ILO member states were not honouring their pledges to implement the 1919 Hours Convention which sought to protect the health and safety of the employed and to ameliorate the worldwide unemployment problem. The target identified in the resolution, however, was not the 48 hours of the 1919 Convention, but '44 hours as a stage towards a more considerable reduction ... for all workers, manual and non-manual, without distinction of sex, race, or nationality ...'. It called for an international campaign 'to secure a shorter working week, for the sake of promoting the welfare of the great masses of the workers.'[21]

A resolution for a maximum 44-hour week (without reduction of weekly wages) and strict limitation of overtime was carried in 1930 by the British TUC. There was the most urgent need, it was asserted, for action to ameliorate unemployment, as 'rationalization' in industry, the trend to 'trustification', 'automation' of production, and the 'increasing intensity of work', all added further to the many job losses caused by the recession. The 48-hour week would not serve the purpose of protecting the jobs of those in work, nor of creating employment for the two million people currently on the dole. No-one, Mr Dukes maintained, opposed improved production methods, better organization of industry, and modern technology, but, unless rationalization could be made to yield a shorter working week and greater purchasing power, it would be the 'greatest curse that has ever beset the working populations of the world'. At the same time, automation was leading to the monotonization of work tasks, which reduced the quality of life.

The economic recession had already lasted eight or nine years and its end was not yet in sight; unemployment would not fall unless the available work could be spread among larger numbers by reducing the length of the working week and cutting out overtime: 'If improved production means anything at all, surely it should mean greater leisure, a greater variety in our lives, that workpeople should not merely have their rest as preparation for further toil, but that we should be able to enjoy a higher and more varied standard of life ...'. The mover and seconder of the resolution produced a battery of statistics on increased output and the marked rise in productivity. With higher productivity per hour and per unit of labour, the employer was faced with three choices: to expand markets, or to reduce working hours, or to pay their employees off. In the prevailing economic climate markets were contracting and employers were averse to reducing working hours. There was extensive resort, therefore, to the third option of terminating employment. Sharing out the work by shortening hours and eradicating overtime was a more humane and civilized solution to the unemployment problem than the dole. The TUC put its faith in the Labour Government to devise an effective policy on these lines. The 44-hour week that the TUC had in mind was inclusive of meal breaks; in effect, it meant an actual basic working week of 39 hours.

At the International Labour Conferences of 1929 and 1930, the complexities of regulating working-time worldwide were beginning to be more fully appreciated. There appeared to be no simple all-embracing solution which could be applied to all occupational groups and in countries with different cultural traditions, at different stages of economic development, and having different political and institutional structures. There were long and heated discussions of working hours for seamen, underground coalminers, agricultural workers, the salaried, railway workers, and the distributive trades. The British Government was not alone in calling for more information on existing practices before the formulation of Conventions for any or all of these groups.

In Britain in 1931, with even higher unemployment, fading hopes of general legislation, and acceptance of the Washington Convention's obsolescence, the TUC set itself a new working-time target and shifted its stance on the question of general legislation.

The New Target: A 40-Hour Week

The General Council's report to Congress in 1931 noted that neither the Washington 48-hour Convention nor the IFTU's 44-hour week was sufficient to ameliorate unemployment at the present time:

> If the shortening of working hours is to fulfil the purpose of effecting a considerable reduction of the present unemployment, hours of work must be curtailed by at least one full working day. The introduction of the 5-day (40-hour) week ... should therefore be made a fundamental demand of the Trade Unions of all countries.[22]

A resolution moved by Mr C. Dukes MP, of the General and Municipal Workers, called for the 40-hour week, without any reduction in the weekly wage, and a strict limitation of overtime to work of agreed urgency. Britain's labour force had been reduced by around one million as a result of casualties suffered during the First World War, yet there were now some three million people without work: 'Only a very drastic and really effective shortening of working hours ... is going to have any effect.' Modern machinery had 'unlimited automative potential' but it was not easing the burden of work; it was intensifying it, and the results were that those in work suffered physical strain and mental stress while many others had lost their jobs. There was another problem: the existence of large pools of surplus labour undermined the bargaining power of the trade unions to negotiate better conditions. To adopt the 'attitude of the Luddites and destroy machines, or even to fulminate against rationalization ... [was] no solution.' Shorter working-time was the only feasible answer.

There was some disenchantment and exasperation over the shorter-hours question at the 1931 Congress. In effect, one delegate observed, the resolution amounted to a demand for a substantial pay rise, which was obviously impracticable at present; and the idea of permitting *any* overtime, *however agreed*, ran counter to the whole principle of the TUC's campaign. The resolution, it was argued, 'savours somewhat of cant' and 'is largely whitewash'. Before 'calling on the Government to do almost impossible things', they ought first to convince their own rank and file members about the detrimental effect of overtime and persuade them to refuse it. There was also the anomaly of the hours differential between manual and non-manual employees. White-collar groups started the working day later and finished earlier than manual wage-earners, and it was the latter who characteristically worked overtime. This problem had not yet been seriously addressed by the trade unions or by the ILO.

Others were less disposed to cynicism. For practical reasons it was impossible to eliminate *all* overtime working. Winning overseas orders for goods in the present climate depended not only on competitive prices but also on an ability to meet early delivery dates. The margin between the successful and the unsuccessful tender was very narrow; some overtime was essential for a 'rush of orders', without which more jobs would be lost. Overtime was often needed also for maintenance work and to deal with machine breakdowns, to permit production to proceed. At the same time, it was problematic for the TUC that many workers were very much in favour of overtime and actively sought a large amount of it; those 'hooked' on overtime 'would no doubt vote for a 40-hour week in the hope of getting a 50-hour time-sheet ...', in some cases from greed but in others from sheer financial necessity. It was a complex problem for which there was no simple solution.

The 40-hour week, proposed by the British workers' delegates at the 1932 IL Conference, met with the united opposition of the employers' groups and the resistance of several governments.

The TUC appointed a special committee to collect information from affiliated unions on hours currently worked in

Britain, to determine the probable effects of the 40-hour week on employers' costs, and to assess the impact of new machinery on workers' health and physical efficiency.

Margaret Bondfield of the Transport and General Workers, in moving a resolution at the 1932 Congress on the 40-hour week in Britain and internationally, acknowledged the difficulties of imposing a rigid upper limit on hours of labour. What was needed, she believed, was a broad framework of legislation which was sufficiently flexible to accommodate the differing circumstances of a diverse variety of trades and industries: 'One of the great difficulties in framing a Bill is not so much a general prejudice ... as the perfectly obvious technical difficulties in applying any cast-iron system to every trade.'[23] Unemployment, whose rate was historically high and whose nature was long-term, created the most intractable of financial difficulties for the state, for the tax-paying public, and all who were obligated to pay national unemployment insurance. Here was another reason to limit hours, for without a most drastic shortening of working-time, the financial burden of maintaining the unemployed would fall ever more heavily upon those still in work.

Yet another line to the argument was added by Mr S. Bradley of the Amalgamated Engineers. He saw the substantial reduction of working hours as providing a path out of the recession. The economy was not self-correcting, and the unions were critical of economic orthodoxy and economic policies for the 'tightening of belts', which had proved totally ineffective. It may be that he was influenced by the Mosley Memorandum[24] which the Labour Party had thrown out, or by the ideas of J.M. Keynes[25] which had been incorporated into the Liberal Party's manifesto. As Mr Bradley saw it, an increase in effective market demand would have a positive effect on the level of employment: 'Every man is a consumer; every man is a market.' The world's warehouses were overflowing with surplus manufactured and agricultural goods which workers had created as producers; but 'every man is more important as a consumer than he is as a producer.' The effect of increasing employment by reducing working hours would be cumulative: 'The newly employed engineer eats more, buys more, wants more; and the more he buys, the more he eats, the more he wants, the greater the number of other workers he throws into employment.' There could be no prospect of an end to the world economic crisis until more people were drawn into employment and spending power was widened.

Miss Bondfield's motion had Ernest Bevin's support, but he reminded Congress of the rank and file's reluctance to practice what their elected union officers preached. Any successes by the Transport and General Workers' Union in negotiating shorter hours were all too often neutralized by transport workers' craving for overtime:

> I have made any amount of agreements for a shorter working day, and what do I find I am getting now? I am finding more fights on overtime than on wages. You have to face up to your own people on the overtime problem.[26]

Mr Bevin blamed neither Conservative nor Labour Governments for failure to ratify the Washington Convention:

> The people who made the Washington Convention impossible of ratification were certain sections of our own Trade Union Movement who would not fall into line.

There were, even so, rational explanations for refusals to fall into line, for the impracticalities of a rigid all-embracing Convention had become only too obvious by now. Ernest Bevin accepted the desirability of a different tack. The need for flexibility within the framework of general legislation in Britain, identified by Margaret Bondfield, was mirrored in Ernest Bevin's view of international legislation. If the ILO were to produce another Convention, it would need to be divided into four or five main parts with subdivisions within each.

A new Convention on working hours, it was emphasized,

would need to be ratified by all ILO member states. Unilateral adoption of the 40-hour week by Britain, regardless of developments in other countries, would disadvantage British employers in both domestic and overseas markets; if the shorter week led to a rise in the costs and prices of British goods, thereby rendering them uncompetitive, the result would be 'a further loss of orders, and more, not less, unemployment'. It had to be remembered, also, that some of Britain's major iron and steel and engineering companies were now international concerns with subsidiaries abroad: Guest, Keen and Nettlefold in Australia, Canada, Brazil and Sweden; Vickers in Japan, Romania and Spain; Stewart & Lloyd in South Africa – to name but three of the many:

> Friends, can you wonder why orders to Britain from these countries have already slumped so badly? If we are to have in this country alone a drastically shorter working week, with its increased costs of production, what do you think these and other firms are going to do? To my mind, this is definitely an international question, and it should be tackled on an international basis.[27]

By 1933 it had been generally accepted by the ILO that, in formulating a new Convention on working hours, the rigidity which had rendered the Washington Convention unworkable would have to be avoided. The ILO's Governing Body and representatives of governments, employers and workpeople expended much time and effort in collecting and evaluating information on the working-time *status quo*, in heated argument on points of difference, and in trying to thrash out workable solutions. It was a slow, cumbersome and frequently frustrating experience, not least because of delay or failure in the return of questionnaires and the vast amount of paperwork that was generated. In 1933 a 'resolution of principle' was moved, to the effect that an international shortening of working-time would ameliorate unemployment, and that wages and standards of living should be maintained when hours were reduced.

Objections were raised by the British Government at the outset. In the Government's view, wages could not be maintained if working hours were reduced, and industrial strife would inevitably follow in the wake of reduced earnings. Britain had a long-established tradition of collective bargaining on pay, hours and other employment conditions; government intervention in such matters was restricted to specific industries with special needs. An international Convention would override Britain's tradition of voluntary bargaining which provided scope for employers and workpeople to devise their own arrangements by mutual consent. The employers likewise voiced their united opposition. As they saw it, there were other important factors, in addition to working-time, which needed to be addressed in devising a strategy to lift the world out of recession and cure unemployment; what was needed, they believed, were solutions to those problems to be considered at the forthcoming World Economic Conference: debts, tariffs, monetary reforms, credits, quotas, and so on.

The ILO's work of holding discussions, gathering information, and issuing reports continued, even so, during the next few years, although progress was painfully slow. The TUC carried resolutions on working time year after year, and was in regular consultation with the Minister of Labour and the Employers' Federation. Already it was feared that the 40-hour week would do little to generate employment, given the formidable productivity increases in recent years, which reduced employers' labour requirement faster than the unions could increase it by negotiating hours downward.

Judged in relation to the amount of time, effort and paperwork devoted to the hours question by the ILO, the outcome was bitterly disappointing for the trade unions. The principle of the 48-hour week was extended to commerce in 1930. A Convention of 1934 established a weekly maximum of 42 hours in automatic sheet-glass works, and a Convention was adopted in 1935 to limit the hours spent underground by coalminers to 7¾ per day.

The 1935 IL Conference agreed a Convention prescribing

the 40-hour week 'in principle'; member states ratifying it were to apply the principle in accordance with subsequent subsidiary Conventions dealing with particular industries, and in such a manner as to maintain standards of living. The British Government, viewing the Convention as a binding declaration of intent, refused to sign it. The TUC, clutching at straws by now, greeted it enthusiastically as 'a public confirmation and acceptance of a principle'; some, it was admitted, might regard it as 'no more than a declaration, having no real effect', but 'its moral and political value is substantial, even if it has no legal effect at the present time'.

For the trade unions, hope triumphed over experience, only to be disappointed again and again. There remained the formidable task of producing industry-specific regulations within the meaning of the general Convention. Of the subsidiary draft Conventions seeking to apply the principle – to glass bottle works in 1935, public works in 1936, and textiles in 1937 – only the first received sufficient ratification as to have any real significance in practical terms. Other subsidiary Conventions proposed in these years – for building and contracting, iron and steel, chemicals, and the printing and allied trades – all failed to secure the majority vote needed for adoption.

The TUC was voicing increasing concern in the mid-1930s about the combined effects on employment of automation, rationalization, trustification, electrification, standardization, the Bedaux system, and the use of oil fuel in manufacturing. At Congress, statistics were quoted indicating substantial productivity increases in coalmining, iron and steel production, heavy engineering, and other major industries. As Arthur Hayday commented at the 1935 Congress:

> If you proceed industry by industry you will make no impression on the unemployment figures ... because the rate of mechanization will be faster than the rate of provision you are making for the reduction of hours to 40.[28]

Economic recovery was underway by 1937, and employment was rising. International Conventions had been too few, too late, and too cumbersome to ameliorate the unemployment of the recent past. Mr Little of the Engineers believed it to be unwise to place too much dependence on Conventions and hopes of legislation from the present British Government. With improving economic circumstances, the shortening of working-time by collective bargaining was once more a practicable possibility. Unemployment could no longer be the main justification for the unions' claims, however. That line of reasoning was now unsustainable in engineering. It had been tenable four years ago, but 'it is about the weakest argument we could adduce today'. The unemployment rate was now less than 2.0 per cent in engineering, and the employers were complaining of a skill shortage. In present circumstances, the only viable line of argument was one based upon productivity improvements. There was a vast amount of statistical evidence, much of it produced by the employers themselves, to show the extent to which productivity had risen. With the rise of profits and dividends, the prospective increase of labour costs, which employers feared, could be absorbed without undue harm to business enterprises, by reducing hours gradually but systematically over a five-year period:

> Unemployment was a powerful argument four years ago. It is a very weak argument today. During the next slump it will be an exceedingly powerful argument again. But there is a consistent thread ... one that is growing stronger, and that is an argument based on productivity.[29]

At ILO meetings in 1937 and 1938, despite the imminence of war in Europe, the struggle to produce workable Conventions to regulate the hours of labour continued. In June 1939, however, it was agreed that further discussions of the issue would have to be postponed, and that the ILO's headquarters would move from Geneva to Canada for the duration of the war.

Notes

1. Bienefeld, M.A. (1972), *Working Hours in British Industry: An Economic History*, London, Weidenfeld & Nicolson, chs 1 and 2; Cunningham, H. (1980), *Leisure in the Industrial Revolution c1780–c1870*, London, Croom Helm, p.85.
2. Evans, A. and Palmer, S. (1985), *Negotiating Shorter Working Hours*, Basingstoke, Macmillan, ch.1.
3. Webb, S. and Webb, B. (1920), *Industrial Democracy*, revised edn, London, Longman Green, p.336.
4. Evans, A. and Palmer, S., *op. cit.*
5. Numerous resolutions recorded in the TUC's annual *Report* up to 1900: for the 8-hour day, elimination of overtime, hours legislation, amendment of existing sectional legislation; see *Report* 1887 pp.41, 84–6; 1888 pp.26–7; 1889 pp.47–8, 54–7; 1890 pp.26, 48–53; 1891 pp.29, 40–2, 44–6; 1893 pp.19–20, 56–7; 1894 pp.36–41; 1895 pp.29, 49, 53–6; 1896 pp.36–7, 68–9; 1897 pp.19, 32–3, 36–7, 39, 41, 56, 1898 pp.53–4, 57–8; 1899 pp.28, 58–60, 62–77.
6. Pelling, H. (1992), *A History of British Trade Unionism*, Harmondsworth, Penguin, statistical table, pp.302–5.
7. Clegg, H.A. (1979), *The Changing System of Industrial Relations in Great Britain*, Oxford, Blackwell, p.31.
8. Trades Union Congress (1900), *Annual Report*, pp.37, 87.
9. *Ibid.* (1905), p.149.
10. *Ibid.* (1906), p.139.
11. *Ibid.* (1912), pp.69–70; Pelling, H., *op. cit.* shows working days lost through strikes in 1912 numbered nearly 41 million.
12. Trades Union Congress (1913), *Annual Report*, p.210.
13. *Ibid.*
14. *Ibid.* pp.210–11.
15. *Ibid.* (1915), pp.312–3.
16. *Ibid.*(1919), pp.318–9.
17. Pelling, H., *op. cit.* statistical table, pp.302–5.
18. Trades Union Congress (1924), *Annual Report*, pp.185–9.
19. *Ibid.* (1929), p.253.
20. *Ibid.* p.213.
21. *Ibid.* (1930), p.355.
22. *Ibid.* (1931), p.128.
23. *Ibid.* (1932), p.420.
24. 'Memorandum by Ministers on Certain Proposals relating to

Unemployment', Cmd. 3331, *BPP* (1929) Vol. XVI; Skidelsky, R. (1975), *Oswald Mosley*, Basingstoke, Macmillan and (1967), *Politicians and the Slump: The Labour Government of 1929–1931*, Basingstoke, Macmillan.
25. Liberal Party (1929), *We Can Conquer Unemployment*; Keynes, J.M. and Henderson, H.D. (1929), *Can Lloyd George Do It?*
26. Trades Union Congress (1932), *Annual Report*, p.420.
27. *Ibid.*
28. *Ibid.* (1935), p.173.
29. *Ibid.* (1937), p.315.

2

The TUC's Quest for Paid Holidays, 1900–39

Introduction

The TUC's quest for paid holidays dates from the second decade of the twentieth century. By long tradition and customary practice reaching back to the mid-nineteenth century, most employers in 1900 were in the habit of paying their salaried professional and non-manual employees for periods of holiday absence, but very few manual wage-workers were thus privileged. Insofar as manual workpeople had holiday leave from work, its duration was much shorter than for their non-manual counterparts and for the great majority it was without pay. According to Pimlott,[1] it was not until the 1880s that the more progressive employers began to provide paid holidays for their manual workforces, but at the beginning of the new century such arrangements still applied to the minority. Characteristically, they were not the outcome of collective bargaining, but 'gifts' bestowed by the benevolent employer. The salaried could expect annual holidays of a fortnight to a full month, according to occupational status and/or length of service.[2] The manual worker's holidays ranged from three to thirteen days annually,[3] and conveniently served the employer's general maintenance and stocktaking purposes.

The weekly Sunday holiday, dating from time immemorial, was observed generally; and with the Saturday half-holiday, which had come to displace St Monday in many industries, the modern weekend had taken shape.[4] Observance of St Monday, the custom of taking Monday, and sometimes also part of Tuesday, off from work, had been widespread in cottage industry and small workshops with their informal work rhythms and desultory work habits. With industrialization, St Monday declined first and fastest where factories and large workshops using steam-powered machinery were established and required the regular attendance of the full workforce for a full six-day working week for purposes of cost-efficient production. The effect of collective bargaining and the Factory and Workshop Acts was the gradual reduction of working hours on Saturday and the establishment of the Saturday half-holiday well before 1900. Apart from the annual holiday of consecutive days and the weekend break, there were the occasional days of holiday. Some of these were local in character, while others were more widely observed as religious feasts and festivals of the Church calendar. The Bank Holidays Act of 1871 and the Holidays Extension Act 1875 had appointed some of the latter as bank and public holidays and added 1 August as an entirely secular holiday.[5] In effect, by 1900 Britain had six officially sanctioned public holidays. Like annual holidays, these were with pay for the salaried and without pay for most of the waged.

Workmen had complained about loss of pay at holiday time before the Royal Commission on Labour, 1892–4: the Warrington Painters' Society objected to 'too many enforced holidays' of this kind, which they could not afford, and the Lancashire Branch of the Gasworkers' Society lamented that their pay for a working week shortened by days of holiday was 'insufficient to keep wife and family'. It was only in districts such as the Lancashire cotton and coal towns which observed 'wakes' holidays, with each town having its own wakes week, that employment was sufficiently regular and family earnings sufficiently high to allow for the dogged accumulation of weekly savings for a holiday at the seaside.[6]

TUC Policy and Action for Paid Holidays

The TUC's policy and action for paid holidays came much later than its initiatives to reduce basic working hours and overtime. For several decades the two issues, working hours and paid holidays, were seen as separate though not entirely unrelated questions. Resolutions dealt with one or the other. It was not until very much later that resolutions began to combine both objectives and to gather other related issues along the way. It seems probable that the similarity in the reasons and justifications argued in support of improvements in both of these spheres explains why the TUC came to see them, in years to come, as inextricably linked.

The first resolutions on paid holidays were carried in 1911 and 1912. It is often assumed that the holidays in question were the consecutive days of annual holiday when firms closed for purposes of repair, installation, maintenance and stock-taking while the workers were 'at leisure'; but, in point of fact, the early proposals called, far more modestly but quite specifically, for payment on the occasion of the bank and public holidays – or what the unions termed 'statute holidays'. The resolutions were not modest in other respects, however, for they were as ambitious as the working-time resolutions as to means, methods and instructions to the TUC's Parliamentary Committee:

> This Congress instructs the Parliamentary Committee to appoint a deputation to wait upon the Prime Minister urging upon him the necessity for introducing a Bill compelling employers to pay all their workers (male and female) for existing statute holidays, as well as for all holidays which may be subsequently proclaimed; and where it may be considered necessary for any workman (including clerks) to be employed on any public holiday, to either give the latter double pay or another day off for each or part of a holiday worked. Further, that neither the Government nor private employers shall compel their employees to work overtime either before or after such holidays in order to make up the time lost.[7]

Evidently at this early stage, the TUC saw a distinction between the holidays voluntarily taken by workers, with or without the employers' authorization, on the one hand and, on the other, those holidays that a third party, the Government, had imposed by Act of Parliament many decades earlier.

The deputation, received by the Prime Minister, reminded him that it was the lowest-paid workers who suffered most from non-payment on the occasion of the 'statute holidays'; and, pushing their argument further, the spokesmen also complained of loss of pay due to 'additional holidays that are forced upon workers because firms shut their doors for several days longer'. The inferior treatment of manual workers, compared with their salaried counterparts, was both unfair and unjust; it was surely ironic that 'bank clerks and people in high places, who can afford to submit to a reduction of wages, do not go short'.

Different treatment of manual and non-manual groups and loss of pay by wage-workers for 'compulsory' holidays were the subject of complaint again at the 1913 Congress. As the London Compositors' delegate expressed it: 'Everyone wants to see compulsory payment for compulsory holidays.' Members of Parliament were paid for their several weeks of holiday, and 'we think that we might be paid for our holidays also'. J.R. Clynes, of the Gasworkers, could see no just reason for better treatment of the salaried, when the manual worker's need was greater:

> Generally speaking, those who work with their coats on – the intellectual workers – work less than eight hours a day, and in the course of the week they have longer spells of rest, and they have longer and more frequent holidays. Holidays extending to a month, three weeks and a fortnight are common among the better-to-do professional men ... We may at least, then, claim for the manual worker as good conditions of recreation and of rest as those enjoyed by the people who perform the lighter work of the country.[8]

Nothing came of the TUC's request for legislation to obligate employers to pay wages for the public holidays. In his reply, the Prime Minister had informed the unions that the bank and public holidays were 'statutory' and 'compulsory' only in the employing establishments specified in the Acts of 1871 and 1875. Elsewhere, taking the days as holidays and receiving pay for them were matters for negotiation and voluntary agreement between employers and their workpeople.

The progress made on that basis evidently raised the unions' sights, for the next resolution on paid holidays, carried in 1919, was far more ambitious than its precursors. Mr A.H. Findlay of the United Patternmakers moved that:

> The Congress affirms that the time has arrived for employers to make provision for and pay to all workmen their wages at the recognized time-rates of the district for at least ten working days' holiday each year, in addition to the Bank Holidays.[9]

The TUC president, at least, was already aware of the pitfalls of gendered language, for he insisted that the word 'workmen' be replaced by 'workpeople'. Nothing daunted by this reproof, Mr Findlay forcefully declared that manual workers were being 'left out' and that it was 'about time that workers were brought into line with ... the clerical and professional classes'. It ought to be within the realms of practical politics, another speaker asserted, to devise a sensible national scheme to benefit all workers in every industry, and to give them an annual holiday of fourteen days. Some employers in the Nottingham area had already got together to agree a local arrangement of that kind. That precedent might be usefully cited by union officers seeking to negotiate a full fortnight's paid holiday for their members.

The subject was not discussed further by Congress until 1925, when the resolution proposed 'not less than a fortnight's holiday with pay'. At the time, the House of Commons was considering a Private Member's Bill on paid holidays, sponsored by Labour members. Again, the main justification given by the delegate at Congress was that manual workers should receive equal treatment with salaried staffs, and now also with 'Government employees': 'Seeing the clerical staffs of firms and Government employees receive this as part and parcel of their employment, it is only right the men who do manual labour should also receive it.' Some workers managed to save enough to take their families away for a holiday at the seaside, but even the thrifty had a struggle to 'get their finances back in order afterwards'.

The 1925 Holidays with Pay Bill did not receive a second reading, but union leaders at Congress the following year, although disappointed, were undeterred in their ambitions, for their claim had been further enlarged. The General Council was called upon to mount a 'national campaign' to secure:

a) an annual summer holiday of two weeks with full pay;
b) payment for all statutory holidays;
c) May Day as an additional statutory holiday.[10]

Up to this time, the TUC's discussion of paid holidays had been largely confined to the British scene and the need to eradicate what the unions regarded as an unwarranted difference in treatment of manual workforces and office staffs. Now the scope of the TUC's vision widened at a time when its representatives were actively and intensively involved in the efforts of the International Labour Organization to regulate working hours in all member states. Congress was informed that 'the question [of paid holidays] is being taken up all over the world'. Employers, in Britain and elsewhere, were resisting claims on grounds of costs; but estimates indicated that the paid holidays sought by the unions would increase labour costs by no more than 4.0 per cent. That, the unions believed, was not exorbitant, and the employers could perfectly well afford it.

It was not until 1929 that the issue came to the fore again.[11] That year it was discussed in depth and at length by the International Federation of Trade Unions at its Prague meeting. Demands for paid holidays were said to be 'gaining ground', for in several countries the principle had been established in collective agreements or embodied in legislation which applied either generally or sectionally. Paid holidays were necessary, it was asserted, to relieve the physical and mental exhaustion caused by the rationalization of industry and the spread of modern production techniques which speeded up the pace of work. National trade union centres were urged to 'use appropriate means and action' to secure recognition in their own countries of the worker's right to be paid for periods of holiday leave authorized by employers. A proposal was carried to request the International Labour Office to investigate current practice and, in the light of its findings, to produce a Convention setting minimum standards to be legally reinforced in each ILO member state.

That year, with a Labour Government in office in Britain, the TUC carried another resolution for 'payment of wages for all statutory and customary holidays, in addition to two weeks' annual holiday.' The issue, it was urged, should be pressed both nationally and internationally, by the TUC, the IFTU, which had made it 'practically its principal question ... to press forward', and by the ILO. In Britain union officers were reported to have concluded 137 agreements for paid holidays during the last twelve months, and Walter Citrine, TUC General Secretary, noted 'with the greatest possible gratification' that one of the first acts of the Labour Government had been to grant a week's paid holiday to all workers in government industrial establishments. However, as in 1925, a Private Member's Bill on paid holidays, introduced that year, met with prevarication in the House of Commons and was lost. Evidence produced by the IFTU disclosed, to the TUC's regret, that Britain lagged far behind most of Western Europe, and even 'our poor friends in Russia', in legislative provision for holidays with pay.

In discussion of the subject again at the 1930 Congress, it was noted that Swedish workers' representatives were pressing the ILO for a Convention. Spokesmen at Congress again lamented the dissimilarity of treatment by British employers of manual and non-manual groups: 'There are very few office workers who do not have about fourteen days' paid holiday every year in addition to payment for public holidays ... Why should the men who work the hardest be denied the same opportunity?'

It was not until 1931, one of the worst years of the depression, that the need to ameliorate unemployment emerged as another strand in the TUC's argument for paid holidays. The TUC was currently advocating the shorter working week to alleviate unemployment; paid holidays would serve the same purpose, particularly at the present time when rationalization was adding to the job losses caused by the depression. As the General Council's report noted:

> Quite apart from its inherent social value and its complete justification as a labour right, the action in favour of paid holidays, considered in connection with the present crisis, may, under certain circumstances, like the wider distribution of work through the reduction of working hours, have a beneficial effect on the labour market ... by facilitating the re-absorption into production of a part of the permanent reserve of the unemployed.[12]

Nearly three million people were now on the dole. It was unacceptable that, while large numbers had no work at all, many of the employed were seriously over-worked: 'We have some men who are working all the hours that God sends, and others who have not worked for years.' Sharing out the available work would benefit both the employed and the unemployed, and would be far better than giving out-of-work pay and allowing those without jobs to become 'absolutely demoralized'.

Congress carried similar resolutions in 1932 and 1933, for a fortnight's annual paid holiday and pay for 'all statutory and customary holidays'. The Minister of Health, it was noted, had recently stated that the working of the National Health Insurance Act had been 'thrown out of gear because of the great increase in sickness absence'. The escalating cost of providing sickness benefit was unsurprising, for they were all aware of the 'enormous increase ... in the number of cases of nervous breakdown and stress-related illness, preventable in many cases, and due entirely to the tension and strain of work...' If there were recognized holidays in industry, there would be a marked fall in the currently high incidence of sickness, which had so upset the financial working of the National Health Insurance Act. Manual work was physically exhausting:

> What the black-coated workers have enjoyed as a right for years, what all insurance clerks enjoy, what all bank clerks enjoy, what all salaried men throughout industry enjoy, ought to be enjoyed by all workers in industry, and more especially by manual workers.[13]

No progress was being made in the unions' negotiations with employers. Appeals to benevolence and philanthropy were futile in the present climate; most employers would only give paid holidays if they were compelled to do so. One possibility, it was suggested, was to have some kind of national insurance arrangement for paid holidays:

> If holidays with pay were laid down by Act of Parliament in the same way as workmen's compensation, and in the same fashion as contributions were made to the National Health Insurance and to National Unemployment Insurance, the employers would not be able to get away from their obligation.

This proposal had little attraction for the Government, in years when disbursements under the health and unemployment insurance schemes were far in excess of contributions. In point of fact, the idea of a contributory scheme for paid holidays for manual workers would be strongly resisted by the TUC in its evidence before the Amulree Committee in 1937.

The ILO's Action and its Effect in Britain

Investigation of paid holidays had been proposed several times by labour representatives at the ILO, but it was not until 1934 and 1935 that the subject was included on the agenda of items for discussion. Congress was informed in 1935 that an ILO committee had already consulted governments of member states with a view to the adoption of an international Convention at the 1936 session.

The Convention adopted that year stipulated an annual paid holiday of at least six consecutive working days after one year's service; public and customary holidays and periods of sickness absence were not to count as part of the annual holiday, and persons dismissed before taking their holiday were to receive pay for every day's holiday due to them. Each government ratifying the Convention was to devise a system of sanctions to ensure that the parties affected fulfilled their obligations within a framework of national regulations set up to implement the terms of the Convention. British workers' representatives at the IL Conference had withdrawn their proposal that agricultural and maritime workers should come within the scope of the Convention, on receiving an assurance that these matters would be placed on the following year's agenda; there was also to be future discussion of paid holidays for domestic workers, home workers, and hotel porters, none of whom were covered by the 1936 Convention.

The Convention was discussed at great length by the TUC in 1936. It was welcomed, even though it stipulated a good deal less than was contained in the unions' resolutions on the subject; and, from past experience, they knew that they would have a formidable struggle to secure implementation in Britain of the regulations formulated by the ILO. The Convention had been bitterly opposed by British employers, and the British Government refused to ratify it.

A third Holidays with Pay Bill, introduced by Mr Rowson on behalf of the Parliamentary Labour Party, had passed its second reading in November 1936. It was the controversy over this Bill in the House of Commons that left the Government with little alternative but to set up a Committee of Investigation. The TUC General Council agreed to give evidence, on receiving the Prime Minister's assurance that the inquiry and report would be completed before the end of the Parliamentary Session. The Committee, set up in 1937 with Lord Amulree as chairman, contained equal numbers of employers' and workpeople's representatives. The six members, nominated from its own ranks by the TUC General Council, were Miss Anne Loughlin, and Messrs Bevin, Hicks, Dukes, Elvin and Hallsworth, all of whom had been actively involved in the ILO's initiative for paid holidays. Written and oral evidence in support of the unions' case was to be presented to the Committee by Sir Walter Citrine and two members of the General Council. They were decidedly optimistic, for in 1937, before completion of the inquiry, a fourth Holidays with Pay Bill was put before the House of Commons, collective bargaining on the subject was making marked progress, and public opinion was becoming favourable.

The TUC's Evidence to the Amulree Committee

In its evidence before the Amulree Committee, the TUC argued that annual holidays of several consecutive days were necessary, that payment of wages at such times was essential, and that general entitlement could be accomplished only by general legislation; moreover, employers could perfectly well afford the expense. It was intolerable that most non-manual employees in Britain enjoyed paid holidays while most manual workers were denied them; and it was lamentable that provision in many other countries was more advanced than in Britain.

The various strands of argument, which the unions had been spinning off and on since 1911, were now woven together into a coherent whole. They were no longer preaching to the converted at Congress, nor word-fencing with small groups of employers at numerous and diverse bargaining tables. All the rehearsals had been held; this was the grand public performance which would be widely reported in the national press. The unions had never before had such an opportunity to plead their case.[14]

The first set of reasons given by the TUC was based on the need to protect workers' physical health and mental well-being, and on socio-cultural considerations such as the development of personality. Both the body and the mind needed regular rest for regeneration, revitalization and recuperation: '... regular annual holidays are an integral part of those admittedly regular periods of freedom from daily toil, commonly described as leisure ...' Without sufficient leisure time, work would be 'at such a cost to health and efficiency as to render it, in the long run, unprofitable ...' The tired worker was an inefficient worker; productivity, total output and product quality were all adversely affected when the worker was physically exhausted and mentally fatigued. The intensification of the work pace and the monotonization of work tasks as a result of the automation of production processes during the last two decades rendered the present amount of leisure totally inadequate. The current daily and weekly rest pauses were insufficient; a worker needed a complete break of several consecutive days at least once a year. In the TUC's view, adequate opportunities for extended rest could not be provided by the free time of the evening, the weekend and the occasional day or two off from work during the year.

The need for more leisure had increased in recent years, for work taxed people's energies far more than in times past. More and more production processes had been mechanized, and in many trades the result was the substitution of 'speedy, repetitive and wholly uninspiring processes for the exercise of individual craftsmanship'. But, even in trades little affected by automation, work had become considerably more onerous: 'The most significant change is that change itself has become more rapid and frequent. Industry today is constantly meeting change. Indeed, it purposely seeks and creates it.' The effect was to impose on workers and managers alike the strain of constant adjustment and readjustment. Change ought not to be obstructed, for it arose 'from the need for new and better products, and industry must always be ready and able to adapt itself to new demands'. Even so:

> If industry is to be able, readily and quickly and with the minimum of wasted material and effort, to turn to new

> products, it must employ workpeople who are not only physically fit but also mentally alert. The continued failure of industry to afford its workpeople proper opportunities for recuperation ... will surely eventually react as unfavourably on the health of industry as it does on the health of its employees.

The health and efficiency argument was pressed particularly strongly by the South Wales Miners' Federation, whose statement contained some detailed statistics of fatalities, serious injuries and sickness absence, along with a graphic description of the arduous and hazardous nature of work underground. The few holidays they had were broken up into a few days here and there, regardless of the recommendations of the Samuel Commission in 1926.

There was some reference, albeit brief, to the socio-psychological benefit of annual holidays; they provided 'for opportunities to engage in activities more satisfying ... to individual inclinations ... [and] for the possibility ... of the freely chosen development of the human personality, often more recuperative than rest itself ... An employed person is not merely a machine to be kept in reasonable working order, but a human being with a life of his own to be lived and enjoyed.'

The TUC countered the claim, made by a few employers, that the postwar reductions in basic weekly working hours were sufficient to offset whatever additional strain had been caused by the intensification of the work pace:

> It is now eighteen years since there was any general reduction in working hours for industrial workpeople. In that time, many industrial processes have changed completely in character, new processes have been developed and the pace of industrial activity has increased. It can hardly be said that a reduction of hours effected eighteen years ago to meet the conditions of that time is a satisfactory off-set to conditions that have arisen since.

On the contrary, the postwar hours reductions had themselves been more than offset by the acceleration of the pace of work and the increases in productivity per person employed.

Holidays, the TUC went on to argue, would be of little use unless they were 'with pay'; without it, the great majority of workers would find it impossible to enjoy proper rest and worry-free relaxation, for being on holiday would be no different from being unemployed: 'No-one thinks of an unemployed person as being on holiday. Leisure without income, in fact, is more often an occasion for added strain and a cause of deterioration than an opportunity for recuperation and development.' Many people on low rates of pay found it difficult to meet their ordinary expenses; to expect them to save enough during the year to pay their normal household bills when on holiday leave was unrealistic; to assume that the average workman could accumulate sufficient savings to take his family away for a seaside holiday was preposterous.

The trade unions accepted that providing paid holidays for workpeople would add to the employer's labour costs, but labour costs, they argued, were only part of total production costs and would be at least partially offset by the increases in productivity and output which would follow. As one of the mining unions asserted in its statement to the Amulree Committee: 'We believe that an annual holiday with pay would not, in the long run, be a loss to the employer or to the industry, as the workers would be more renewed with increased vigour, and the result would be increased efficiency in their work, and less loss of time in consequence of sickness.' The point was reiterated, in the TUC's memorandum of supplementary evidence:

> The costs to a concern which does not grant ... holidays with pay and the benefits to a concern which does, may not always be directly perceived ... but they are real nonetheless. If the benefits of adequate holidays in the form of healthier and more efficient workpeople could be directly perceived and measured, it would probably be seen that holidays with pay, far from being a disadvan-

tage in competition with others, yield, in fact, a competitive advantage.

The aggregate cost of providing paid holidays for the nation's workforce, according to estimates produced by the financial experts, would add roughly 4.0 per cent to the total wages bill. This, the TUC witnesses argued, was not an exorbitant amount, and was not beyond the employers' present means. Moreover, the actual increase in labour costs would probably be less than 4.0 per cent.

The estimated increase had taken no account of the number of wage-workers already receiving a fortnight's paid holiday, nor of the number whose period of paid holiday simply needed to be increased to the full fortnight sought by the TUC. Around four million manual workers already received pay at the time of their annual holidays, and the estimated cost ought to be correspondingly reduced. Another important point, given some emphasis by the TUC's witnesses, was that the nation's total wages bill included all the cash components of the worker's pay packet; but the calculation of holiday pay was usually related to basic or regular earnings – supplementary components of pay, such as overtime earnings and special bonuses, were usually excluded when employers calculated the worker's holiday pay. At the same time, it was standard practice for the employee to work at his or her place of employment for a qualifying period of time before becoming eligible to receive holiday pay; again, the cost to be borne by employers would be reduced by a corresponding amount. In other words, the actual total cost would be less than 4.0 per cent of a sum smaller than the total wages bill.

The TUC's representatives offered further elaboration. Drawing upon statistical evidence contained in *Further Facts in Industrial and Commercial Efficiency*, they pointed out that in 1928 the lowest wage costs, as a proportion of total production costs, were 4.7 per cent in the manufacture of steel billets and 7.6 per cent in the production of steel ingots. The highest wage costs, amounting to 74.3 per cent, were in coalmining; and the next highest, at 46.1 per cent, were in the gas industry. In the spinning and weaving branches of the textile trades, the range was from 12.8 per cent to 21.5 per cent. These, and many other figures cited by the TUC, related to the situation which obtained in 1927 and 1928; today's figures would be lower, as a consequence of recent productivity improvements. The Fourth Census of Production in 1930 had disclosed that total wages relative to the sales value of total output varied from 4.7 per cent in the drink and tobacco industries to 31.0 per cent in mechanical engineering; industries with wage costs in excess of 40.0 per cent were rare; the average was somewhere in the region of 20.0 per cent. Even in coalmining, the main exception, wage costs had fallen to 64.0 per cent by 1936. In industries with wage costs as high as 50.0 per cent, an additional 4.0 per cent on the wages bill would increase total costs by only 2.0 per cent; where wage costs were as low as 10.0 per cent, the effect of a 4.0 per cent rise would be a fractional 0.4 per cent increase in aggregate production costs.

Cost increases such as these, the TUC believed, were neither excessive nor unaffordable for British industry. Even if paid holidays were to add the full 4.0 per cent on wages, the cost was not beyond the realms of practical possibility, given the steady rise in profits in recent years. An analysis of costs and profits in industries covered by the Import Duties Inquiry disclosed that profits, as a percentage of the wages bill, had increased in those industries from 54.5 per cent in 1930 to 66.9 per cent in 1934. An article in *The Economist*, analysing the performance of over 2000 manufacturing companies, indicated an increase in average dividend on ordinary shares from 5.8 per cent in 1933 to 8.2 per cent in 1936. There was similar evidence of the rising trend in profits in contemporary issues of *The Times*.

A second set of reasons, mentioned only briefly and tentatively at first, embodied the unions' resentment that employers discriminated against the manual worker in the matter of provision for paid holidays, whereas non-manual groups were treated preferentially: 'Commercial and professional people and well-to-do sections of the community have long enjoyed [paid holidays] ... as a matter of course. The working class has not, unfortunately, as a general rule, possessed such an advantage.' The advantaged groups were identified as 'the majority of salaried employees, clerks and, to a lesser extent, employees on "standing wages" in industry, commerce and public services generally, shop assistants ... and the staffs of hospitals and institutions'. Difference in the treatment of manual and non-manual grades was thus acknowledged, but there was no direct demand at this stage for equalization as a principle of social justice, and it seems likely that the TUC thought it wise to lead with arguments calculated to be most persuasive and appealing. Its testimony, couched in firm but respectful terms, suggested that employers had a great deal to gain by providing paid holidays for their manual workforces who, in consequence, would be more efficient, alert, cheerful and productive; the company's profits and competitiveness would improve.

The representatives of the National Federation of Colliery Enginemen, Boilermen and Mechanics were rather more outspoken.[15] At present, they noted, all officials, foremen and office staffs in the mining industry had paid holidays but other workers were denied them; in other words, 'those ... who are earning the highest wages, and are best able to afford holidays, get holidays with pay' whereas 'those who cannot afford holidays get none at all'. Salaried employees in industry, manufacturing and commerce generally received paid holidays, and did so at a cost to the employer and at manual workers' expense: 'The cost of their holidays is a charge on their industry ... and other workers who do not get holidays must ... contribute to the cost of giving holidays with pay to others. This, we believe, is unfair ...'

There was even less reticence on the part of the South Wales Miners' Federation, whose spokesmen explicitly demanded equality with the salaried as a matter of social justice. The declaration, that unequal provision of paid holidays was no longer socially justifiable, was simple and direct, and devoid of reassuring assertions about the improved productivity that employers stood to gain. Their class-conscious resentment at their treatment as second-class citizens was cogently expressed:

> We see no reason why the men who usually do the hard physical work of our community, and who are generally paid the least wages, should be treated in this respect less favourably than men who are usually much better remunerated, who are generally employed in more congenial work, and who live in more pleasant surroundings. We think that the time has arrived when the traditional idea, that only salaried persons should have holidays with pay, must be eradicated from our minds, and it should now be accepted that persons who render useful service to the community should, in this respect, receive equal consideration.[16]

The South Wales miners wanted the boon that their regional industry's office staffs had enjoyed for many years: 'It is generally the practice in the South Wales coal industry to grant under-officials and all the clerical staff two weeks' holiday with pay. The higher officials probably get ... longer holidays.'

The convictions, forcefully expressed by spokesmen for workers in coalmining, were given further emphasis in the TUC's memorandum of supplementary evidence, submitted on 1 December. The tone of the supplementary memorandum was quite different from the tenor of the first statement made on behalf of the TUC; it was more aggressive, more assertive, and a good deal less apologetically polite. The probable cause of the change of mood was twofold. First, Walter Citrine had been subjected to rigorous cross-examination in which some committee members had asked penetrating questions with a view to exposing the weaknesses of the unions' case; sharp questioning needed to be countered by even sharper answers, and by stronger statements in order to give punch to their argument. Second, the opponents' case had now been given; the TUC now knew exactly what it was up against, and the social justice aspect was clearly a weakness in the employers' defence of the status quo:

> The General Council are entirely unable to accept the view that existing holiday periods for the great majority of industrial workpeople are sufficient to enable them to take the amount of rest and recuperation they require. If comparison is made between the manual wage-earner and the non-manual salaried employee, it will be found that non-manual employees generally work less hours, receive higher pay, perform less physically exacting and onerous tasks, and are more secure and permanent in their employment than are manual workpeople. In addition, they are paid for holidays considerably in excess of those granted to manual workpeople ... It is difficult to see how this persistent and comprehensive distinction between the manual and the non-manual worker can be justified. If the existing holidays of manual employees are sufficient to enable them to take the rest and recreation they require, it is clear that there are very many people indeed whose holidays are far too excessive to be good for themselves, or for the country.[17]

The demand for equal treatment surfaced again when workers' representatives were asked their opinion on the idea of financing paid holidays by a contributory arrangement. The proposal was resisted on the ground that such a scheme would 'perpetuate the undesirable distinction between black-coated workers and productive workers.' Their view was that manual wage-earners should 'receive holidays with pay as a right, exactly in the same way as salaried employees', and that there was 'no justification for making the one class achieve it only by a contributory scheme'.

If the TUC's spokesmen made effective use of their evidence in comparing holiday provision for manual and non-manual grades in Britain, they made far more extensive use of evidence comparing provision in Britain with arrangements in many other countries. Here lies a third set of reasons to support their demand for action by the British Government. Much was made of the fact that a supposedly advanced country such as Britain was lagging far behind; not only were countries at a similar stage of economic development ahead of Britain in terms of arrangements for paid holidays, but even so-called backward countries had better standards. Britain, it was urged, ought to be in the van of progress, not trailing in the rear: 'We cannot fail to note that 38 other countries have legislation ... for at least some categories of workers, whilst we are without any such legislation at all. We do not think it a wise policy ... for Britain to continue to lag behind other countries in this matter.' Most of the legislation currently in operation elsewhere had been passed in response to the ILO's Convention on payment for holidays: 'By 1936, 38 State members of the ILO had passed legislation ... for all or certain categories of workpeople.' The leaders in continental Europe were Belgium, France and Italy, but even China, Peru, Latvia, Mexico and Uruguay had taken action to comply with the standards established in the international Convention.

Some critics had argued, on the Government's behalf, that Britain's comparative backwardness in the matter of legislation for paid holidays was to be explained, and excused, by her more advanced national insurance arrangements to assist the unemployed, the sick and the elderly. The TUC was not convinced by this argument, for the ILO had released statistics which showed that the contribution from employers to social insurance, as a percentage of wages per insured worker, was less in Britain than in France, Germany, Austria, Poland and Czechoslovakia, all of which had some form of legislation for paid holidays. National arrangements for paid holidays and national arrangements for social insurance against unemployment and ill health could not be convincingly represented as alternatives; a progressive country with an enlightened government ought to have both.

The TUC's witnesses provided long and detailed descriptions of legislation in other countries. In doing so, they probably missed their intended mark, for some of the governments, including those of Nazi Germany and Communist Russia, whose 'enlightened' paid holiday arrangements were presented as models to be emulated in Britain, were anything but enlightened in other respects.

The TUC had learned from the struggle over the 1919 Hours Convention, however, and had accepted by now that attempts to secure compliance with rigid regulations to control hours of work were doomed to failure. With this in mind, they sought to persuade the Committee, and the Government, of the flexibility of a proposed measure whose underlying principle was intentionally coercive and anything but flexible.

The legislation they outlined was intended to apply to the country's workforce in general. Although collective bargaining had made some headway, the majority of manual workers were without paid holidays. Certain groups – the unorganized, the weakly organized, and those in trades where employment was characteristically taken up with a succession of different firms – would never gain paid holidays unless the employers in question were statutorily obligated to provide them. Perhaps the TUC weakened its own case; for in focusing on the disadvantage of trades without, or with only weak, trade union representation to reach collective agreements on the issue, it undermined its argument for general legislation to cover all and sundry. Unions that had proved themselves capable of negotiating collective agreements for the first week of paid holiday were presumably equally capable of gaining the second week on the same basis.

The TUC's witnesses recognized that it would be necessary to have special arrangements for some industries, such as building and construction, where workers were not permanently attached to one firm but took jobs with a series of different building contractors, often shifting from one locality to another. They asserted that this problem could be resolved without too much difficulty; the Ministry of Labour could set up a centralized fund for the industry in question, along the lines of arrangements already in operation in France and Belgium, and with an administrative structure similar to Britain's unemployment insurance scheme for the collection of employers' contributions and disbursement of workpeople's holiday pay. The TUC's recommendation exposed yet another weak spot in its argument for a general statutory measure, whose regulations would be administered, monitored and even implemented by a government department. In some of the trades with shifting employment, such as building, engineering, construction and dock work, both the employers and the workers had long traditions of organization and of collective bargaining. The two sides were surely capable of negotiating on paid holidays and of setting up centrally administered funds themselves. The absence of paid holidays across large sections of these industries reflected bargaining priorities. As the Amulree report acknowledged, the question of paid holidays was inextricably entangled with the question of wage rates. The TUC was well aware that such was the case. Relatively good rates of pay in engineering and parts of the building industry, by the standards of the time, suggest that the bargaining preference had been increased rates of pay rather than paid holidays.

All of this directed attention to the propriety, or otherwise, of government intervention by Act of Parliament in the settlement of wages. Wages were normally set by collective agreement or by a statutory wage-fixing body where organization was weak. Employers asserted that government intervention would undermine the British tradition of voluntary negotiation; in other words, it was not the Government's place to intervene nationwide in settlement of wages. The TUC's counter-argument was not entirely convincing, for it amounted to little more than an assertion that, as the state already intervened in several spheres of social welfare, a bit more intervention was neither here nor there. They were on firmer ground in pointing to the extensive intervention from the Government in response to employers' demands for assistance; for there was 'scarcely an industry which has not sought and received direct help from the state since 1930'. If the Government was prepared to intervene on behalf of employers, it should be prepared to do likewise for labour.

The TUC had a fair point in claiming that the distinction between state intervention for paid holidays and state intervention in other matters affecting the welfare of a large portion of the community was one of *degree*, not one of *principle*. This, in fact, was crucial to their case for legislation to generalize holidays with pay, and it needed to be argued cogently, lucidly, and, most of all, logically. In the event, their resort was to hector and bluster. The declaration, that 'workpeople have a right to expect from the state protection and assistance at least comparable to that which is nowadays accorded to the great majority of employers', conveniently overlooked the extension of social insurance, the jobs created by public works schemes, and the retraining programmes, introduced by the Government during the recession. The logic that linked state intervention to compel parents to send their children to school, with state intervention to compel employers to grant paid holidays, is dubious to say the least.

The legislation proposed by the TUC contained all the main provisions of the ILO's Convention and Recommendations of 1936. The main difference lay in the amount of holiday, for the unions sought twelve working days exclusive of bank and public holidays, instead of the one week prescribed by the ILO. Unless circumstances were 'exceptional', the fortnight's holiday was to be taken in one unbroken spell, and paid at not less than the minimum wage rate set by collective agreement or the relevant wage-regulating body. The full holiday with pay would be conditional upon twelve months' continuous service; and service would not be deemed 'broken' if employment was interrupted by 'sickness, accident, family events, military service, the exercise of civil rights, involuntary unemployment, or change of management ...' Another important clause stated that: 'Any agreement to relinquish the right to, or to forego, such holiday shall be void.' There were two other major clauses, one to permit voluntary agreements for better than the legal minimum, and another to impose penalties on employers failing to comply with their legal obligation: they would be compelled to keep proper records so that their compliance could be monitored.

The TUC was optimistic about the likely outcome of the Amulree inquiry. The unions had presented a great deal of carefully researched factual and statistical evidence in what was for the most part a cogently argued case for legislation on paid holidays; and they were heartened by the fact that their own nominated representatives on the committee were not outnumbered by the employers' nominees.

Notes

1. Pimlott, J.A.R. (1976), *The Englishman's Holiday: A Social History*, Hassocks, Harvester, ch. 8.
2. Information on holidays for these groups is given in: Select Committee on Bank Holidays, *BPP*, 1867–8, Vol. VII, Minutes of Evidence, May 4, 11, 18, 25; *Report of the Select Committee on the Bank Holidays Bill*, 22 June 1868; Civil Service Inquiry Commission, *First Report*, 1875, C. 1113–1, Appendix G.
3. Board of Trade (1906), *Earnings and Hours Inquiry*.
4. Bienefeld, M.A. (1972), *Working Hours in British Industry: An Economic History*, London, Weidenfeld & Nicolson; Reid, D.A. (1976), 'The Decline of Saint Monday, 1766–1876', *Past and Present*, No. 71, pp. 76–101.
5. The full titles of the two Acts were: 'An Act to make provisions for Bank Holidays, and respecting obligations to make payments and do other acts on such Bank Holidays [25th May 1871]' and 'An Act to extend to the Docks, Customs Houses, Inland Revenue Offices, and Bonding Warehouses in England and Ireland certain provisions of the Bank Holidays Act, 1871, and to amend the same [13th May 1875]'. Both Acts listed the scheduled days; Scotland's schedule of bank holidays included: Christmas Day, New Year's Day (or the next following Mondays to be taken in lieu, if these two fell on a Sunday), Good Friday, the first Monday of May, and the first Monday of August.
6. Walton, J.K. (1981), 'The Demand for Working-Class Seaside Holidays in Victorian England', *Economic History Review*, 2nd Series, Vol. XXXIV, No. 2, pp.249–65; Walton, J.K. and Poole, R. (1982), 'The Lancashire Wakes in the Nineteenth Century' in Storch, R.D. (ed.), *Popular Culture and Custom in Nineteenth Century England*, Manchester, University Press.
7. Trades Union Congress (1912), *Annual Report*, p.288, repeats the previous year's resolution; TUC Parliamentary Committee (March 1912), *Eleventh Quarterly Report*, TUC Parliamentary Deputations to Ministers (Thursday 15 February 1912), Discus-

sion with the Prime Minister on Pay for Statutory Holidays, pp.20–2.

8. Trades Union Congress (1913), *Annual Report*, p.320.
9. *Ibid.* (1919), p.375.
10. *Ibid.* (1925), pp.529, 574; (1926), pp.471, 506.
11. *Ibid.* (1929), pp.224–5, 390–1.
12. *Ibid.* (1931), p.128.
13. *Ibid.* (1933), p.278.
14. The TUC's case was outlined in two major written statements. See Departmental Committee on Holidays with Pay, *Minutes of Evidence* (1937–8), Memorandum of Evidence by the Trades Union Congress, 8 June 1937, pp.22–8, and Memorandum of Supplementary Evidence by the General Council of the Trades Union Congress, 1 December 1937, pp.394–7. Quotations are from these two documents, unless otherwise indicated.
15. Memorandum of Evidence by the National Federation of Colliery Enginemen, Boilermen and Mechanics, 3 November 1937, pp.294–7.
16. Memorandum of Evidence by the South Wales Miners' Federation, 16 November 1937, pp.309–10.
17. Memorandum of Supplementary Evidence by the General Council of the Trades Union Congress, 1 December 1937, pp.394–7.

3

Change in the Basic Working Week and Paid Holidays, 1900–39

Introduction

Circumstances in the first four decades of the twentieth century did not provide the best of contexts for the shortening of the standard working week and the introduction of paid holidays. There were brief periods conducive to gains through collective bargaining, before and immediately after the First World War and again towards the end of the 1930s; but otherwise the TUC's struggle to reduce working time made little headway. Conservative-dominated governments were not won over by the proponents of general legislation to reduce the basic working week and to give entitlement to paid holidays to the working population as a whole; only the Labour Party, which was never in a position to act effectively on these issues, was sympathetic to the unions' claims.

Government and the Question of General Legislation to Shorten the Working Week

The Government was not driven to legislate for shorter working hours across the whole of Britain in the first decade and a half of the twentieth century, despite the unions' demonstrations, rallies, petitioning and lobbying of Members of Parliament. During the First World War, the Health of Munition Workers Committee, headed first by Seebohm

Rowntree and later by Dr Collis, advised, among other things, regular rest pauses and avoidance of excessively long working hours in order that the vital work of the war effort might be maintained for as long as the emergency lasted.[1] Workpeople and the trade unions were afterwards 'rewarded' for their wartime sacrifices with hours reductions and pay increases in the immediate postwar years when circumstances were favourable to the negotiation of improvements.

Following the First World War, a number of pressures during the brief period of economic prosperity led to the quite widespread adoption of the 47- or 48-hour week; numerous agreements to reduce the basic working week, often in combination with substantial pay rises, and in some cases paid holidays also, were reached in 1919 and 1920. There seem to have been four main factors conducive to the shortening of basic working time.

First, the boom, brief though it was, created a favourable economic environment. With encouraging profit performance, employers could more comfortably absorb any cost increase resulting from the shortening of the basic working week, and productivity rises, by reducing unit costs, had a similar effect. The same environment gave the trade unions a stronger labour market position to secure improvements, for the sudden upsurge of unemployment which they had expected did not immediately materialize.

Second, following the Whitley Committee's recommendations on the means to create peaceable industrial relations and general well-being in the workplace, joint industrial councils and similar bodies, termed interim industrial reconstruction committees, were set up in several industries, and trade board regulation was extended to greater numbers under the 1918 Trade Boards Act. Voluntary agreements and trade board directions for hours reductions were therefore given wider application. Automation and rationalization, which further raised productivity,[2] permitted the retention during the depression of most of the hours cuts gained in the good years.

Third, the idea of the shorter basic working week was broadly supported by the government of the day; it was 'viewed as a concession worth making to the unions in order to assist in the reconversion of industry to peacetime operations and to aid postwar industrial recovery'.[3] Industrial unrest in 1917, which escalated in 1919, 1920 and 1921 with around 35 million, 26½ million and nearly 86 million days lost, respectively, through strike action, underlined the need to pacify industrial relations; and the investigations into industrial fatigue, conducted by the Ministry of Munitions during the war, had disclosed some of the problems caused by prolonged hours of labour. All of this may explain the Government's initially favourable attitude to the 1919 Washington Hours Convention before the rosy glow of postwar relief and euphoria over the termination of the war faded. Interwar British governments did not ratify the Convention, but they were not obdurately against hours reductions where circumstances permitted. Although, with the exception of Labour governments, they were unwilling to impose a statutory upper limit on working time generally, they were prepared to pass a certain amount of sectional legislation for specific groups, to allow hours improvements negotiated in the process of collective bargaining, and to condone hours cuts in government establishments on that basis. It was the Government that presided over the establishment of the 7-hour day for underground coalminers by legislation in 1919, superseding the 1908 Act for the 8-hour day; and, again, the Government intervened to increase the miners' day to 8 hours after the 1926 General Strike, before adjusting it to 7½ hours in 1930. It was the Government, also, that endorsed the 8-hour day for railway workers in December 1918 soon after the cessation of the war and while the railways were still under government control.[4]

Fourth, shorter working time was being strongly pressed by the trade unions after the war, and some were prepared to back their claims with industrial action. There were strikes in the main heavy engineering and shipbuilding centres for the 44-hour or the 40-hour week, but many major industries managed to negotiate a basic week of 47 or 48 hours without disputes.

It was not until 1924, when postwar progress seemed to have run its course, that the TUC began its campaign for ratification of the 1919 Washington Convention by the British Government. The 1924 Labour Government, precariously and briefly in office, was in no position to give practical expression to its sympathies on the hours question.

Conservative governments' representatives at the ILO's annual meetings either opposed working-time Conventions or abstained from voting, although they were prepared to support Recommendations which would leave ILO member states free to introduce measures appropriate to their own social, cultural, institutional and administrative traditions. The 1919 Hours Convention was subsequently felt to be too rigid and far too simplistic to be effectively, fairly and equally implemented worldwide. The Government's concern to preserve British sovereignty, coupled with an unwillingness to have British employers constrained by a yoke constructed externally when there was no guarantee that employers in other countries would be similarly yoked, goes some way in explaining its caution. The London Conference of the labour ministers of leading European countries, convened by the British Government in 1926, attempted to resolve the very real difficulties likely to arise in attempting to put the Convention into effect. There were problems of defining terms and concepts, of interpreting the wording of the various clauses, and of identifying the means of implementing, administering and organizing the specifics in diverse and often variable types of employment.

Agreement was reached on all the major points raised at the London Conference, but the British Government was still not prepared to take the risk of introducing general legislation. To pass an Act of Parliament in the face of universal opposition from employers would have been politically suicidal. The risk of alienating the working class electorate by failing to legislate on working-time was not alarmingly great; the TUC's own evidence showed that, through collective bargaining, many workpeople already had the Convention's basic working week of 48 hours, and that some had even shorter hours. The

Labour Government of 1929, it is true, did introduce an Hours of Industrial Employment Bill, but the prospective legalization of the terms of the Washington Convention did not arouse enthusiastic excitement among the unions, for they recognized that the Convention and the Bill were already outdated and unlikely to be effective as a means to ameliorating unemployment, whether in Britain or anywhere else. The Bill failed.

When, in 1933, the British Government refused to support a new International Convention for the 40-hour week, its main objection was that British employers would find it impossible to shorten the basic working week while at the same time maintaining basic weekly wages at their current levels; if wages fell as a result of a Government-enforced hours reduction, there would be industrial strife. Moreover, legislation would override and weaken Britain's system of voluntary collective bargaining. The Government was not persuaded that a general limitation of working hours would have a major impact on the general level of unemployment. It was for this reason, among others, that the Minister of Labour called for more investigation, more information and more discussion, both internationally and in Britain, of current hours of work, the probable cost of reducing them without also reducing wages, and of the composition of the unemployed.

In the 1930s the Minister of Labour was in frequent consultation with the Employers' Confederation and the TUC. The question of hours reductions, he frequently asserted, needed to be tackled industry by industry. At a meeting with the full General Council of the TUC in January 1935, he raised several pertinent questions on the means to absorb the unemployed into work:

(i) Could it be said that every vacancy, however created, could be filled from the ranks of the unemployed, no matter what craft or special skill was involved?
(ii) What were the facts regarding the efficiency of unemployed men today, after, in many cases, long periods of unemployment?

(iii) How far was there any real shortage of skilled workers in the different trades?
(iv) Had industries themselves fallen behind in their provision for training young people for skilled occupations?
(v) What would be the real effect upon unemployment of raising the school-leaving age?[5]

On the question of working hours, the Minister of Labour requested precise information on TUC policy with regard to wages in the context of hours reductions. In February of 1935 he notified the TUC General Council of a number of questions he wished to discuss industry by industry:

(i) the extent to which existing vacancies cannot be filled owing to the geographical distribution of the unemployed and inability to secure workpeople of the kind required where vacancies exist;
(ii) the actual or potential shortage of trained workpeople and the steps being taken or required for remedying this position, both as regards the present and the future;
(iii) the extent to which, for other reasons such as age or physical fitness, vacancies had not been filled;
(iv) the determination of the effective labour supply among the unemployed nominally attached to various industries;
(v) the possibility of increasing the number employed by reducing hours of work, limitation of overtime, rotation of shifts, standing off at intervals, or by regular holidays, and the probable effect on wages and costs of such measures;
(vi) special problems affecting the employment of women and juveniles, including the question of the age of recruitment in the various industries.[6]

The British Government's investigations of hours of work and unemployment petered out with gradual recovery of the economy and the fall in the numbers out of work. The annual wrangle on hours Conventions continued at ILO conferences, until the issue was abandoned with the onset of the Second World War.

Many of the issues raised by the Government on the question of general legislation to limit hours of work were fundamentally important and in need of sensible and sensitive attention; but government ministers were all too often guilty of procrastination and of fobbing the TUC off with weak and time-wasting excuses. The Board of Trade, the Ministry of Labour and the Labour Exchanges already had much of the information alleged to be 'not yet available' or requiring 'further investigation'. The possibility of using a statutory limitation of working hours to ameliorate unemployment was never considered seriously – even as a temporary, short-term emergency measure. There were interwar attempts at job creation through public works schemes, but, for the most part, the Government relied on the national unemployment insurance scheme to deal with the problem. Most of the reductions in working time from 1900 to 1939 were the outcome of collective bargaining. The unions would never again pin such high hopes on general legislation to regulate the hours of labour.

The Shortening of the Basic Working Week

From the beginning of the century trade union action to shorten working time was extensive, intensive and continuous, particularly during the interwar recession. The main gains were confined to years of comparative prosperity, with the coincidence of rising productivity, buoyant trade, and labour market circumstances which gave the unions some bargaining clout.

The basic 54-hour week had become widespread in the late nineteenth century. Although by 1906 a working week of 55 hours or more still obtained in some spheres of employment, many workpeople had gained a basic week of 52 or 53 hours (Table 1). In most major centres of the printing industry, compositors, who had begun the new century with a working week of 52 or 53 hours, had gained reductions to 50 or 51 hours by 1914 on the basis of local agreements; soon after the

TABLE 1
Average Hours, Excluding Overtime, Worked in a Full Week: All Manual Workers, 1906

Industry	Hours worked
Cotton	55.5
Woollen & worsted	55.6
Linen	55.1
Jute	55.0
Silk	54.5
Hosiery	53.9
Lace	53.2
Carpet	55.3
Hemp	54.1
Smallwares	54.0
Flock & shoddy	55.7
Bleaching, printing, etc.	55.7
Dress, millinery, etc.	53.4
Shirt, blouse, underclothing, etc	50.2
Tailoring (bespoke)	53.8
Tailoring (ready-made)	51.2
Boot & shoe	53.5
Road, sanitary, etc. services (Borough & U.D. Councils)	54.4
Road, sanitary, etc. services (County & R.D. Councils)	55.6
Gas supply	52.6
Electricity supply	51.9
Water supply	55.1
Saw milling, etc.	54.4
Cabinet making, etc.	53.1
Pig iron	55.2
Iron & steel	54.4
Tinplate	47.8
Engineering & boilermaking	53.1
Ship & boat building & repair	52.9
Railway carriage & wagon building	53.6
Light iron castings, etc.	53.8
Electrical, telegraph, etc. apparatus	52.4
Brass & allied metal trades	52.7
Grain milling	58.1
Baking & confectionery	55.9
Malting & brewing	54.9

TABLE 1 – continued

Industry	Hours worked
Cocoa, chocolate & sugar confectionery	51.9
Sugar refining	58.7
Aerated water & general bottling	54.1
Spirit distilling	57.4
Tobacco, cigarettes	49.6
Paper manufacture	56.9
Printing	51.6
Bookbinding	51.0
Paper stationery manufacture	52.1
Porcelain, china & earthenware	52.5
Brick, tile, pipe, etc.	55.4
Chemical manufacture	55.9
Explosives	50.5
Leather, tanning, fellmongering, etc.	55.4
Coach, carriage, van, etc. building	54.5
Harbour & dock services	57.1
Laundry service	54.7

Derived from: *British Labour Statistics: Historical Abstract, 1886–1968*, London, HMSO, 1971, Table 36, pp.94–5.

war the 48-hour week became standard, and remained so until the establishment of the 45-hour week in the late 1930s (Table 2). In the engineering industry, there was very little change from the 53 or 54 hours worked per week in 1900 in the main towns and cities, until the achievement of a standard 47-hour week by 1920; there were no further reductions to the end of the 1930s (Table 3). In the footwear industry, the 54-hour week, which was general in the larger centres of the trade in 1906, was reduced to 52½ hours by 1910; the basic week of 48 hours, established soon after the war, had been further shortened to 46 hours by 1938 (Table 4). Normal hours worked in the furniture trade varied from place to place quite widely in 1900, ranging from 48 hours in Manchester to 54

TABLE 2
Normal Weekly Working Hours in the Printing Industry: Compositors, 1900–38

	1900 January	1906 October	1914 October	1920 April	1930 April	1938 April
London	54	52½	50	48	48	45
Manchester	50	50	50	48	48	45
Liverpool	51	51	51	48	48	45
Birmingham	52	52	51	48	48	45
Newcastle	53	52	51	48	48	45
Hull	53	53	51	48	48	45
Leeds	52½	52½	51	48	48	45
Glasgow	52½	50	50	48	48	45
Aberdeen	51	50	50	48	48	45
Dundee	51	50/51	49	48	48	45
Edinburgh	52½	52½	50	48	48	45
Cardiff	52½	52½	51	48	48	45
Belfast	52½	52½	51	48	48	45

Derived from: *British Labour Statistics: Historical Abstract, 1886–1968*, London, HMSO, 1971, Table 4, pp.34–5.

TABLE 3
Normal Weekly Working Hours in the Engineering Industry: Fitters and Turners, 1900–14; Fitters, Turners and Labourers, 1920–38

	1900 January	1906 January	1910 October	1914 October	1920 April	1938 April
London	54	54/48	54/48	54/48	47	47
Manchester	53	53	53	53	47	47
Liverpool	53	53	53	53	47	47
Birmingham	53	53	48	50/53	47	47
Sheffield	54	54/48	53/48	53/48	47	47
Glasgow	54	54	54	54	47	47
Cardiff	53	53	53	53	47	47
Belfast	54	54/56½	54/56½	54/56½	47	47

Derived from: *British Labour Statistics: Historical Abstract, 1886–1968*, London, HMSO, 1971, Table 1, pp.28–9.

TABLE 4
Normal Weekly Working Hours in Footwear Manufacture: Adult Male Workers, 1906–38

	1906 October	1910 October	1914 October	1920 April	1930 April	1938 April
London	54	52½	52½	48	48	46
Northampton	54	52½	52½	48	48	46
Newcastle	54	52½	52½	48	48	46
Kettering	54	52½	52½	48	48	46
Leeds	54	52½	52½	48	48	46
Leicester	54	52½	52½	48	48	46
Bristol	54	52½	52½	48	48	46
Glasgow	54	52½	52½	48	48	46

Derived from: *British Labour Statistics: Historical Abstract, 1886–1968*, London, HMSO, 1971, Table 6, p.37.

TABLE 5
Normal Weekly Working Hours in Furniture Manufacture: Journeymen Cabinetmakers, 1900–38

	1900 January	1906 January	1910 October	1914 October	1920 January	1924 January	1938 January
London	52½	50/52½	50	48/52½	47	47	47
Manchester	48	48/53	48	48	44/46½	46½	46½
Liverpool	50	47/54	47	46½/54	46½	44	44
Birmingham	54	54	54	54	47	47	47
Newcastle	50	50	50	50	44	44	44
Halifax	53	53	53	53	47	–	–
Preston	49½/54	52	49½/54	49½/53	46½	–	–
Leeds	49½	49½/51½	49½	49½/52½	47	44	44
Glasgow	51	51	51	51	47	47	47

Derived from: *British Labour Statistics: Historical Abstract, 1886–1968*, London, HMSO, 1971, Table 5, p.36.

hours in Birmingham. The range had been reduced to between 44 and 47 hours by 1920, and remained unchanged thereafter up to 1938 (Table 5). In the building industry, the bricklayers' working week varied locally from 49½ hours to 54½ hours in 1900. There was very little change until after the war when the 44-hour week became common, with, later, slightly longer hours during the summer months in a few places (Table 6).

Widespread, and in many cases substantial, hours reductions were achieved in 1919. In the *Ministry of Labour Gazette*[7] it was observed: 'Perhaps the most marked feature of the industrial situation in 1919 was the reduction which was effected in weekly working hours in the principal industries.' The hours commonly worked in these industries in 1918 ranged from 48 to 60 hours per week; by the end of 1919 the most usual range was from 44 to 48 hours. In that year alone, some 6½ million workpeople were reported to have received hours reductions amounting on average to 6½ hours per week. The long list of 'principal industries' thus affected

TABLE 6
Normal Weekly Working Hours in the Building Industry: Bricklayers, 1900–38

	1900 January	1906 October	1910 October	1914 October	1920 December		1926 April		1938 April	
	a	a	a	a	a	b	a	b	a	b
London	50	50	50	50	44	–	44	44	44	44
Manchester	54½	54½	54½	49½	44	44	46½	44	46½	44
Liverpool	49½	49½	46½	46½	44	–	44	44	44	44
Birmingham	54	54	51	49½	44	44	46½	44	46½	44
Newcastle	50	50	50	50	44	–	44	41½	44	41½
Leeds	49½	49½	49½	49½	44	44	46½	44	46½	44

a = summer months; b = winter months; there was considerable local variation in normal working hours in the winter period.

Derived from: *British Labour Statistics: Historical Abstract, 1886–1968*, London, HMSO, 1971, Table 2, pp.2–3.

included building, coalmining, iron and steel, engineering and shipbuilding, textiles and clothing, transport, paper and printing, glass, bricks and pottery, chemicals, and the public utility services. The Ministry of Labour's assessment of total numbers receiving hours cuts was undoubtedly an underestimate, for the calculation did not include agricultural workers, shop assistants, and the police, all of whom had also gained a shorter working week.

The most substantial reduction, of 13.7 hours per week on average, occurred in the iron and steel trades; other major reductions were won in transport, the public utility services, and textiles, amounting to cuts of 8.7, 7.6, and 7.0 hours respectively. A reduction of 6.3 hours was gained in the glass, brick and pottery trades, in the chemical industry, and in engineering and shipbuilding. In the printing trades the adoption of the 48-hour week involved a cut of 2 or 3 hours from the 50 or 51 hours worked formerly; the introduction of the 48-hour week in the cotton industry represented a 7-hour reduction from the 55-hour week worked before the war.

The wave of postwar reductions began in the engineering and shipbuilding trades whose working week of 53 or 54 hours was cut to 47 hours as from 1 January 1919, followed shortly by the introduction of similar arrangements in other metal-working industries. The 48-hour week was adopted in railway services at the beginning of February.

The shortening of hours was generally accomplished without a fall in wages. In almost every case the reduction in hours was subject to the condition that weekly time wages should not be reduced. For workers paid by the hour, the rates were either enhanced in the proportion by which the weekly hours were reduced, or increases in hourly rates were given, which resulted in a net increase in weekly wages. Piece rates were enhanced in proportion to the reduction in hours, while in other cases a small percentage increase was given. Likewise, for shift workers, the shift rate was either maintained or even slightly increased with a reduction of shift hours to 8. Other lesser cuts in working time, for smaller numbers, occurred in 1920.

TABLE 7
Normal Weekly Working Hours, 1924

Normal Weekly Working Hours of:	No. of trade union members covered by agreements:
40	24,500
42	800,600
44	305,687
46	8,500
46½	11,590
47	964,224
48	1,409,613

Total trade union membership: 4,688,609
Total members covered by agreements for 48 hours or less: 3,524,714
Percentage covered by agreements for 48 hours or less: 75.0%

Derived from: TUC, *Report*, 1924, p.188

Evidence, forwarded to TUC headquarters by affiliated unions, disclosed that by 1924 roughly three-quarters of the total trade union membership were covered by agreements for a basic working week of 48 hours or less (Table 7). Of the slightly more than 3½ million thus entitled, roughly 67.0 per cent had a normal week of 47 or 48 hours, and around 31.0 per cent had 42 or 44 hours. By 1935 a standard week of less than 50 hours was worked in all the major sectors of employment (Table 8).

Holidays With Pay: Early Advances

At the beginning of the twentieth century, holiday periods for the vast majority of manual workers were short and without pay. The paid holidays, given to the privileged minority by some of the paternalistic employers, were essentially a form of largesse – gifts 'benevolently' bestowed at the employers'

TABLE 8
Average Weekly Hours Worked: All Manual Workers, 1935

Industry	Hours Worked
Mining & quarrying (except coal)	45.7
Treatment of non-metalliferous mine & quarry products	49.6
Brick, pottery, glass, cement, etc.	48.0
Metal, engineering, etc.	48.2
Textiles	47.7
Leather	48.8
Clothing	45.4
Food, drink & tobacco	48.5
Woodworking	48.3
Paper, printing, stationery, etc.	48.6
Building, etc.	46.9
Other manufacturing industries	48.2
Public utility services	48.0
Government industrial establishments	49.7
Transport and storage	48.6
All the above industries	47.8

Derived from: *British Labour Statistics: Historical Abstract, 1886–1968*, London, HMSO, 1971, Table 38, p.96.

discretion; and they were usually conditional upon impeccable time-keeping, avoidance of unauthorized absence, and often upon 'good conduct' or 'satisfactory service'. The boon could be given or denied, according the supervisor's subjective assessment of the worker's worthiness. Evidence suggests that employers found arrangements of this kind instrumentally useful in curbing lateness and reducing absenteeism.[8] Days of holiday, whether paid or unpaid, were few. The Board of Trade's 1906 Earnings and Hours Inquiry disclosed that, on average, workpeople had 11 or 12 authorized days off annually, and that holidays ranged from 8½ days in chemicals, paper-printing, and food, drink and tobacco, to 9 days in the building trades, 10 in textiles, and 13 in engineering and iron and steel.[9]

It was not until the early twentieth century that provision for holidays with pay began to feature in, usually local, district or private, collective agreements in a few industries. This was a significant departure, for it acknowledged paid holidays as an appropriate subject for negotiation; the length of the holiday and the associated holiday pay became part of the wage-work bargain, and were no longer a 'gift' arbitrarily bestowed on the 'deserving', but a component of income earned by workers who chose to take part of their wage rise in the form of pay for the holiday period. An agreement gave 'entitlement' to all workers covered by its provisions for as long as it remained in force. Some of the earliest agreements, predating the First World War, were reached in certain sections of the railway industry, newspaper printing, and in the road, sanitary, and maintenance departments of local authorities.

A few more such agreements were made during the First World War, and significantly more followed in the period of relative prosperity from 1918 to 1922. It was at this stage that regional and national agreements began to appear alongside the local variety. This development was undoubtedly encouraged by the spread of Whitleyism, for there was a marked tendency for the principle of paid holidays to be adopted in industries in which national and regional joint industrial councils had been set up.[10] In 1919, when manual workers in most industries gained 'considerable wage increases and a substantially shorter standard working week', a number of agreements made that year included provision for paid holidays. In all, an estimated one million manual wage-workers were currently covered by such arrangements.[11] By 1920 the numbers had risen to an estimated two million.[12] At the close of 1922 the Ministry of Labour reported that there had been 'a further extension' of agreements on the subject since 1920, although no estimate of the total numbers with entitlement was given that year. The numbers had fallen to 1.5 million by 1925, and did not begin to rise again until 1937. The decline suggested by the 1925 figures[13] may be illusory, for while the 1920 estimates included those covered by 'less formal arrangements' as well as those with provision by 'formal collective agreements', the 1925 statistics exclude the former group. What is not in doubt is the failure of further growth during the decade and a half following 1922. During that time, new agreements were largely offset by the lapsing or abandonment of others. The decay of many of the joint industrial councils during the depression meant a weakening or dismantling of structures that had fostered the spread of agreements for paid holidays.

There was no wholesale abandonment of the practice of paying wages for the holiday period, even so. It was observed in the *Ministry of Labour Gazette* in 1929 that, although some of the earlier arrangements had now been modified or allowed to lapse, 'in the majority of cases the provisions have remained in force without alteration'.[14] This did not alter the fact, however, that 'the great majority of wage-earners in many of the largest industries are not paid for holidays'. Further investigations showed that the level of coverage obtaining in 1925 remained unchanged in 1932, 1934 and 1936.[15]

Many of the early agreements had been reached in industries and utility services operating under conditions of rising demand, or in relatively stable 'sheltered industries' unaffected by foreign competition, or industries where wage costs as a proportion of total production costs were comparatively low.[16] They were conspicuously absent, Cameron claims, in the otherwise favourable years from 1919 to 1922, in industries that had not set up a structure of joint industrial councils; these included all the major industries: textiles, iron and steel, engineering, shipbuilding, coalmining, building and construction, and agriculture. However, the hours restrictions and pay increases gained in these industries during the years in question suggest that it was the order of bargaining priorities rather than non-existence of joint industrial councils which explains the lack of payment for holiday periods.

In the absence of collective agreements and other kinds of formal arrangements, there were in many industries 'recommendations', which left employers with the flexibility of 'free choice' in the matter. Industries subject to the Trade Boards Acts of 1909 and 1918 did not issue formal 'directions' for paid holidays in the interwar years, but the trade board authorities for the brush and broom trade and one or two others did issue recommendations to that effect. In the 1920s and early 1930s several employers' organizations and the surviving joint industrial councils issued similar recommendations, leaving individual employers to act on their own initiative. Such recommendations, numerously cited in the *Ministry of Labour Gazette*, testify to the fact that many employers favoured paid holidays in principle but fought shy of making firm commitments on the basis of formal industry-wide or region-wide agreements, requiring their signatures on the dotted line, to introduce paid holidays at a specified time. The Minister of Labour noted in 1932 that 'provision for holiday payments is recognized by some employers' associations, although not actually embodied in agreements effected with workpeople's organizations'.[17] It was this random and diverse system, which benefited far too few workpeople, that the TUC was keen to replace by arrangements providing greater standardization, formalization and security.

If the limited extent of coverage of agreements for paid holidays was characteristic, so also was the diverse nature of the arrangements in operation. The majority of agreements provided payment for 'public holidays', usually six in number, and several provided for additional periods ranging from as few as three days to as many as twelve. Most of them had conditions attached. Payment was usually conditional on six or twelve months' continuous employment, and the amount of paid holiday sometimes varied according to length of service. The service qualification was occasionally 'linked with a stipulation regarding good time-keeping, absence without sufficient cause for more than a specified number of days during the qualifying period resulting in loss of payment for the holiday'. There were instances also of payment being made 'conditional on good conduct and the rendering of satisfactory service'.[18]

Such conditions persisted throughout the 1930s. The practice of making formal agreements through negotiation was forward-looking in its early indication of what would become general in years to come; but it was backward-looking in retaining vestigial traces of practice in times past. Apart from the Victorian style of 'good conduct' proviso, there were self-help kinds of schemes with holiday pay based entirely on workers' contributions or on joint contributions from the worker and the employer. The London type founders, for example, who worked a 50-hour week for fifty weeks in the year, were paid for only 48 hours per week, pay for the two extra hours accruing towards payment for a total of twelve days of holiday, including six public holidays and one full week's holiday. Similarly, in the baking trade in parts of Scotland, payment for holidays was made in lieu of payment for 'Sunday sponging'. In the boot and shoe trade, holiday pay was made up of equal weekly contributions, to a holiday fund, by the worker and the employer. Another such arrangement for joint contributions operated in lambswool and worsted yarn spinning in Leicester; and a similar, and in this case 'voluntary', scheme was in operation in the tanning and currying trade in London. In a few cases the amount of holiday pay was at a specified 'flat rate'; in most cases the worker received the basic weekly wage for the basic working week.[19]

It was the diverse and unequal nature of schemes for paid holidays, coupled with the failure of collective bargaining to increase coverage beyond the one-and-a-half million mark, that prompted Labour members in the House of Commons to take up the trade unions' case for general legislation on the subject.

Initiatives to Secure Legislation for Paid Holidays

Four Private Members' Bills, seeking to generalize annual paid holidays in Britain by Act of Parliament, were introduced into the House of Commons by Labour members: in 1925, 1929, 1936 and 1937. There was little enthusiasm at first; and, although sympathy with the idea increased in the course of time, amendments had the effect of defeating the intentions of the Bills' sponsors. With greater pressure from the TUC and Labour members for government action in the later 1930s, a committee of inquiry was set up to conduct a full investigation of the extent of holidays with pay in Britain and to make recommendations.

The 1925 Bill, to entitle all workpeople to an annual paid holiday of not less than eight consecutive days after twelve months' continuous service with the same employer, did not receive a second reading.[20] The 1929 Bill, which had similar objectives, proved equally contentious in discussions in the House of Commons. Its sponsors argued that an annual paid holiday would increase productivity by improving workpeople's physical efficiency, and would boost employment in the seaside resorts and the holiday catering trades; employers, it was alleged, would not necessarily be burdened by the cost, given their capacity for reorganization and rationalization of their businesses. Moreover, a number of other countries already had, or were actively considering, legislation on the matter, and Britain ought to be among the leaders.

The Bill's opponents were not won over by these arguments. They asserted that to impose a general statutory obligation on employers to provide paid holidays for all workpeople would 'interfere with the long-established custom of employers and employees to settle conditions in their own industries'; the House should not entertain such a Bill 'unless it was presented by a government which is in a position, after full consultation with all the interests concerned, to give the House authoritative information on the costs and effects of the proposal, and the measure of agreement thereon throughout the industries affected.' The House was not opposed to the Bill *in principle,* but there were many practical difficulties, not least of which were the lack of information on the probable costs for different industries and the means to ensure provision for the many 'vulnerable' groups who would not be affected by the Bill in its present form. The general feeling was that the matter could not be dealt with in such simple terms as the proposed measure contained. A full investigation was required before proceeding further. This was accepted and the Bill was withdrawn, but, because of the deepening economic crisis of the early 1930s, the intended inquiry was deferred.

In 1930, 1931 and 1932 the TUC continued to press for statutory enforcement of annual paid holidays to ameliorate unemployment by effecting a more equitable distribution of the available work. Ernest Bevin was urging the need for a 'National Holiday Scheme', with holiday pay provided by means of a national fund on the lines of the unemployment insurance scheme. The introduction of arrangements for paid holidays as a means of spreading the available work was mentioned, albeit briefly, in the House of Commons in March 1933, when policies to deal with the unemployment problem were under discussion. The member for Gravesend asked the House to consider whether it would be possible to frame some kind of scheme, in conjunction with unemployment insurance, by which insured workers would go on 'holiday benefit' for two periods of two weeks each year. The proposal, intended as a temporary expedient for the duration of the recession, was not favourably received by the Government as a practicable solution to the unemployment problem. With the unemployment insurance scheme running into deficit in these years, there was little enthusiasm to set up a similar kind of arrangement for paid holidays, and one, moreover, that would set a 'dangerous' precedent.

Resolutions on holidays with pay had come before the International Labour Organization from time to time since 1921, but it was not until 1935 that the subject was placed on the agenda for discussion at that year's conference. In response to a questionnaire, sent out to member states by the International Labour Office, the British Government declared that it would oppose a rigid Convention but was perfectly willing to support a Recommendation on the question:

> The Government are of the opinion that holidays with pay should be provided wherever circumstances permit. They feel, however, that apart from other difficulties attendant on an attempt to deal with this matter by

means of international regulations, the consideration which has so far been given to the problem has not yet taken into account the great problem presented by the large proportion of workpeople who during the year work for different employers or who are not continuously employed. It does not appear, therefore, that it would be possible to adopt the international regulations in the form of a draft Convention. The Government, however, would be prepared to support the adoption of a Recommendation, which would have the object of encouraging all practicable steps to be taken to extend the provision of holidays with pay and of stimulating further consideration of this subject.[21]

In 1936 the ILO produced a Convention for an annual holiday with pay of at least six consecutive days for workers in industrial and commercial undertakings, and adopted Resolutions to discuss the possibility of producing similar regulations for domestic servants, hall porters, homeworkers, agricultural workers and seamen. The British Government abstained from voting on the 1936 Convention, and expressed its opposition to a proposed Convention to regulate paid holidays for seamen. Again, the main objection was that the Convention in prospect would be of no benefit whatsoever to the large numbers not permanently employed by one concern. The Government's implied view was that permanent employees were able to settle the matter with their own employers when circumstances permitted; the ILO's Conventions did nothing to assist those who would never be in that position. Holidays with pay for seamen were already granted in the UK 'in pursuance of agreements arrived at by the National Maritime Board, in the case of deck and engineer officers'. The agreements did not apply to the 'lower deck' seamen, however, who worked for a succession of different shipping companies, sometimes changing their employment frequently during the year. The British Government was prepared to support a Recommendation for 'a reasonable amount of leave with pay', but was opposed to a Convention which proposed legislation 'giving benefits only to the most favourably placed seamen...'[22]

The British Government abstained from voting on the two Conventions. The principle of paid holidays was not at issue; but the Government would not ratify rigid international measures which would bind British employers hand and foot and impose a general increase in costs across the economy as a whole.

As Labour members saw it, the Government was obstructing an important social reform which was intended to improve the lot of the manual worker. Their reaction was to introduce another Private Members' Bill into the Commons in 1936, again seeking to establish a statutory minimum of eight consecutive days of annual paid holidays in Britain. Drawing on the ILO's investigations, Conventions and Resolutions, they argued their case more cogently and more eloquently than in 1925 and 1929, but opponents mounted an equally well-reasoned case. Again, there was no opposition in principle to paid holidays; the main stumbling block was the idea of statutory enforcement without first conducting a thorough investigation of the current extent of paid holidays, the likely costs of extending them further, and the 'pros and cons' of legislation. Mr Grimson moved to reject Mr Rowson's Bill.[23]

The Bill's sponsors refused to given in. It was 'inopportune', they admitted, to attempt to press for such a measure in 1929 when the industrial outlook was bleak, but at the present time of industrial recovery and subsiding unemployment, employers could better afford the cost. The Bill ought not to be seen, as some people tried to misrepresent it, in terms of 'Socialism'; rather, it should be understood as 'enlightened and sensible Capitalism'.

The sceptics remained unconvinced; they had very little information on the extent of paid holidays in Britain, and even less on probable costs for different industries of extending them generally. There had been marked progress, during the last few years, through voluntary collective bargaining: 'Is the failure of the voluntary system so complete that we ought to proceed by legislation, for that will surely deal a blow to the system of voluntary collective bargaining?'

The Bill received a second reading, even so, and was referred in February 1937 to discussion by a Standing Committee which proceeded to amend it. The amendments had the effect of robbing the measure of its obligatory character; for, in stipulating that annual paid holidays should be legally sanctioned only where the Minister of Labour was satisfied that wages and terms of employment made it impossible for workpeople to make their own provisions, and that paid holidays should not be given 'to the detriment of trade or industry', a large loophole was created to permit employers to escape any obligation. The Bill's sponsors, condemning the amendments as 'stupid and vicious' and destructive of the entire purpose of the measure, would have nothing more to do with it. Liberal members refused to take upon themselves any responsibility for wrecking the Bill.

The Standing Committee had, however, urged that the Government should undertake a full and detailed investigation of the matter. Evidently, feelings were running high in the House of Commons, especially among Liberal and Labour members, for a Committee on Holidays with Pay, chaired by Lord Amulree, was set up towards the end of March 1937. Its brief was:

> To investigate the extent to which holidays with pay are given to employed workpeople, and the possibility of extending the provision of such holidays by statutory enactment or otherwise; and to make recommendations.

A fourth Private Members' Bill for paid holidays was presented by another Labour member, Mr Malcolm Macmillan, in October 1937, while the Amulree Committee was still conducting its investigation, and at a time when Labour members had become cynically disenchanted with the Government's attitude. The Parliamentary Secretary at the Ministry of Labour intervened to calm those who were outraged at further delay in what they regarded as a long overdue social reform, by reminding them that the now well-advanced inquiry demonstrated the Government's awareness of strength of feeling in the House; they were given an assurance of the Government's preparedness to act upon the Committee's recommendations. The Government was 'sincerely anxious to deal with the problem in a more comprehensive manner than was provided for in the Bill', which was 'so badly constructed' as to exclude certain groups, such as agricultural workers and anyone not in regular full-time work with one employer. Another member of the House complained that the measure now before them was 'exactly the same as the Bill on which the Commons had previously failed to agree'; it was 'a thoroughly bad Bill, which would fail entirely to achieve the object suggested by its title'. The Bill was lost at its second reading, by the narrowest of margins. There was now little to be done, but to await the Committee's report.

In his address to Congress late in 1937, when the Amulree Committee's investigation was nearing its conclusion, Ernest Bevin, a member of the Committee, showed a sagacity and discernment of thought which, up to that time, had been lacking in the TUC's attitude to the question of paid holidays. He made a special plea on behalf of casual, seasonal and temporary workers who, as a 'great asset to the nation', ought to have the same opportunity as everyone else to 'enjoy periods of recreation with their families.' Congress, he continued, wanted *all* workers to have holidays with pay; the TUC had long regarded legislation as the most effective means of generalizing the benefit, but where should the line be drawn between statutory enforcement and voluntary agreement?

> We must carefully consider the question as to how far the state should be permitted to interfere in the regulation of wages and conditions. Our movement is a voluntary one, and the claim for state regulation must not be carried too far. It might easily lead us on to the slippery slope of the totalitarian state under capitalist control, by which our very liberty may be destroyed. There are some industries in which, to prevent sweating, state regulation is essential. In other industries the legalizing of voluntary agreements

is all that should be accepted. In the remainder it is better to maintain standards by trade union action wherever we can.[24]

In making these observations, Bevin was undoubtedly influenced by the evidence uncovered by the Amulree Committee, and it seems probable that he was trying to forewarn the TUC of the Committee's forthcoming recommendations to which he and other trade union representatives on that body would fully subscribe. The report recommended a good deal less than the TUC wanted – and it was unanimous.

The Investigation and the Outcome

Witnesses representing the TUC and certain individual trade unions, as we have seen, argued the case for general legislation to give statutory entitlement to paid holidays. The counter-case was presented by witnesses on behalf of the National Confederation of Employers' Organizations and by several individual employers.[25] For the vast majority of these the principle of paid holidays was not at issue; it was the imposition of a general statutory obligation that they resisted.

One of the most telling of the employers' arguments against general legislation on the subject was that the question of payment for holidays was inextricably entangled with the much wider issue of the settlement of wages and other terms of employment. By long and well-established tradition, wage and related matters in Britain were usually settled by negotiation between employers and workers' representatives. Legislative intervention by the Government in what was essentially a wage issue would cut across agreements and undermine the very foundations of Britain's long-established system of voluntary collective bargaining. It was only by voluntary negotiation that pay could be properly determined and settled in such a way as to take account of each industry's particular circumstances and of workpeople's preferences as to whether any available monies should be allocated for weekly wage increases or earmarked for other purposes such as payment for holidays. A statutory imposition of payment for holidays would take away the freedom of bargaining groups to determine their own priorities. If employers were forced to pay wages for holidays, regardless of their own or their workers' preferences, some would take steps to offset the imposed cost rise by reducing weekly wages or by refusing wage increases at the next negotiation, or by conceding smaller wage increases in the near future. The result would be discord, and possibly conflagration, in industrial relations.

An alternative to offsetting the cost increase by clawing back wages was to project it on to prices. Price increases induced by government interference would reduce the competitiveness of British goods in both home and overseas markets. Foreign markets would be lost; in the home market there would be reduced demand for British goods and a shift to cheaper 'substitute products' imported from abroad. The outcome would be a rise in unemployment. Another alternative was for employers to absorb the cost by introducing mechanized processes to raise productivity; unit costs could thus be reduced and prices maintained at their current levels, but again the outcome would be unemployment for those technologically displaced.

The opposition case was thus partly based on the need to preserve the practice and principle of free collective bargaining which, it was argued, was more advanced and efficient in Britain than anywhere else, and partly on the need to protect the competitiveness of British firms in domestic and overseas markets and the jobs that British industries provided for British workers.

Another point of some significance raised by employers was that the financial burden imposed on them by statutorily enforced paid holidays would fall unequally on different industries and different business enterprises; and that workpeople would also be unequally affected. First, as labour costs were proportionately high in labour-intensive industries, the extra funds to be found would be much greater than in capital-intensive industries where labour costs were relatively low.

Labour costs varied from below 10.0 per cent to over 60.0 per cent of total production costs. Some of the labour-intensive industries, such as coal and textiles which were also heavily dependent on export markets, had been particularly badly affected by the depression; many employers had gone out of business with the contraction of these industries, and the remaining firms were only recently showing signs of recovery. For many of them, an imposed cost increase at this stage would be the last straw. Second, a statutory measure would affect workpeople unequally and, therefore, unfairly. In effect, general legislation would mean that workers without paid holidays would get a statutory pay rise, while those who already received them by collective agreement would get nothing. The latter had accepted a portion of their wage increase in the form of holiday pay, thereby suffering a financial cost which would not be offset by the legislation proposed. In contrast, the former had chosen to take the whole of their increase in the form of additions to weekly wages and to forego payment for holidays; these people would receive both the higher wages already agreed, and also holiday pay at the instigation of the Government.

Employers produced impressive and highly detailed statistical analyses of costs, prices, wages, profits, dividends, output and employment in different industries, and estimates of the costs of providing paid holidays for all. There would be much confusion and great administrative difficulty in attempting to adjust the formidably complicated local, district and national wage rates to take account of payment for holidays. Similarly, adjusting production processes so as to meet output targets while at the same time accommodating a fortnight's holiday leave for all would create serious difficulties in organizational terms.

Employers in the cotton textile trades asserted that it was generally understood in the industry that payment for holidays was already contained in the existing wage rates agreed with the workpeople's organizations. Holidays, amounting to thirteen and a half days in the year, had been taken into account in wage settlements; the fact that so many cotton operatives regularly took their families on holiday to the seaside during local wakes weeks confirmed the sufficiency of wages to meet both ordinary and holiday expenses. Holidays were a normal part of the working year and were covered by normal wages; this was confirmed by the fact that, under the Workmen's Compensation Act, annual earnings were divided by 52 for the purpose of computing the amount of compensation due. The cotton workers saved weekly amounts from wages in insurance clubs in anticipation of holidays; would the employers be expected to deduct those holiday savings at source and act as a banker, or would the Government require them to make annual lump sum holiday payments in addition to the holiday-pay component already contained in weekly wages?

There were obvious difficulties, the employers argued, in industries such as civil engineering contracting, building, and port transport, where workers took up jobs with a succession of different employers: which employer would be obliged to pay the workers' wages for the holiday period?

The majority of employers subscribed to the principle of paid holidays, but they asked to be allowed to work out the practicalities of the matter through the existing machinery for negotiation, which had the advantage of providing sufficient flexibility to accommodate the special needs of particular industries, the different circumstances of individual firms, the bargaining priorities of the trade unions, and the ability of the employer to meet the costs. Employers with arrangements for paid holidays already in operation were against legislation to force others to make similar provision. Some had no objection to legislation for their own industries but were opposed to its imposition on other industries. All believed that a simple, rigid, all-embracing statutory measure was altogether inappropriate to the diverse nature of British industry. As the Amulree Committee observed in its report, the problem was one of great complexity, for which there was no simple solution.

The employers' case, like that of the unions, had weak points as well as strong features. They applauded the flexible system of voluntary collective bargaining as the best means of introducing paid holidays, but suggested no alternative means where organization and collective bargaining structures were weak or non-existent.

Pretentious claims about the 'robust system' of voluntary bargaining as a 'great asset' and the 'pride' of industrial relations in Britain amounted to little more than empty rhetoric. The long-run recession, structural change in the economy, automation, rationalization, and a persistently high unemployment rate had exposed that system's weakness and the vulnerability of workpeople and their trade unions in such circumstances.

The employers' objection on grounds of cost, although impressively argued and supported by a battery of statistical evidence, invited sympathy, but was less compelling in 1937 than it would have been in 1931. They did not seriously address the possibility of absorbing the cost by more efficient methods of management, by diverting a portion of profit to holiday-pay purposes, or by insisting that those holding stocks and shares in companies accept smaller returns on their capital to the same end. There were ways, other than price rises, lower wage settlements, and job cuts, of affording any increase of labour costs that holidays with pay might cause. Enlightened employers, who had introduced paid holidays long ago, spoke confidently of the improvements which had followed: better time-keeping, reduced absenteeism, lower labour turnover, calmer industrial relations, more co-operative attitudes, and greater productivity – but the majority were not disposed to become equally enlightened, either by negotiation or by Act of Parliament. Little was said in defence of the custom of granting paid holidays for the salaried while denying them to manual grades – although logical reasons could have been given.

When the Amulree Committee produced its report in April 1938, it summarized the results of what has been described as the most detailed investigation, up to that date, of the extent to which workpeople in Britain were covered by arrangements of various kinds for holidays with pay. A year earlier, when the Committee had held its first sitting, the Minister of Labour had reported that between 1.5 and 1.75 million manual workers were currently covered by general or district collective agreements providing payment of wages for annual holidays. In addition, large numbers of clerks, 'other salaried employees', shop assistants, workers on 'standing wages', and workers in individual firms, were covered by arrangements other than collective agreements between employers and trade unions. In March 1938 the Amulree Committee found that of a total workforce (whether currently employed or unemployed and including both manual and non-manual employees earning £250 or less per annum) of roughly 18.5 million, an estimated 7.75 million (slightly more than 40.0 per cent) received holidays with pay (Table 9).

The number of manual workers covered by collective agree-

TABLE 9
Number of Workpeople with Consecutive Days of Annual Holiday with Pay, March 1938

Manual wage-earners covered by collective agreements	3,000,000
Clerks, draughtsmen and typists	1,250,000
Shop assistants	1,000,000
Other salaried groups and workers on standing wages	500,000
Manual workers with arrangements other than collective agreements	250,000
Employees in public administration and defence	1,000,000
Domestic staff and miscellaneous	750,000
Total with annual paid holidays	7,750,000
Total number of workpeople	18,500,000
Total without annual paid holidays	10,750,000

Percentage of workpeople with annual paid holidays: 42%
Percentage of workpeople without annual paid holidays: 58%

The definition of 'workpeople' adopted by the Amulree Committee was 'those coming within the employment field, including the unemployed, who are either manual workers, or non-manual workers, in receipt of not more than £250 a year'.

Derived from: Departmental Committee on Holidays with Pay, *Report*, 1938, Cmd. 5724, Appendix 1.

ments providing for paid holidays had increased during the preceding twelve months from less than two million to around three million; another quarter of a million were covered by arrangements other than collective agreements, and a sizeable group of some three-quarters of a million, described as 'domestic staff and miscellaneous', received paid holidays by custom.

The remaining majority, amounting to around 10.75 million of mainly manual wage-earners, were without paid holidays. These, the Committee observed, fell into five main groups. First, there were people the nature of whose work or employment contract presented difficulties in making arrangements for holidays with pay; these included agricultural workers, outworkers in certain branches of industry, and those engaged in contract work in building and construction, public works, painting and decorating, shipping and canal transport, and the entertainment trades. Second, there were workpeople in industries said to be subject to keen foreign competition, where there was the problem of passing on to export prices the cost increases resulting from the introduction of paid holidays: coalminers and workers in a wide range of industries such as cotton and woollen textiles, bleaching, dyeing and finishing, flax, hemp and jute, hosiery, india rubber, felt hat, iron founding, and the shipping industry. Third, there were workers in industries where the issue was said to be currently 'under consideration': iron and steel manufacture, ship building and repairing, and dock labour. In point of fact, before the Committee's report was printed, general agreements had been reached in the iron and steel trades and in shipbuilding and repairing. Fourth, there were 'small and miscellaneous' firms and industries such as those subject to Trade Board regulation, where employers and workpeople were weakly organized. Fifth, there were large numbers of manual wage-earners who did not have continuous employment throughout the year, casual workers, and those who hired themselves to a succession of different employers.

Even so, the 60.0 per cent increase in the numbers covered by collective agreements on the subject during the twelve months spanning the investigation was both impressive and reassuring. Growth seems to have resulted from four main causes. With industrial recovery, employers were better able to afford the cost. The prominence given to the issue by the inquiry, and the associated publicity, had an effect on negotiators and on public opinion generally; it received centre-stage spotlighting. Employers were now far more willing to make concessions in the process of collective bargaining in order to win the goodwill of their workpeople and the trade unions in circumstances of declining unemployment and tightening labour markets; growing numbers were keen to demonstrate their willingness to abide by the principle endorsed by their representatives: that annual paid holidays were 'a good thing' and should be freely negotiated wherever circumstances allowed. At the same time, more workpeople had reached a threshold in the level of weekly earnings at which they were prepared to accept a portion of the next wage rise in the form of payment for holidays. It is absurd to argue, as do Pimlott and Cameron, that employers pre-emptively hastened to introduce their own schemes on the assumption that they could negotiate terms more favourable to themselves than would otherwise be inflicted on them by Act of Parliament. General legislation to make annual paid holidays obligatory nationwide was extremely unlikely, given successive governments' past performance in the matter of general legislation to impose maximum weekly working hours. Labour governments had toyed with the idea but their attempts had been obstructed in the House of Commons; likewise, Labour-sponsored Private Members' Bills for paid holidays had been pruned of their obligatory character in committee. It was inconceivable that the Government would take an entirely different line at this stage; and, in the final analysis, the Government was under no obligation to implement anything that the Amulree Committee might recommend. In any case, in the unlikely event of a general measure being passed, employers who had existing arrangements providing less than the minimum standards set under an Act of Parliament would have to revise their schemes to comply with the new regulations. The only obvious advantage for employers in introducing paid holidays before the Committee's report was published was greater goodwill on the part of their workforces and a better industrial relations climate.

The Government was not taking any great risk in intimating, prior to the completion of the investigation, that the Committee's suggestions would receive the most serious of considerations; for even the most extreme of recommendations could be implemented in a diluted, delayed or deferred form, so as to satisfy employers' insistence on 'flexibility' without repudiating the validity of the unions' case for generalizing paid holidays.

The Government passed the Holidays with Pay Act in July 1938 within a few months of receiving the Committee's report in April of that year, and, in doing so, it followed the main recommendations contained therein. The Act was simply an 'enabling' measure; it was 'permissive' in that it did not obligate the entire employer population, or any section of it, to do anything. It was targeted, most obviously, at industries where basic terms of employment were fixed by the statutory wage-regulating authorities; and even those bodies were 'enabled', but not required, to introduce arrangements to provide paid holidays. The full title of the measure makes this perfectly clear: 'An Act to enable wage-regulating authorities to make provision for holidays and holiday remuneration for workers whose wages they regulate, and to enable the Minister of Labour to assist voluntary schemes for securing holidays with pay for workers in any industry.'

The wage-regulating authorities included the trade boards set up in certain industries under the Trade Boards Acts of 1909 and 1918, the agricultural wages committees set up in England and Wales under the Agricultural Wages (Regulation) Act 1924 and in Scotland under the Agricultural Wages (Regulation) (Scotland) Act 1937, and the Road Haulage Central Wages Board set up under the Road Haulage Wages Act 1938. By implication, any other statutory wage-regulating body created in the future would be similarly affected. Once a wage-regulating authority had reached a decision and issued a direction for paid holidays, an employer failing to comply with it would be 'liable on summary conviction in respect of each offence to a fine not exceeding twenty pounds'. It would obviously be prudent for the employer to make holiday payments amounting probably to less than £5 per worker than to risk a fine which might amount to £20 per unpaid person.

For workpeople in industries where employment was typically intermittent and taken up with a succession of different employers, the Committee recommended the establishment of 'holiday trust funds', like that recently set up by the engineering industry, to which the employer would make weekly contributions for as many weeks as the worker was employed by the firm; each worker would have a 'holiday card' which would be accordingly stamped with 'holiday credits', and which would be taken from one employer to the next; holiday pay would be disbursed from the central fund at the time of the holiday. The Minister of Labour would assist, with advice and administration, where an industry could not manage under its own steam.

In the case of workpeople in spheres of employment not subject to regulation by statutory authorities, the Minister of Labour was to assist and encourage voluntary collective agreements between employers and workers' representatives. Progress in provision for paid holidays, the Committee had advised, should be 'largely by voluntary arrangement in the first place, since wage issues are regularly settled in the ordinary course of collective bargaining.' This did not mean that the idea of general legislation was to be completely abandoned, now and forever; a main and immediate problem was that the task of framing a comprehensively and pervasively suitable measure was highly complex and would involve much delay which might seriously disturb industrial relations. It was for this reason that the Committee advised immediate moves on the basis of voluntarily negotiated settlements for those whose terms were not regulated by the statutory wage-fixing bodies. To assist negotiators, the Minister of Labour, early in 1939, issued a booklet containing some general guidelines for negotiators and the detailed texts of numerous agreements on paid holidays, which had already been implemented.

Crucially important at the time, however, was the Amulree Committee's recommendation that there should be a 'probationary period prior to the introduction of general legislation' to provide a breathing space for voluntary advance; the situation should then be reviewed in the Parliamentary session, 1940–41, with a view to framing a measure in the light of any deficiencies and anomalies that still remained.

The length of the paid holiday period, whether collectively agreed or directed by a wages board, was to be left entirely to the parties concerned. The minimum, it was suggested, should be one week; the holiday 'should consist of at least as many days as there are in the working week, and these days should, as far as practicable, be taken consecutively...' except in agriculture where the full holiday might be split into two spells. There was nothing here to discourage negotiators from agreeing a longer holiday.

The 1938 Act did not contain the provisions which the Committee had recommended for domestic servants; and those employing only their own family members or one or two workers were left to work out their own arrangements. With these exceptions, the Act closely followed the main recommendations contained in the Amulree Committee's report. That the report was 'unanimous' seems somewhat perplexing at first, for the six committee members nominated from its own ranks by the TUC's General Council had endorsed a document which recommended substantially less than the union movement was advocating on the basis of its own evidence. It seems likely that Ernest Bevin and his five colleagues were disposed to comply, given the prospect of a second chance in 1940–41, and the marked success of collective bargaining for paid holidays during the preceding twelve months. At the same time, they were perhaps anxious to show, after the humiliating fiasco of 1926 and the low prestige that their movement had suffered for several years, that the trade unions did not invariably act irresponsibly in their own blinkered self-interest, but were prepared to wait a while longer if employers and the Government were willing to meet them halfway.

Some disappointment was expressed at the 1938 Congress, but there were no scathing recriminations nor harsh accusations of treachery against those who had served on the Committee; nor did turbulence in industrial relations ripple across the country as a result. As the TUC saw it, the investigation and the Act had, in a very real sense, provided them with a new and higher baseline for future negotiation; one of the most important outcomes was that employers had publicly subscribed to the principle and practice of annual paid holidays. Even the mine-owners, who had formerly ridiculed the South Wales miners for claiming paid holidays at the bargaining table,[26] were now prepared to negotiate on the issue. Labour members in the House of Commons were far more incensed than the trade unions about the Government's niggardliness in giving workpeople so little.

The half-a-loaf that the unions gained was much less than the whole loaf they wanted, but it was much better than no bread at all. Whereas in the few relatively prosperous years following the First World War the main improvements in working time had taken the form of reductions in basic weekly working hours, the main changes in the years of industrial recovery prior to the outbreak of the Second World War were in the form of increases in holidays with pay. If the 1938 Act did not turn out to be the millstone that at least some employers had feared, neither did it represent the milestone that the unions had had in view. In a very real sense, however, it served as a touchstone in the history of holidays with pay in Britain.

Notes

1. Whiteside, N. (1980), 'Industrial Welfare and Labour Regulation in Britain at the Time of the First World War', *International Review of Social History*, Vol. 25, pp.307–31; Reports of the Health of Munition Workers' Committee in *Ministry of Munition Papers*, 4/6338, PRO.
2. Pollard, S. (1992), *The Development of the British Economy, 1914–1990*, London, Edward Arnold, pp.37–43; May, T. (1993),

An Economic and Social History of Britain, 1760–1970, London, Longman, pp.328–37.

3. Evans, A. and Palmer, S. (1985), *Negotiating Shorter Working Hours*, London, Macmillan, p.7.
4. *Ibid.*
5. Trades Union Congress (1935), *Report*, p.173.
6. *Ibid.*
7. *Ministry of Labour Gazette* (January, 1920), p.4.
8. Musson, A.E. (1965), *Enterprise in Soap and Chemicals: Joseph Crosfield & Sons, 1815–1963*, Manchester, University Press, p.151; Cadbury, E. (1912), *Experiment in Industrial Organization*, Birmingham, Cadbury Brothers, p.19; Phelps Brown, E.H. (1959), *The Growth of British Industrial Relations*, London, Macmillan, p.86; Departmental Committee on Holidays with Pay (1938), *Report*, Cmd. 5724, pp.7–9.
9. Board of Trade (1906), *Earnings and Hours Inquiry*.
10. Departmental Committee on Holidays with Pay (1938), *Report*, Cmd. 5724, p.8.
11. *Ministry of Labour Gazette* (1920), August, pp.421–2, (1922), December, pp.474–5.
12. *Ibid.*
13. *Ibid.* (1925), March, pp.76–7.
14. *Ibid.* (1929), August, pp.275–6.
15. *Ibid.* (1932), July, pp.242–3; (1934), July, pp.232–3; (1936), April, pp.125–6; (1938), March, pp.86–9.
16. Cameron, G.C. (1965), 'The Growth of Holidays with Pay in Britain' in Reid, G.L. and Robertson, D.J. (eds), *Fringe Benefits, Labour Costs and Social Security*, London, Allen & Unwin, p.277.
17. *Ministry of Labour Gazette* (1932) July, p.242.
18. *Ibid.* (1929), August, p.275.
19. Contributory and other types of schemes are variously recorded in issues of the *Ministry of Labour Gazette* for 1920, 1922, 1925, 1929, 1932, and 1934.
20. Information relating to this Bill, and the Bills of 1929 and 1936, is outlined in Departmental Committee on Holidays with Pay, *Report* (1938), Cmd. 5724, pp.24–5; see also *The Times* (1925), 2 April p.8, 20 May p.13 and (1929), 2 November p.7, 13 November p.13, 15 November p.14 and 16 November p.7.
21. Quoted in Departmental Committee on Holidays with Pay, *op.cit.* pp.15–16.

22. Quoted *ibid.* pp.17–18.
23. *The Times* (1936), 21 November, p.14.
24. *Ibid.* (1937), 7 September, p.6; TUC, *Report* (1937), p.416.
25. Employers' views are given in Departmental Committee on Holidays with Pay, Minutes of Evidence, (1937–8) and are summarized in the Committee's *Report*, paras 67–79.
26. *Ibid.* Memorandum of Evidence by the South Wales Miners Federation, 16 November 1937.

PART II
1939–69

4

The TUC's Wartime Concessions and Postwar Expectations, 1939–59

Introduction

The onset of hostilities presented the Government and workpeople with the most formidable of difficulties, both strategic and financial. Initially, there was mutual distrust between the Government and the trade unions, and that situation did not improve during the first few months of the war. The TUC General Council, asked for an assurance of support for the war effort, requested an amendment of the 1927 Trades Disputes Act as a *quid pro quo*; the Government had replied, provocatively, that it depended on the unions' behaviour during the wartime emergency – although there was little sense of urgency as yet. The situation changed in May 1940 when the Chamberlain Government collapsed and the Coalition Government was formed under Churchill's leadership. The Parliamentary Labour Party had played a significant role in Chamberlain's downfall, and it was unsurprising, therefore, that Churchill should invite leading Labour members, Attlee and Greenwood, to join his five-man War Cabinet. Labour members were given charge of other Ministries; and Ernest Bevin, a Member of Parliament for the first time, was made Minister of Labour and National Service.[1] The direct involvement of Labour members at important levels of decision-making, and Bevin's competence in performing the onerous and challenging duties at the Ministry of Labour and National Service, were important factors in reconciling the leadership and rank and file of the trade unions to the privations and sacrifices they would endure during the war.

After the war, with a Labour Government in office until 1951, the TUC resumed its campaign for legislation for the 40-hour week and a fortnight's holiday with pay. The unions expected their proposals to be greeted favourably, for during the interwar period Labour Members of Parliament had advocated ratification of the Washington Convention and had introduced Bills on holidays with pay. The unions' hopes remained unfulfilled, however; their requests were said to be unaffordable. There were two main problems with which the Government had to contend. First, foreign borrowing and gifts from abroad, which had enabled Britain to live beyond her means for several years, came to an end in the summer of 1945; second, the disruption and diversion of production for the needs of war had been so extreme that it would take several years of austerity to restore the economy to a state of peacetime efficiency and stability. Britain had a 'dollar problem', sterling crises, balance of payments difficulties, and the ever-present threat of inflation.[2] At the same time, the Government was committed to a policy of nationalization of certain industries and services, full employment, and major reforms in the spheres of social insurance and social welfare, including the creation of the National Health Service as part of the modern Welfare State.

A Conservative Government was elected in 1951, and the Conservatives remained in office for the next thirteen years. Britain entered the 'age of affluence'. Full employment and the steady rise of earnings permitted rising standards of living which encouraged even higher aspirations.[3] After the TUC's confrontations with the Labour Government on the question of legislation to shorten the basic working week and increase paid holidays during the second half of the 1940s, there were few further debates at Congress on these matters to the end of the 1950s.

The War Years

The TUC's activities on the question of holidays with pay during wartime were largely confined to monitoring progress following the 1938 Act, to seeking resolution of anomalies resulting from the interplay of the Holidays with Pay Act and the unemployment insurance scheme, and to noting the Government's directions for the cancellation, postponement or rearrangement of holiday leave for the civilian workforce. The campaign for a general reduction of the basic working week and curtailment of overtime working was discontinued; official TUC policy was to accept the long working hours necessitated by the wartime emergency, the needs of national security, and the maintenance of essential services. There was some concern to control hours of work, but the reasons were quite different from those which had been argued in peacetime Britain. The main anxiety was that the high levels of production of munitions and manufactured goods vital to the war effort could not be maintained for long by a workforce suffering from fatigue and exhaustion caused by excessively long working hours. The TUC was particularly concerned for some control over the hours of work of the large numbers of women drawn into full-time employment, for the earlier closing of shops made shopping difficult. It was not until 1944, when it was becoming apparent that the war would soon be at an end, that the unions resumed their campaign for the basic 40-hour week and legislation for annual paid holidays.

The 1938 Holidays with Pay Act had empowered the statutory wage-regulating authorities to make provision for annual paid holidays, and in 1939 the TUC General Council informed Congress that the Trade Boards Advisory Council had circulated individual boards with a model scheme which was recommended for implementation. At the time when the TUC's annual report was being compiled, a total of 37 trade boards had already issued directions, all but three of which had received confirming orders, to introduce a full week of paid holiday that same year.[4] Other trade boards were said to have the matter under 'active consideration', but had not yet issued proposals. The General Council was somewhat troubled that, despite this prompt and encouraging start, several trade boards had excluded outworkers from their arrangements. It was heartening, however, that all of the directions and confirming orders issued so far were 'without prejudice' to any future decision to raise the level of holiday pay or to grant longer holidays than those currently authorized. Congress was informed in 1940 that all but four trade boards now had schemes for holidays with pay in operation, and that the new Furniture Manufacturing Trade Board proposed to introduce a scheme shortly.

The General Council[5] had frequent meetings with the Unemployment Insurance Statutory Committee on the question of unemployment insurance and holidays with pay. Certain anomalies had arisen, including the matter of unemployment insurance contributions and benefits during periods of unpaid holiday and the significance of unpaid holidays for 'continuity of employment' and the 'waiting period', both of which affected the worker's entitlement to unemployment benefit. These, and other problems in the relationship between the two arrangements, were of a highly technical and complex nature, and their resolution required certain amendments to the unemployment insurance scheme.

In 1940, with the collapse of France, the difficulties encountered by the British Expeditionary Force, and the urgent need to replace vital equipment lost at the fighting front, the General Council, in consultation with the Minister of Labour and National Service, agreed variously to the cancellation, postponement and staggering of public and annual holidays. Many civilians were working a seven-day week of twelve-hour shifts during the national emergency in order to maintain essential services. With the prospect of the war continuing much longer than anticipated, it was recognized that very long working hours could not be sustained indefinitely without the risk of falling productivity and declining output of equipment vital to the war effort. After extensive consultation with TUC representatives, Ernest Bevin, Minister of Labour in the wartime Coalition Government, advised that actual hours of 70 or 80 per week, currently being worked, should be reduced to 58 or 60, and then to 55 or 56. Various methods of shift and rota working were suggested as means to meet production needs while avoiding 'excessive strain'.[6]

Insofar as complaints were voiced at Congress, it was with two objectives in view: to avoid extreme fatigue and gross physical strain which might affect Britain's performance in the conduct of the war and her ability to provide for the civilian population; and to protect the many women who had joined the workforce for the duration of the emergency. A resolution, moved at the 1941 Congress, urged that women workers should be allowed at least 'one day's rest in seven', that 'work should be reorganized so that the machinery of production can be kept continuously in operation and the human element afforded time for rest and recreation', and that 'adequate travelling facilities' should be provided to reduce the time which women spent travelling to and from work. The main purpose of the resolution, the speaker asserted, was to ensure that women's 'spirit of determination' and their willingness to 'give their utmost' to the war effort, which had been fully demonstrated during the dark months after Dunkirk and the even darker months of the 'black-out', should not be 'frittered away, weakened, and stultified' by the lack of proper planning and organization of working time:

> Directly after Dunkirk, we all of us agreed voluntarily to shut our eyes to any question of the hours that were being worked. Women, together with their men colleagues in the great engineering factories, worked twelve, thirteen, fifteen, and in some cases eighteen, hours on jobs which they felt were urgent and necessary, in order to re-equip the Forces ... The trade unions concerned could see, and the employers and government departments admitted, that if such long hours continued, production would decline. You can keep up long hours – a spurt such as we made after Dunkirk – for a limited period, and production rises, but you cannot go on for one, two, or three

years under these conditions and still keep production at its maximum.[7]

It was not only a question of working hours; it was also a question of shopping hours. Most of the shops were shut by six o'clock in the evening before women working a six- or seven-day week left the factories. Women used to live close to their place of employment and do their shopping on the way home; but now, 'with the concentration of industry, with the changeover and transfer of women from the textile mills ... to the filling factories and engineering factories ... they have to travel some distance to get to and from work'. At the same time, under wartime regulation, the shops closed earlier; and, with wartime shortages, some items of grocery were sold out early in the day. The difficulties of transport and shopping were accentuated by air-raids, bomb damage and petrol shortages, which often meant fewer, and sometimes re-routed, bus services, or a long walk home in black-out conditions. The Minister of Labour, through the Welfare Officers, had issued some guidelines, and it was up to trade union leaders to ascertain that those instructions were being carried out. Advance planning and full consultation with the trade unions could save a great deal of energy, time and trouble, and ease the burden that so many married women had taken on.

Congress recognized that there was a 'transport problem', owing to shortages of buses, manpower and petrol, and the difficulty of drawing up workable rosters for drivers and conductors, many of whom were women. The transport unions were in favour of improving passenger services for the travelling public, but they were also concerned about the working hours of transport workers. At present the women, like the men, were 'not only working a seven-day week, but working spread-overs of anything up to twelve, fourteen and fifteen hours'. The unions, in consultation with the Minister of Transport, were seeking better arrangements of working time, which would also improve passenger services. Transport workers, it was protested, were doing their best in the most challenging of conditions. In the winter of 1940–41 transport workers had had to contend with both the black-out and the blitz:

> Many of them who had worked through the black-out and the blitz could not get home ... Next morning, the people who should have taken out the early turns could not get in, but the men and women who had not been home were there to man the vehicles in order that production in the factories should go on.

Better transport services, it was argued, ought not to be at the cost of a worsening of the transport worker's working week.

There were similar protests from the distributive trade unions in response to complaints about shopping difficulties. Congress, in point of fact, had carried a resolution in 1940 urging the Home Secretary to issue an order for an earlier compulsory closing hour for all shops. In effect, the request was for an even earlier close than that fixed by an order of 1939. The experience of the winter of 1939–40 had shown that the shops did very little business after the hour of the black-out; there was no point, therefore, in keeping the shops open. Another consideration was the safety of the assistants, many of whom did not have ready access to air-raid shelters when the warning sirens sounded, and, like other workers, faced a difficult journey home at the end of the day. Here, too, it was argued that to keep the shops open later for the convenience of shoppers would lengthen working hours for those who served them.

The whole contentious issue was referred to the General Council for further consideration. The general feeling was that an emergency Act of Parliament would do little to improve matters, and that local initiatives by agreement between trade unions, employers and local authorities would be more effective in districts where the problem was found to be particularly acute.

The number of workpeople covered by arrangements for paid holidays, either by collective agreement or directions issued by the trade boards, increased during the war years, although holiday leave was frequently cancelled, postponed, or surrendered in the circumstances of the time. Some industrial workers responded positively to the Government's appeal for those temporarily 'at liberty' to work on the land, others took their holidays at times other than summer, and the majority had to make do with the 'holidays at home' initiatives which were encouraged by the Government and locally organized in years when the needs of war took priority in railway transport and there was little accommodation and entertainment to be had at the seaside holiday resorts.

The paid holiday most commonly gained by manual workers during the war amounted to one week plus six public holidays. This was far short of the TUC's target. The 'probationary period', recommended by the Amulree Committee before further legislative action, elapsed, but because of the wartime emergency, the Government, otherwise preoccupied, did not reinvestigate the extent of coverage in 1940–41, nor discuss the form that legislation on the matter should take. There was no outburst of protest from the TUC in the early years of the war about the Government's failure to act on the Amulree Committee's recommendations. The unions' acceptance of the situation undoubtedly owes something to Ernest Bevin's presence at the Ministry of Labour.

It was not until 1944, with signs of an approaching conclusion to the war, that the TUC resumed its campaign for the shortening of working time, with a resolution at that year's Congress seeking legislation both for the 40-hour week and a minimum of a fortnight's paid holiday for all workpeople.

The Resumed Campaign

The exercise of 'power with responsibility'[8] by Labour members in the wartime government and by the TUC increased public confidence in, and respect for, the Labour Party and the trade union movement, and contributed in no small degree to the election of a landslide Labour Government in 1945. In 1944, with public opinion felt to be already favourable, Congress gave overwhelming support for a resolution for an approach to the Government for 'the legalizing of agreements which establish a 40-hour week', and for legislation to provide all workpeople with a minimum of a fortnight's holiday with pay; and it was further pressed that 'both these reforms should be brought into operation as soon as possible after the termination of hostilities, and that the Government should urge the application of these principles throughout the world by inclusion in the peace settlement'.[9]

The unions now found a new and additional justification for their claims, in the Government's recently published statement on economic policy. William Beveridge had produced two seminal works: his report, *Social Insurance and Allied Services*, and his book, *Full Employment in a Free Society*.[10] At the same time, expansionary economic theory, developed by J.M. Keynes, was attracting the interest of policy-makers. The Government had issued a White Paper on social insurance, and had committed itself to a policy of full employment in peacetime Britain. There was no more effective means of achieving full employment, the unions believed, than by establishing a maximum 40-hour week, so as to 'stop some people having too much work imposed on them while others are unable to find any employment at all'. The spectacular productivity gains achieved in manufacturing industry during the war made a nationwide shortening of the basic working week affordable for employers in terms of cost, and feasible from the viewpoint of maintaining output. The last general reduction in basic hours of work had occurred over 20 years before, and, given the tremendous sacrifices made by workpeople in the recent past, a further general shortening of working time was now merited. In other words, the time was believed to be ripe for the advancement of the unions' cause.

The speaker reminded Congress that workpeople now had higher standard of living expectations. Their aspirations were not confined simply to more time off from work so as to give them more leisure time; they included higher earnings to enable them to *enjoy* their leisure and to permit them to take their families off to the seaside for a holiday away from home:

'If holidays are to be enjoyed, people need the money to enable them to do so, and that means negotiating higher pay.'[11]

The subject of increased leisure and full employment, to be achieved on the basis of the 40-hour week and a fortnight's annual holiday with pay, was discussed at great length by Congress in 1945; and in the light of replies to a questionnaire which the General Council had circulated to affiliated unions, the TUC set up a special Forty-Hour Week and Holidays with Pay Committee to develop policy and strategy and to monitor progress. The proposed approach was one based on a combination of legislation and voluntary collective bargaining; the Government was to be requested to give legal backing to agreements on the 40-hour week, and the trade unions were to bring the matter forward for discussion by joint negotiating bodies at industry level as soon as possible after the termination of hostilities. Several unions, Congress was informed, had already approached the employers on the matter, and a number of others were preparing their cases and giving notice of their intention to raise the issue at the bargaining table. There was little to suggest, however, that the employers' attitude was other than 'hostile'.

On the question of paid holidays, the TUC's special committee could see no good reason for modifying the proposal which the unions had put to the Amulree Committee in 1937 for general legislation for a full fortnight of annual paid holiday for all workpeople. The General Council was urged to approach the Minister of Labour to ascertain whether the Government intended to take any steps to legislate on paid holidays now that the war in Europe had been brought to a conclusion.

The whole working-time issue was reviewed at some length at the 1945 Congress, by Sir Mark Hodgson, a member both of the General Council and of the Committee on the Forty-Hour Week and Holidays with Pay. It is clear that, after the privations, shortages, sacrifices at the fighting front, and the prolonged working hours endured at home, the TUC was now mustering its forces to secure some reward for Britain's working population. The Committee envisaged the two-day work-free weekend as part of the reforms it was seeking. As Sir Mark Hodgson put it: '... the present proposals ... for a 40-hour week, comprised as far as possible within five days, with a fortnight's paid holiday, is the culmination of the long movement to improve the conditions of the worker in this country.'[12]

The nineteenth-century movements to reduce the hours of work had been motivated by the need to protect the worker 'against conditions so severe that almost all of his life ... was taken up by labour', to the detriment of physical health, social life and standard of living. The success that had attended the efforts of past generations to reduce the hours of labour had removed the immediate oppression of excessively long working hours for the majority. With the ending of the war, the unions could return to the question of shorter working-time with the objective of 'enabling the worker to develop himself in an efficient manner to become a full citizen in a modern community'. Increased leisure was both 'a necessary thing in itself and an essential part of efficient industrial organization'.

For the next few years, Hodgson continued, the aim would be to ensure that no obstacle impeded full employment of the country's resources for the needs of reconstruction; but the high levels of output required for that purpose ought not to be achieved at the expense of workpeople's standard of living and conditions of work. The workers needed more time away from their place of employment in order to recuperate, relax, enjoy life, and grow to assume full citizenship. With everything 'in the melting pot' after the war, the time would be opportune for the reforms they sought: 'Unless a stimulus is given to industry to revise its outlook on the utilization of labour, that opportunity might be lost, and, with it, the opportunity to raise industry to a new level of social and productive efficiency.' As the proposed hours reduction was a substantial one, it might be preferable in some cases to phase it in, in two stages. The industrial re-equipment and increased production needed after the war could be achieved by the application of science, automation, and more efficient methods of production. The responsibility for innovations of this kind lay with employers and managers, who should be reminded that higher production could be achieved by means other than long hours of labour and the curtailment of workpeople's leisure time. There were good reasons for maintaining and raising wages; for 'just as a reduction of hours is part of an efficient production policy, so the maintenance of earnings is part of it if the purchasing power of working people is to be adequate to take up the increasing supply of goods for a full employment policy'.

Legislation was likewise believed to be the most direct and effective means of increasing annual holidays with pay. It was intended to approach the Minister of Labour to discuss the introduction of a measure to establish a fortnight's paid holiday as a statutory minimum:

> The necessity of a clear and adequate break in the year's work is underlined by the period of intense effort through which we have passed, and extended legal provision is an urgent matter. The extension of holidays with pay does not stand or fall with the general reduction of working hours, and the nature of the claim is to a certain extent different. Nevertheless, in combination they represent a programme for the widening of the social opportunities of the worker. Such an improvement in the human status will provide the best foundation on which a future of industrial technological development can be advanced. This programme we now hope to see initiated as a vital part of the industrial and social reconstruction of the country.

When in 1946 the TUC's Committee on the Forty-Hour Week and Holidays with Pay outlined its main observations on hours of work, it advised distancing of the unions' policy from international initiatives, and dissociation of the 40-hour week from the question of unemployment:

(i) that the establishment of a 40-hour week in this country should be pursued principally as a matter of internal industrial and economic policy, i.e. that it should not be allowed to become too closely associated with any movement for the reduction of hours by international agreement;

(ii) that the approach in this country should be by a combination of voluntary and legislative methods, i.e. an approach by individual unions to their appropriate employers' organizations, together with an approach at an appropriate time by the TUC to the Government with a request for legislation;

(iii) that the case for the 40-hour week should be based principally upon workpeople's need for increased leisure for rest, recreation and personal development, and the ability of industry to provide this improvement in working conditions, i.e. not to associate the case for the 40-hour week with the problem of unemployment.[13]

The General Council's role would be to encourage and assist affiliated unions in collective bargaining for the 40-hour week, to approach the Labour Government for legislation to obligate employers to devise and implement 40-hour week arrangements, and to prepare a public statement that would outline the case for a 40-hour week, the extent to which hours had already been reduced below 47, and the nature of the TUC's proposals for legislation.

In March 1946, representatives of the TUC General Council, led by Sir Walter Citrine, met with certain members of the Labour Government, including Aneurin Bevan, Herbert Morrison and Hugh Dalton. The trade union group had, not unreasonably, expected a sympathetic and favourable response to its proposals for the regulation of working hours, but they met with polite yet firm resistance. The TUC's demands were said to be 'too precipitate'; the effect would be to reduce output and to increase production costs. Legislation to establish a general 40-hour week was out of the question, they were told; moreover, they were warned, there would be adverse repercussions on the economy if those industries which could afford to reduce hours with comparatively little inconvenience to themselves were to do so in advance of the rest. Evidently, the unions were being advised to exercise moderation in their claims at the bargaining table; the Labour Government appeared, on the hours question at least, to be 'siding with the employers'. The union delegates were reminded that the Government was already taking steps to raise standards of living by the reform of the national schemes for social insurance, the introduction of certain non-contributory benefits, encouragement of house-building projects by local authorities, and various kinds of subsidies – all of which required the maximization of production.

These arguments did not immediately convince the TUC's spokesmen of the impracticability of their proposals. Their reply was that the increased output and containment of production costs sought by the Government did not depend entirely on the retention of a prolonged working week; advancing technology had the capability of increasing both production and productivity. The Committee on the Forty-Hour Week and Holidays with Pay was quite emphatic on this point:

> It is therefore *not* the view of the committee that the TUC should abandon the pursuit of the 40-hour week because of the fact that the immediate industrial and economic situation of the country is one that calls for increased and sustained production. It is *not* admitted that an early reduction in working hours would necessarily lead to loss of output.[14]

There seems to have been some, albeit slight, relaxation of the TUC's position, even so, for it was conceded that the immediate acceptance of the principle of the 40-hour week as a general rule in industry did not assume an immediate hours reduction to 40 nationwide. They anticipated its gradual achievement over a period of years, in a flexible manner and with due regard for the special circumstances of particular industries. The consultative and legalistic stages might take up to two years. This would give employers a breathing space to plan ahead for the reduction of basic working hours in stages.

Following the first and fruitless discussions with Labour ministers, the TUC's committee had decided to make a further approach to the Government, for legislation to give legal force to voluntary agreements on the 40-hour week and, where industries were weakly organized, to impose a statutory obligation on them to prepare appropriate schemes for submission to the Minister of Labour within a stated period of time; the envisaged legislation would also empower the Minister of Labour to draw up appropriate arrangements for those industries failing to devise their own schemes, and would enable the statutory wage-regulation authorities to issue directions for the implementation of the 40-hour week.

On the question of holidays with pay, the 1946 Congress was reminded that the Amulree Committee, in its report of 1938, had recommended reconsideration of general legislation in the Parliamentary session, 1940–1, but that because of the war the matter had been shelved. The Committee on the Forty-Hour Week and Holidays with Pay believed that the time was now ripe to approach the Minister of Labour for general legislation for annual paid holidays of at least twelve working days, exclusive of bank and public holidays. At the meeting, which took place on 17 May 1946, the Minister expressed his willingness sympathetically to consider the possibility of introducing new legislation on holidays with pay at an early date if a suitable measure could be prepared in time, but he intimated that, as the views of both employers and trade unions on the scope and details of such an important Parliamentary Act should be obtained and discussed, the matter would be referred to his Joint Consultative Committee.

Congress noted that some hours reductions had been won in the process of collective bargaining, but many employers, it was regretted, remained resolutely hostile and refused to negotiate on what they claimed was 'a matter for the Government'. As one speaker at Congress expressed it:

Some lead will have to be given by the Government

> before they [the employers] are prepared to negotiate for a reduction in the hours of the working week ... We are justified in saying, give us legislation which will enable us to ensure that all engaged in each industry will fit in with the new hours ... Workers have a moral and social right to a reduction in their working week. Their greatest gain will be that they will live longer and be able to enjoy the new social services which the Government has brought in ... What could be a more opportune time for it than now, when we have a Labour Government at our disposal, and with whom we are working hand in hand? Production and more production are the only means for full employment. Full employment can only be got with the co-operation of the workers. I cannot see, in view of the fact that the Government needs *our* co-operation, why we should not ask for *their* co-operation in implementing this long overdue reform.[15]

It was noted, again, that greater output did not depend solely on the hours of labour, and that, in large part, productive efficiency was a matter of effective management, organization and administration of industry; what was needed was 'an intensive examination ... to see if those in control of industry are operating it in the most efficient manner and making the best use of the available manpower'.

The TUC was making no progress in its efforts to persuade the Labour Government to legislate on working-time, but, as it was observed at the 1947 Congress, many unions had now succeeded in gaining 'appreciable hours reductions' through voluntary negotiation with employers. Workpeople in a 'wide range of industries' now worked a normal week of 44 or 45 hours, usually over five days. Other industries were said to be 'coming into line'; the first stage of the TUC's policy on the 40-hour week had thus been 'accomplished over a wide range' by means other than general legislation. The previous year, 1946, was acknowledged to have been 'a difficult year'; and the problems caused by the fuel crisis, the severe winter, dwindling dollar credits, and an adverse balance of payments, had not yet been resolved. It was decided, therefore, to defer the matter of a further approach to the Government for legislation to regulate working hours.

The TUC also deferred its proposal for legislation on paid holidays. The Minister of Labour, as promised, had investigated the extent to which holidays with pay were currently being provided on the basis of voluntary agreements; evidence showed that most workpeople had entitlement to one week of annual paid holiday plus six public holidays with pay. When the matter was reviewed by the TUC's Committee on the Forty-Hour Week and Holidays with Pay, its advice was that, in view of present economic circumstances and the urgent need to boost production, and taking into account the pervasive shortening of the basic working week by voluntary agreements, the question of legislation for longer paid holidays should be postponed.

At the 1948 Congress, a resolution for legislation to establish two weeks of annual paid holiday as a statutory minimum was withdrawn on the advice of the General Council. The TUC's Economic Committee likewise believed legislative action to be inadvisable, for it would have unfavourable repercussions upon the economy, the export trades and the balance of payments.[16]

The TUC, therefore, yielded to the Government's plea for moderation, and refrained from further pressurizing Government ministers on the hours question, thereby avoiding the embarrassment of a head-on clash with the Labour Party. Any ill-feeling that the unions harboured about the rebuff with which the Government had met their overtures was tempered by satisfaction with the policies for nationalization and the creation of the welfare state, and with the modest hours reductions gained by negotiation with employers. With the Labour Government out of office in 1951 and the election of a succession of Conservative governments to the end of the decade, the unions abandoned the idea of general legislation and concentrated their efforts on collective bargaining for hours reductions.

Back to the ILO

Spokesmen at Congress in the later 1940s had more than once insisted that reductions of working-time in Britain should not be tied to international movements on hours, and there are few references in Congress reports in these years to the work of the ILO on the subject. A similar situation obtained in the case of paid holidays. It was not until 1953, when the fortnight's paid holiday appeared on the ILO's agenda, that the unions became actively involved again. Early in the proceedings, the workers' group narrowly failed to secure agreement that the proposed international standard should take the form of a Convention rather than a Recommendation which would carry considerably less weight. The Recommendation raised little comment and even less excitement at Congress, for it was unlikely to have much influence on the Conservative Government; and, in any case, the unions were already making collectively bargained progress on the fortnight's paid holiday.

There was much greater interest from Congress in the ILO's initiatives to set a minimum holidays with pay standard for agricultural workers. When in 1951 the ILO's Committee on Agricultural Labour was considering provision for a minimum wage, it had been agreed that paid holidays would be put on the agenda the following year. Neither the Convention nor the Recommendation adopted in 1952 offered a great deal.[17] The Convention simply contained some broad outlines of ways and means of 'regulation'; governments, in consultation with employers and workpeople, would decide which undertakings, occupations, and kinds of agricultural employment would be covered by the Convention, and whether provision would be by legislation, collective agreement, or 'special bodies' representative of all the interests concerned. The annual paid holiday would exclude public and customary holidays and the regular weekly rest day. Other main provisions were more favourable treatment of young workers, longer holidays related to years of employment, and a proportionately shorter holiday period, or payment in lieu, for those who did not qualify for the full holiday by minimum length of service.

The Recommendation, which supplemented the Convention, proposed that the annual holiday period should consist of at least one full week after one year's continuous service; and that a fortnight's holiday might be provided for agricultural workers below 16 years of age in order to ease the transition from school to paid employment and to avoid over-strain during the years of physical growth. In 'exceptional circumstances' the holiday might be split into two spells, but wherever possible it should be taken as a full unbroken week in order to ensure that it fulfilled the purpose of enabling the worker to 'recuperate'. The British Government, Congress was informed in 1953, abstained from voting on both the Convention and Recommendation.

The matter was discussed at some length by Congress in 1954. The British Government's stance was inexplicable; for most agricultural workers in Britain already had paid holidays equal to, or even better than, those stipulated by the ILO. The 'technical difficulties' which seemed to be at the root of the Government's objection, were resolvable, and Britain ought to 'set a much needed example to those countries, particularly in Asia, where agricultural workers' conditions leave much to be desired'.[18] Ratification of the Convention would make little difference to the amount of the agricultural worker's paid holiday in Britain, but it would give legal security for current arrangements. In England, Wales and Scotland, the existing agencies for fixing holidays with pay and other employment terms and conditions were the wages boards set up under the various Agricultural Wages Acts. The boards were 'empowered' to make provisions for paid holidays – and they had done so. The British Government had refused to ratify the international measures, for the effect would be to *require* the boards to make provisions rather than to *enable* them to act, as at present. In other words, the minimum standards would be *obligatory* and not dependent on the decisions of the various statutory wage-regulating bodies to take action under authorization of Acts of Parliament permitting them to do so.

Concern was voiced at the 1955 Congress that the British Government had still not ratified the 1952 Convention and Recommendation, despite the approaches made by the General Council to the Minister of Agriculture and Minister of Labour. Government spokesmen had admitted that the international regulations would not substantially alter the present position in Britain. The main difficulty was the wording of the Convention which could be held to limit the discretion of the regional Agricultural Wages Boards; however, the Minister of Labour was 'at present reconsidering his earlier decision'. Evidently the TUC's argument prevailed, for in 1956 Congress was informed that: 'During this year, the Government has ratified the Convention.'[19]

During the war years, the TUC's main concern about working-time had been to control excessively long hours of work in order to avoid the decline of production due to bodily fatigue and mental stress. Apart from that, its initiatives to shorten working hours were suspended. During the first five years following the war, the trade unions mounted a major campaign to secure legislation on the 40-hour week and a fortnight's paid holiday. In a very real sense, this was not a new campaign, but merely a resumption of its interwar drive, and it met with no more success than in the 1930s. The gains – reductions of the basic working week to one of 44 or 45 hours in some industries and an increase to a fortnight's paid holiday by a few trade unions – were the outcome of collective bargaining. The campaign generated considerable heat in the second half of the 1940s. Thereafter resolutions on working-time became fewer, and discussion less protracted and less impassioned to the end of the 1950s.

Notes

1. Pelling, H. (1992), *A History of British Trade Unionism*, London, Penguin, ch.11.
2. Pollard, S. (1992), *The Development of the British Economy, 1914–1990*, London, Edward Arnold, ch.6.

3. May, T. (1993), *An Economic and Social History of Britain, 1760–1970*, London, Longman, ch.13; Goldthorpe, J.H., Lockwood, D. *et al.* (1968), *The Affluent Worker in the Class Structure*, Cambridge, University Press.
4. Numerous directions and confirming orders issued by the trade boards are recorded in the *Ministry of Labour Gazette* in 1939 and 1940.
5. Information on the views and action taken by the General Council is recorded in wartime *Reports* of the TUC; see, for example, TUC, *Report*, 1939, pp.146–8, 195–7; 1940, pp.114–5, 334–5; 1941, pp.110–11, 177–9, 207–8.
6. *Ibid.* 1941, p.290.
7. *Ibid.* p.291.
8. Pelling, H., *op.cit.* ch.11.
9. Trades Union Congress (1944), *Report*, pp.306–7.
10. The first was published as a Government White Paper, *Social Insurance and Allied Services* (1942), Cmd. 6404; Beveridge, W.H. (1944), *Full Employment in a Free Society*, London, Allen & Unwin.
11. Trades Union Congress (1945), *Report*, pp.173–4, 427–31.
12. *Ibid.* p.428.
13. *Ibid.* (1946), p.183.
14. *Ibid.* p.185.
15. *Ibid.* (1947), p.252.
16. *Ibid.* (1948), p.253; (1949), p. 252.
17. *Ibid.* (1951), p.213; (1952), pp. 200–201.
18. *Ibid.* (1954), pp.150, 441–2.
19. *Ibid.* (1956), p.124.

5

The TUC's Targets, 1960–79: Priorities and Preferences

Introduction

The period from 1960 to 1979 has been termed the 'era of the unions'. The growth in trade union membership was a salutary development for the TUC, but, with the escalation of friction in industrial relations, the press became ever more critical of trade union actions as manifestations of irresponsible self-interest which inconvenienced the public at large and threatened business competitiveness. Union membership grew from around 9¾ million in 1960 to an all-time peak of some 13¼ million in 1979. Whereas industrial relations were 'troubled' in the 1960s, they were 'turbulent' in the 1970s. Whereas (except in 1962) the number of working days annually lost through strike action were less than 3 million up to 1967, they rose and remained high thereafter (except in 1976) to reach over 13 million in 1971 and 1974, over 23 million in 1972, and over 29 million in 1979.[1]

Near-full employment during the 1960s, as in the preceding decade, put the trade unions in a relatively strong bargaining position. From 1948 to 1968 the official unemployment rate for males and females combined was consistently less than 3.0 per cent and rose above 2.0 per cent in only seven years. In the 1970s the average annual unemployment rate ranged from 2.6 per cent to 6.9 per cent, with the most marked rise occurring in the latter half of the decade.[2] Tight labour markets advantaged the trade unions at the bargaining table; but collective bargaining was not entirely unconstrained, for successive governments intervened to curb pay and price inflation with a series of incomes policies which variously urged voluntary restraint in pay claims, or set guidelines, or imposed statutory limits and the occasional pay freeze. There were exemptions, however; pay rises above the norm were permissible where wages were especially low and where workpeople's acceptance of new production methods and working practices gave rise to significant improvements in productivity. The latter exemption encouraged 'productivity bargaining'.[3] Although some productivity agreements were later disparaged as phoney deals, which raised wages but had little or no effect on productivity, one result was to introduce a new style of 'something for something' bargaining in which both parties to an agreement might gain.

People's lives, some contemporaries observed, were becoming less work-centred and progressively more leisure-oriented. Parker,[4] Roberts[5] and others postulated 'the emergence of the leisure society'.

These were years in which sociological researchers discovered 'the affluent worker'.[6] For much of the period money incomes were rising rapidly; basic wage rates increased in what was rapidly becoming the annual pay round, shop stewards and local union negotiators were able to secure a variety of wage supplements for the groups they represented,[7] overtime work at premium rates became more abundant, and the earnings of married women, drawn into paid employment in ever larger numbers, augmented family incomes. Affluent working class families now acquired spending habits, consumption patterns, and material living standards formerly characteristic of the middle class. There was increased spending on household durables of all kinds: refrigerators, gas or electric cookers, washing machines, electric irons and kettles, television sets and record-players, along with telephones, fitted carpets, cars, home-ownership, and holidays abroad.[8] Attitudes were changing, aspirations were rising, and horizons were widening.

The prosperity of the 1960s gradually subsided and gave

way to the uncertainties of what Coopey *et al.* term 'the troubled economy' of the 1970s. Unemployment began to rise. The shrinking manufacturing sector, Britain's declining competitiveness in world trade,[9] and technological advance which changed and reduced employers' labour requirements, brought an unwanted form of leisure for the growing numbers who lost their jobs.

Priorities and Preferences in the Age of Affluence

Working-time had been discussed infrequently and with little sense of urgency during the 1950s, but in 1960 the TUC returned to the issue with renewed interest. The 40-hour week had not yet been established as the norm, but large numbers of workpeople now had entitlement to a full fortnight of annual paid holiday plus the public holidays with pay.

A succinctly worded resolution moved at the 1960 Congress called for the third week of paid holiday. The further intensification of work in recent times, it was asserted, requiring ever greater mental concentration and ever more strenuous physical effort, necessitated a longer break in the working year for relaxation, recuperation and revitalization. The recent increases in production and productivity, which brought the benefit of rising profits for employers, ought to provide workpeople with the benefit of longer holidays. With modern production techniques, workers were 'burning themselves up twice as fast as they did in years gone by ...' and the result before long would be falling productivity. The three-week holiday was therefore a 'vital and essential need for both sides of industry, not only for the workers' welfare, but also for the productive capacity of the nation'. The speaker observed, cynically and class-consciously, that 'the farther you get from the workshop floor, the farther you get from the real job ... and the nearer you get to managerial status, the longer the holiday you get'.[10] There was no good reason, in his view, for employers to withhold from manual workers what was allowed for office personnel whose jobs were considerably less exhausting.

The delegate who had raised the subject had claimed that the resolution was 'a short and simple one', but a member of the General Council disagreed. The matter was far from simple. A longer paid holiday was only one of several benefits which workpeople desired. Individual unions would be well advised to list the various choices in order of preference, according to the wishes of their members and in the light of circumstances prevailing in the particular industry. Priorities could never be the same in all industries and for all sections of the country's workforce. In many industries there was an urgent need to negotiate for the introduction of occupational pension schemes: 'and rightly so, because when you give a pension, you give a reward to the men who have done the work and borne the heat and burden of the day.' If Socialism meant anything, it meant 'rewarding the older people by giving them pensions, so that in the eventide of their lives they might have contentment and a happy retirement'. In the quest for increased leisure time, there were many workpeople who might prefer a shorter working week to a longer holiday. That would be a sensible choice; for with a reduction of the basic working week from 44 to 42 hours, an employee would gain around 100 more hours of leisure per year without loss of pay, but with an extra week's paid holiday the gain would be only 42 to 45 hours. Negotiators ought to make such calculations in ordering their bargaining priorities. Other workers might prefer the guaranteed week; in good times it was easy to forget the guaranteed week and the security it provided, but it was 'an important priority' in some spheres of employment; so also was occupational sick pay:

> These are the benefits that the General Council have in mind ... and maybe I am going to shock Congress, because I am going to say that if the unions themselves accept the fact that the unions in the individual industries must decide the priorities, then the General Council will view with more favour a third week's holiday with pay ...[11]

It seems probable that members of the General Council were more aware than some delegates at Congress of the currently favourable opportunities to win for manual workers some of the fringe benefits which had long been available for white-collar groups and the salaried in general. Along with markedly high pay increases, items such as occupational pensions and sick pay were coming within the grasp of manual workforces in these years. The 1960s and 1970s would witness the unprecedented spread of arrangements providing benefits supplementary to the national insurance schemes for pensions and sick pay.[12] The main difference between pay increases, the shorter working week and paid holidays on the one hand, and special pay supplements, and occupational sick pay and pensions on the other, is that the former were normally negotiated at national industry-wide level while the latter were more usually agreed at the level of the company; insofar as there were national agreements on the latter items, they tended to be confined mostly to public sector organizations, including the nationalized industries.

Evidently the mover of the resolution was none too happy with the line taken by the General Council, for he went on to insist that 'the whole Congress' should 'without reservation' give support to those unions proposing to negotiate on paid holidays; most European and Scandinavian countries had better provision than Britain. The same point was pressed again in 1962, with statistics given to show the extent to which other countries were ahead.

In general workpeople in Britain currently had no more than 18 days of paid holiday each year: 12 days of annual holiday plus six public holidays; those working a 5-day week had only 16 days. If this was compared with the 25 to 31 days of holiday with pay in France, 25 to 28 in West Germany, 31 in Italy, 29 in Sweden, 22 in Belgium, 28 to 30 in Finland, 26 to 27 in Denmark, and 28 in both Holland and Norway, 'we get a powerful indication that when British employers opposing longer holidays argue the necessity of being able to compete with foreign producers, they are in effect attempting to reap an advantage from the relative cheapness of British labour'. In other words, it was asserted, British employers were maximizing their own advantage by sacrificing workpeople's leisure in order to raise output and profits.

There had been talk at the previous year's Congress of prioritizing choices 'because we cannot do all things at once', and union officers had been advised to 'make calculations'. In making such assessments, negotiators ought to bear in mind that, while the value of wage increases, pensions, sick pay, and the guaranteed week could be eroded by price inflation and rising taxation, the benefit of increased leisure was enduring. Before Congress was tempted to echo 'the Macmillan mythology of never having had it so good', it should be remembered that, as far back in history as 1552, around 27 days were legally sanctioned as holidays. It was a sobering thought to reflect that sixteenth-century society had holidays that the twentieth century, 'with all its vaunted technology and economic achievements', was unable to afford.

Another speaker, who described himself as 'a humble foundry worker', pressed socio-cultural reasons for longer holidays: 'Holidays are for the mental peace of the worker, so that he can begin to feel relaxed and give deeper appreciation to the things around him, the beauties of nature and so on ...'. They would enable people to visit and admire the country's great castles and cathedrals:

> I do not profess to visit cathedrals for religious purposes; but I do appreciate the tremendous work of construction and the great beauty that a cathedral can represent. And I can look at an old castle and think in terms of its beauty ... Workpeople on holiday would visit museums, listen to good music, read good books ... One has to think in terms of holidays giving workers the opportunity to enjoy such things.[13]

An additional two public holidays would bring Britain more into line with leading European countries, most of which had far more occasional days of holiday than Britain. Observance of May Day, a centuries-old traditional holiday, had lapsed in

Britain, but it was widely celebrated in continental Europe; a Labor Day was observed in September in the USA, and yet Britain, the birthplace of trade unionism, did not celebrate the trade union movement on any specific day: 'Surely the time has now arrived to get back to the principle that May Day should be a national holiday.'

The following year the General Council outlined its main observations on the holiday question, reminding Congress that opportunities to extend paid holidays varied from industry to industry, and that individual unions would have to determine their own negotiating priorities accordingly. It was resolved that the best means of assisting those unions seeking the third week would be to provide them with information about the present position in Britain and other countries, together with statistics and arguments which might be used effectively at the bargaining table.

Another aspect of the more generous provision abroad was the practice of offering additional paid holidays to young employees and to workers in physically arduous and hazardous occupations. This, the General Council noted, had no parallel in Britain. In West Germany and Austria, for example, where adult workers received from 22 to 25 days' paid holiday, those below 18 years of age were allowed an extra 12 days; young workers in France and Belgium had an extra 4 or 5 days; and additional days of holiday leave were provided for underground workers in Norway, Sweden and Belgium. British trade unions, the General Council suggested, might seek similar concessions in their negotiations with British employers.

The General Council was not convinced of the advisability of seeking additional public holidays nationwide, for it would require amendment of existing legislation relating to bank and public holidays and involve a great deal of time and effort which would not necessaily meet with success. There was nothing to prevent individual unions from negotiating additional occasional days for their own members, however, if they so desired. Negotiators might prefer to focus their efforts on securing the shorter working week or the third week's holiday, or even both, for there was a greater chance of success in these areas than in gaining extra public holidays. There were already three public holidays in the spring and early summer months; should Congress decide sometime in the future to act on the proposal to secure more public holidays, these might be better spaced if one of them were to be appointed in autumn rather than at the beginning of May. The question, it was felt, required further thought.

The 1963 Congress reaffirmed the need for longer paid holidays and the 5-day 40-hour week, both of which were now being justified in terms of forward-planning as the means to prevent future unemployment, and in terms of the worker's 'rightful share' in the fruits of present prosperity. No-one could predict how long full employment would last: 'We believe in planning ... If you do not get a shorter working week and longer holidays as a cushion, you are going to have unemployment.' At the same time: 'Workpeople should reap some benefit from industrial progress ... And let us stop talking of fringe benefits in these things. They are not fringe benefits but essential priorities.'[14] It was all very well to talk of differing aims and varying preferences, it was argued, but the resolution had quite rightly recognized a 'general need' and a 'universal priority' which superseded 'individual choice':

> It expresses our common and united interest ... Fundamentally, the claim ... rests on common ground. It is this: that workers have a right to share in the benefits of increased productivity which industrial and commercial progress has made possible, and to take part of their share in the form of leisure.[15]

The General Council's report to Congress in 1964 contained a summary of recent change in basic working hours and holiday entitlements in Britain. It was noted that during 1963 there had been a quickening of the trend to the 40-hour week for manual workers and that the trend had continued in 1964 with little sign of abating. A noteworthy feature of the last 18 months had been the growing number of long-term agreements covering periods of two or more years, which provided for the shortening of hours and lengthening of holidays in stages, little by little. A few industries and several large companies were already operating a basic 40-hour week, and others had definite plans to do so in the near future. An estimated one million manual workers – around 7.0 per cent of workers covered by collective agreements or wage-regulating orders – now worked a basic week of 40 hours or were covered by arrangements to introduce the 40-hour week by a specific date. Certain other industries, including building, civil engineering, cotton, footwear, and glass, had agreements to reduce the working week to 41 or 41½ hours. In addition, there had been some reductions in industries where longer-than-average working hours were characteristic: in agriculture from 46 to 45 hours, and in baking (other than the multiples) from 44 to 42 hours. In the matter of basic working hours, Britain did not now lag quite as far behind other major European countries, apart from France, but was still far behind the USA, Australia and Canada. The extent to which Britain had now moved into line with major European countries was no cause for complacency on the part of the trade unions, however, for there were already clear signs of moves towards even shorter basic working hours in parts of Europe, especially in West Germany. In other words, the trade unions were chasing a moving target.

The basic working week of manual workers in other economically advanced countries provided an important yardstick against which to measure progress on the hours front in Britain, but it was not the only comparison that could be made. Manual grades in general had a longer working week than salaried staffs. The General Council noted that, although no comprehensive statistics were available, it was 'well known that many non-manual workers have a 35 to 38 hour week.' Civil servants were to have their working week reduced by one hour in 1964, and by another hour in 1965. Evidently, the leadership of the TUC was already thinking in terms of a new target, before the 40-hour week had been established as the norm.

If the unions were making headway in reducing basic working hours, they were also gaining ground in increasing paid holidays. About 96.0 per cent of manual workers covered by collective agreements or Wages Regulation Orders were currently entitled to an annual paid holiday of two weeks, around 4.0 per cent had a basic entitlement of more than a fortnight, and an estimated 15.0 per cent were covered by arrangements providing extra days according to length of service with the same employer. During 1964 several national agreements had been reached to phase in the third week by one-day or two-day increases per year; and more agreements were in the pipeline for additional days for workers with longer service. The overwhelming majority had six public holidays with pay, and some received extra occasional days.

It remained true, nevertheless, that manual workers in Britain were disadvantaged in comparison with their counterparts in most European countries, where the fourth week was becoming increasingly common. Sweden now had legislation for the fourth week, which would come into operation in 1965. France had legislation which gave workpeople statutory entitlement to a minimum of three weeks, and collective bargaining had secured the fourth week for around six million workpeople. In some European countries holiday pay was higher than basic wages; workers in Belgium and the Netherlands, for example, received double pay for each holiday week. In Britain some industries had agreements for holiday pay based on 'average earnings' as opposed to 'basic rates', and similar arrangements were under discussion elsewhere; but most workers received only the basic rate for the standard working week at holiday time. In effect, for many people income was lower when they were on holiday leave than when they were at work, yet holidays were times of peak spending in the year. The trade unions, the General Council advised, ought seriously to consider the possibility of negotiating higher holiday pay rates or special holiday bonuses.

The General Council's investigation disclosed much less progress on working time in sectors where conditions were set by the statutory wage regulating authorities. A broad approach to the Wages Councils, however, was believed to be impracticable, for priorities and preferences had to be taken into account, and many of the Councils were currently considering other improvements, such as wage increases, which workpeople wanted more urgently. The TUC's Advisory Committee was to keep developments in the Wages Councils under review.

New Targets: The 35-Hour Week and the 4-Week Holiday

In the quest to reach European standards, the TUC's working-time targets in 1964 were 'a progressive reduction of working hours to 35 per week without loss of pay, and longer holidays of not less than three weeks'. Substantial progress had been made recently, but the unions could not afford to rest on their laurels. They had 'shown amazing moderation' in their claims, and the time had come to be more ambitious: 'We are rapidly becoming the most backward nation in Europe' and should 'declare that we have no intention of remaining at the back of the queue for very much longer'.[16] British employers had been 'niggardly in the extreme in dealing with the unions' claims, particularly those for increased holidays'. It was regrettable that the manual worker's holiday was being lengthened 'on the instalment plan – one day a year ... and extra days for long years of service'. Service-related entitlements benefited relatively few and disadvantaged those who left their place of employment to work elsewhere; but: 'with the spirit of determination at Congress, the four-week annual holiday will be won before long.'

There were cogent health reasons for longer holidays. The rising incidence of sickness absence, of which both the Government and the employers complained, could be checked if people had more leisure time to restore their energies and their morale. Of the 24 million persons paying in to the national health insurance scheme, about a million were off sick at any one time and claiming sickness benefit, 'thus costing the nation something in the region of £130 million a year'. At the same time, the technological displacement of labour, which was in prospect, could be countered in advance by the 'preventive medicine' of shorter working time.

A report from the ILO in 1960, Congress was reminded, had shown that where working time had been reduced, employers had often been able to raise production and productivity by increased investment, better plant utilization, greater plant capacity, and improved methods of management; and it had been suggested that companies could benefit from the reduction of sickness absence, labour turnover, and absenteeism when holidays were increased and working hours shortened. Rising productivity was welcome, a member of the General Council believed, if consumer markets could continue to absorb all that was produced, and so long as it brought greater leisure for workpeople rather than lost jobs. A recent government report had said of the motor industry that, despite the considerable increase in production during the last few years and the higher output levels projected for the near future, employment in the industry was expected to rise only moderately. It was well known that the car manufacturers were taking full advantage of the automated techniques that were now available. Whereas, in 1961, 401,000 workers had produced 1,640,000 vehicles, it was forecast that by 1966 a workforce 'moderately increased' to around 459,000 would be producing an estimated 2,582,000 vehicles. In effect, there would be an increase of about 15.0 per cent in the numbers employed but a rise of some 60.0 per cent in production over the five-year period. In the chemical industry, which again was capital-intensive and highly automated, a projected 38.0 per cent increase in production would be achieved with a workforce reduced by 2.0 per cent. The implications for employment in these and other industries were perfectly clear. If jobs were to be preserved in the future, it was of 'paramount importance ... to move quickly forward to further [hours] reductions'.

The unions, another delegate observed, might seem to be acting prematurely in advancing claims for a 35-hour week before the 40-hour week had been fully established as the norm. But past experience showed that it took several years from the declaration of an objective to the moment of achieving it. To set new and ambitious targets was therefore perfectly reasonable. The fact remained, however, that 'the real job of the British trade unions' was to obtain for their members a sufficient wage to enable them to dispense with the large amount of overtime currently being worked: 'How many men on the basic rate,' he asked rhetorically, '... can afford their families a holiday in Blackpool, never mind about abroad, unless they work a substantial number of hours overtime, including Sundays, most weeks' without being 'a bit of a magician?' There was a need for a widespread campaign to raise basic pay rates, coupled with the demand for increased leisure. The time 'must come when every worker ... can afford to take a proper holiday, not by working Saturday mornings and Sundays, but by working the bare minimum of a 35-hour week'.

The General Council's 1966 report to Congress showed that further progress had been made in the basic working week and annual holidays in the last few years. Some 30.0 per cent of manual workers were now entitled to a basic holiday of more than a fortnight, 33.0 per cent had extra service-related days, and around 50.0 per cent had gained the basic 40-hour week, often under long-term agreements.

New international Conventions on hours and holidays in these years seem to have been few and appear to have generated only lukewarm interest at Congress. The 1970 Convention for the three-week holiday, revising the Conventions of 1936 and 1952, prompted the General Council to ask the Employment Secretary what steps the Government would take to ratify it. As the Government had again abstained from voting on the issue at the IL Conference, the Secretary's reply, that holidays, like wages, hours and other terms of employment, were matters for voluntary negotiation and not state intervention, came as no great surprise to the TUC. The inconsistency of this non-interventionist stance with the Government's heavily interventionist past and future policies to curb improvements in pay and other items in the total remuneration package, seems to have caused no comment. The unions were now deeply involved in a drive for more public holidays; to channel their efforts in that direction would benefit far more workpeople than to expend their energies in a campaign for legislation for the three-week holiday which for many had already been won by negotiation.

Flexitime working, publicized in the press following its introduction in the Civil Service and certain other organizations, was discussed at Congress in the early 1970s. The General Council reviewed the system's advantages and disadvantages, and concluded that it might be acceptable in offices where the work was usually done by individuals acting alone, but that it was less suitable in manufacturing work. Union negotiators meeting with employers' proposals to introduce flexitime were advised to ensure that any agreement they reached contained safeguards for employees. As virtually all the currently available information on flexitime working came from employers and their consultants, it might be biased; but employers' proposals to introduce it might provide the occasion for the unions to gain improved job security for the employees affected, along with higher pay, a shorter basic week and longer paid holidays, as a *quid pro quo*.

Another change in working patterns, and one sought by the unions rather than employers, was the four-day working week and the three-day weekend. In identifying the 'many factors' currently influencing its policy on working time, the TUC noted in 1972: recognition that a high rate of economic growth would not necessarily produce a correspondingly increased demand for labour and more employment opportunities; a marked decline in job satisfaction, arising from the repetitive, routinized and monotonized nature of many work tasks; increased stress and fatigue caused by technological advance and the introduction of new performance-related pay structures; deterioration of the working environment as a result of cost-cutting by employers; and greater purchasing power that enabled people to take up leisure activities for which they needed more leisure time. With widening horizons, people were increasingly looking outside the working environment for personal fulfilment and social satisfaction; a major socio-cultural transition from a work-centred to a leisure-oriented society was underway. In this context the General Council urged the need for more rapid progress in shortening working time: moves towards a 32-hour 4-day normal working week, the fourth week of annual paid holiday, sabbatical leave, time off from work in preparation for retirement, opportunities for early retirement in combination with a substantial increase in the state retirement pension, and leave of absence for attendance of adult education courses – reflecting the concept of lifetime education. These would be targets for the unions to the end of the 1970s and beyond.

More Public Holidays

The question of more public holidays was raised at Congress again in 1965, at a time when the Government had the re-arrangement of some of the six existing public holidays under review. A resolution carried that year proposed that when the General Council was 'consulted on the projected re-arrangement ... it should urge upon the Government the desirability of creating an additional public holiday on May 1st'.[17] Public holidays had been 'much in the news recently' due to the experimental change, initiated by the Government, in moving the August Bank Holiday to the end of the month. Here was a 'golden opportunity' for an approach to the Government to appoint May Day as a regular national holiday.

The subject appears to have generated little enthusiasm, for it was discussed neither at length nor in detail, and was treated with equal brevity the following year in the General Council's report, which noted somewhat dismissively that affiliated unions did not seem to be advancing claims for May Day at the bargaining table. By implication, there was no point in approaching the Government for something which did not seem to be high on union members' list of priorities.

The question was not raised again until 1970, when the General Council reported its concurrence in the Government's declared intention to amend the law on bank holidays.[18] An interim order had been issued, with effect to 1973, and legislation would follow to make the change permanent. The only change, however, would be to shift the August Bank Holiday and to sanction a day in lieu when Christmas Day fell on a Sunday. Evidently, feelings were now running high, for a resolution carried by Congress that year called for 'at least two' additional public holidays – May Day plus New Year's Day (and an alternative day in Scotland). The tenor of discussion suggests exasperation as much as dissatisfaction with the *status quo*: 'There are six public holidays that the British worker has to stick to, and that is that.' In contrast, workpeople had 10 to 13 public holidays in West Germany, 16 in Italy, 10 in Belgium, Australia and Luxembourg, 11 in Austria and Sweden, 8 in Switzerland, France and the USA, 9 and 9½ in New Zealand and Denmark respectively, and 8 to 10 in Canada. To compound Britain's inferior position, most other countries had longer annual holidays as well.

The speaker reminded his audience that when the May Day holiday had been proposed at Congress in 1961 and 1965, they had been more or less fobbed off with the excuse that most of the existing public holidays were already crowded into a few short months, and that not one single union had sought May Day at the bargaining table. The General Council's rebuff, that it was 'not even intelligent to spread holidays in this way in a period of two months', had been accepted uncritically and without protest. Spreading the public holidays was not the main problem; the main problem was that Britain had 'too few days to spread'. Other countries, most of which observed May Day, managed to spread from 10 to 16 public holidays over the year; and if they could do it, so also could Britain.

In addition to May Day, which was a centuries-old traditional holiday and also, as Labour Day, an important date in trade union history, Britain ought to have a public holiday on New Year's Day. That day was an officially sanctioned holiday only in Scotland, but most workpeople now wanted to celebrate New Year's Day in the 'real spirit', as the first day, the birthday, of the year, and many were taking it regardless:

> And yet look at the hue and cry we have had over the past few years. The British worker is failing to turn up at the docks, the car industries, and all the rest. All the Press boys have a field-day, the industrialists have a field-day, about the loss of production that occurs ... But no one has outlined, or has tried to talk about, the number of giants of British industry and the shareholders who do not turn out on New Year's Day – and I do not think they are *all* Scots.[19]

Evidently, many workpeople were awaiting neither legislation nor collective agreements for the New Year's Day holiday, but were resorting to wilful absenteeism on the day in question. In certain districts, May Day was similarly treated. There had been May Day demonstrations in London the previous year, and even larger rallies were expected in the near future: 'They will take May Day without any legislation or any urging from the Trade Union Movement,' a delegate observed, 'and progressively more will take New Year's Day.' The situation provided strong evidence of workpeople's preferences, and of employers' resistance to trade unions' claims at the bargaining table: 'We do not seem to be able to negotiate these days, despite pressure from the shop floor.' If the Government were to give 'official recognition' of the two extra public holidays, the problem would be resolved, and 'at least it would be some incentive to get the production we are always being told about'.

The arguments and evidence aired at the 1970 Congress convinced the General Council that the question must now be given serious and immediate attention. The bank holidays and public holidays, Congress was reminded the following year, were scheduled by legislation, and that legislation applied only to certain spheres of employment specified in the relevant Acts of Parliament. They had become widely extended to other trades and occupations, mainly by collective agreement and Wages Council Order, to become extensively observed in most, if not all, industries and services. Since employers would be more disposed to concede the unions' claims for May Day and New Year's Day if these were officially sanctioned as bank holidays, the General Council had made an approach to the Government and was to meet the Employment Minister to discuss the matter. The Government rejected the General Council's proposal that the additional bank holidays should be designated under the Banking and Financial Dealings Bill of 1971. A reply from the Treasury stated that the Bill sought only to consolidate and slightly amend existing legislation on bank holidays, and was not intended for the appointment of new holidays.

The General Council raised the question with the Employment Secretary early in 1972, but again received a negative response. The following year, it was reported to Congress that large numbers of people had stayed away from work on New Year's Day, and that employers were beginning to concede the day's holiday in collective agreements. At a further meeting with the Employment Secretary, the General Council reminded him that, of all EEC member states, only the UK and Eire did not observe New Year's Day as a national holiday. There was also the problem of inconvenience which the present uncertain position on New Year's Day caused for employers who were unable to predict how many employees would report for work on that day. Managers had to make contingency plans and run their plant at reduced capacity, which, in terms of overheads incurred, could be as expensive as closing for the day. The Employment Secretary repeated his earlier counter-argument, that more public holidays were inconsistent with the Government's economic policy, although he did acknowledge that the case for New Year's Day was a strong one.

In discussion of the subject at that year's Congress, the question of living standards was raised. It was argued that no standard of living was 'decent enough' without 'adequate opportunities ... to enjoy sufficient time with our families and engage in social pursuits'. The rise of earnings during the last decade and a half enabled people to be better fed, clothed and housed; but the 'more material comforts' which were now affordable were at the cost of the social dimension of family life, for many married women had been drawn into paid employment. The general rise in living standards, which politicians credited to their economic policies, was somewhat illusory, for the 'average family' now spent 'a darned sight more hours at work than they used to, because of the increased number of married women who are now working'.

Congress was aware that the United Kingdom had fewer public holidays than were observed in other EEC countries; arrangements in the UK ought to be brought into line, as the harmonization of standards was one of the EEC's objectives: 'Having been forced into Europe, some people think against our will, it is only right that we should look over our shoulders to see what is happening ... in the European Economic Community.' The Government's publication, *The Common Market and the Common Man*, which listed the statutory and public holidays of the various EEC countries, showed 'not surprisingly that the United Kingdom is at the bottom of the league'. The TUC's case for more public holidays was, therefore, 'absolutely overwhelming'.

The General Council met with the Employment Secretary in June 1973 to press the TUC's case. In October of that year the Government issued a consultative document on prices and incomes which indicated its preparedness to designate, with effect from 1974, New Year's Day as a public holiday in England, Wales and Northern Ireland, and an alternative day in Scotland. The request for May Day also, subsequently pressed by the General Council in November, was refused however.[20]

The Government's willingness to concede New Year's Day as a public holiday owed much to the fact that many workpeople were already entitled to the day off with pay under the terms of collective agreements, and many others were absent without authorization and without pay. Something was owed also to employers' complaints and press reports that a fair proportion of those who turned up for work on that day, following New Year's Eve celebrations running on well beyond midnight, arrived late or were in no fit state or frame of mind to function productively. Workpeople had already captured New Year's Day as a holiday in advance of any official declaration from the Government to that effect. Legislation simply sanctioned what was already more or less achieved as a *fait accompli* in much of the private sector where companies and whole industries were free to make their own arrangements within the now less rigid restraints of government policy for prices, incomes and productivity. The main effect of legislation declaring New Year's Day a public holiday was upon the business and commercial activities of the City, the banks and other financial institutions, and certain public offices, which could not be suspended at will.

Following the election of a Labour government, the General Council wrote to the new Employment Secretary in April 1974, requesting that May Day be designated as an eighth public holiday. The question was considered by Labour Cabinet Ministers, who decided 'with regret' that the creation of a new holiday must wait until economic circumstances were more favourable. The matter would be reconsidered later in the year. The Labour Government's response to the General Council's request for May Day had been disappointing. The explanation, that the extra day could not be allowed in present economic circumstances was a 'mere pretext'; and there was little reassurance in the 'empty promise' of reconsidering the question when the state of the economy improved. As it was expressed by one delegate:

> Now I, for one, cannot accept this. I would make the comparison, that if the last Conservative government could allow us under their Stage III of the Price and Pay Code the provision of an extra day of statutory holiday, then, even in the light of the present economic situation, a Labour government could make a concession within the Social Contract and stipulate that, from next year and henceforth, 1st May will be a statutory holiday.[21]

There followed further consultations between the General

Council and the Employment Secretary, and a compromise was reached to declare May Day a public holiday, not immediately, but with effect from a specified future day. The Employment Secretary wrote to the General Council in March 1976 to confirm that the Government had decided to designate May Day as a public holiday to be observed in and from 1978. Exactly which day in May would be appointed as the eighth public holiday was yet to be decided. The General Council believed that, given the historical significance of May Day for the Labour Movement, the new holiday ought to be on the first day of May, or the next following Monday when 1 May fell on a Saturday or Sunday. The Employment Secretary, on the other hand, took the view that the first Monday in May was preferable, for it would provide workpeople with a long weekend and avoid the disruption of production that a mid-week holiday might cause. In his letter of 30 March 1976, the Employment Secretary also informed the General Council that the Government had decided to make provision, with effect from Christmas 1976 and New Year's Day 1977, for days in lieu (the next following Monday or Tuesday) when those two public holidays fell on a Saturday or Sunday.

British workers' eight official public holidays were still fewer than those available to workforces in several other countries at a comparable stage of economic development, but the TUC did not conduct further campaigns for more such days. Instead, unions in individual industries and companies would negotiate additional one-day holidays, to be taken at various times in the year, according to the priorities and preferences of their members.

Signs of Recession and a New Working-time Campaign

The 40-hour week had become the norm by the end of the 1960s. In the mid-1970s, with rising unemployment, the TUC turned its attention more emphatically to the 35-hour week and drastic curtailment of overtime as a means to ameliorate the problem. In 1976 there came the first signs of a campaign that would begin in earnest in 1978.

In years when negotiations were still constrained by incomes policy, a resolution, carried in 1976, called on Congress to 'give high priority to reducing the working week as soon as ... normal collective bargaining is resumed', asked the General Council to 'lead a campaign for a 35-hour week', and urged affiliated unions to 'reduce overtime working and oppose moonlighting'. The TUC, it was argued, needed to devise and implement policies which would effect a return to full employment, for statistics and graphs depicting unemployment trends in Britain and comparable industrial economies indicated that the current 'deplorable level of unemployment' was 'no one-off freak wave' which would 'recede before some tidal movement of recovery from the recession in world trade'.[22] Moonlighting and overtime working had to be discouraged, for the effect was to deprive the unemployed of job opportunities.

The currently rising unemployment rate was said to be largely caused by the 'violent inflationary cost upheaval in world trade in 1974–5', which had plunged the British economy into 'the worst recession for forty years', but there were other contributory causes, for 'underlying and underpinning this surge of unemployment, generated by the retrenchment of world trade, is the permanent threat ... arising from structural and technological change'. To ignore the inevitable effect of such pressures on employment would be an act of folly. Denis Healey had recently stated that the world recession reflected conscious decisions by governments to give overriding priority to the task of curbing inflation and correcting payments imbalances at the cost of jobs. The rise of unemployment was therefore reversible:

> First, we must all understand that unemployment, like inflation, is not a biblical plague visited as a judgment on a licentious and sinful nation by a vengeful god. It is man-made, and we can resolve it ourselves.

The Government could, and should, intervene 'with different

priorities and different policies', but unions could help to reverse the situation by drastically reducing working-time so as to share out the available work, thereby promoting a return to full employment.

The following year Congress again called for strenuous efforts by negotiators to reduce working time, and urged the Labour Government to implement co-ordinated measures to boost the economy: increased investment from the proceeds of North Sea oil, more funds for the National Enterprise Board, subsidies for youth training and employment schemes, and expansion of the public sector programme.

All were aware that the Labour Prime Minister had recently spoken cautiously of reflating the economy, emphasizing the advisability of 'driving up through the gears in order to avoid the risk of stalling the engine by trying to get away in top gear'. That made a certain amount of sense, but too much caution, the speaker believed, had led to the downfall of former Labour governments. The postwar Attlee Government had 'clung to siege-economy methods' up to 1951 at a time when world commodity prices were moving in Britain's favour. The result was that an incoming risk-taking Tory Government 'got the prize through taking the risk, and had thirteen years of rule as a reward for it'. In 1970, a Labour Government which had 'transformed a record Tory trade deficit into a substantial credit balance continued with its hard-slog policies right into the election period, and lost the prize in consequence'. Too much caution at the present time would lead to a 'repeat performance'.

There had been some reference the previous day to 'Heath's ill-fated boom which went bust in 1973'; the Tory Government had presided over a doubling of the money supply in roughly three years. In theory, the speaker explained, investment would flow into productive industries, an export-led boom would follow, and Britain's 'economic miracle' would provide higher standards of living for all. That was not the result, however, because the money flowing through the secondary banking system did not go into productive investment but into speculation in land and property; and, in consequence, 'large areas of our manufacturing industry ... could not meet the demands made upon them because they were "clapped out" through years of investment drought', and other areas were 'raped by asset-strippers and financial spivs'. The subsequent increase in the price of imports, coupled with a vastly expanded money supply, created 'the inflationary troubles we have been fighting ever since'. Prime Minister Callaghan's caution was perfectly understandable, but imaginative policies, skilfully applied and backed up by the TUC's working-time initiatives, could help to ameliorate both inflation and unemployment. The trade unions were urged to renew their efforts: 'We need ourselves to restrict overtime, to start negotiating reduced working years.' These, Mr Basnett continued, were desirable objectives in themselves, but 'absolutely essential if we are to return to full employment ... If we do not pledge ourselves to pursue these objectives, we forfeit the right to tell others what they should be doing.'

Much more could be done by the Government, it was asserted. The TUC's Economic Committee had suggested 12 ways in which taxation policy, including VAT, could be used to increase consumer spending, which would help to preserve and generate employment; and investment in, and expansion of, public sector services would help to offset the mounting job losses in Britain's shrinking manufacturing sector: 'The surest way of creating employment is to reverse the present programme of cutting public expenditure.' Every advanced industrial nation seeking to achieve and maintain full employment in the future would have to rely on expansion of the service sector. The level of unemployment in Britain, now approaching two million, was 'intolerably high' and the problem was compounded by the 'long-term change in the character and composition of the labour force', which reflected structural change in the economy as a whole. Such developments, coupled with the onward rush of new technology which reduced employers' labour requirements, suggested that unemployment would get worse unless the Government and trade unions took positive steps to ameliorate it.

A nationwide reduction of the basic working week, it was

generally recognized, would do little to increase employment unless overtime working could be strictly limited. Some overtime was unavoidable, essential to maintenance and repairs, and occasionally unanticipated and of an emergency character; but it tended to be 'minimal if the staff complement is right'. It was 'systematic overtime', regularly used by some employers as a cheaper alternative to taking on more workers, that was the main problem. Three main difficulties would be encountered by negotiators seeking to eliminate it. First, where overtime suited employers' purposes, they would surrender the practice neither readily nor lightly; second, many workpeople were in favour of overtime and actively sought it, either from poverty or cupidity; and, third, there were many collective agreements, with in-built provision for 'acceptance of overtime working', which could not be dismantled easily. Negotiators were urged to rise to the challenge and use every opportunity that arose to eradicate regular overtime.

The fact that growing numbers had no work at all, while others had 'excessive amounts' of it, lowered the quality of life both for the employed and unemployed; for while the former had the money but lacked the leisure time to enjoy life, the latter lacked the money to enjoy their free time and had a constant struggle to make ends meet. It was this situation in 1977 that prompted Clive Jenkins to call for 'a fresh look at the whole capsule of working life', and to ask:

> Why should our people only be leisured when they are too old to enjoy it, and on a lower standard of life? Why should not we have much longer holidays, and why should not we say that our people are entitled to a couple of slabs of time off in a lifetime ... to reflect and rejuvenate? And why not examine the whole question of retirement? ... What we need is to promote a balance between the working life and the personal life.[23]

The TUC began a major campaign in 1978 to reduce working time.[24] The General Council voiced its disappointment at that year's Congress at the Labour Government's unilateral imposition of a further stage of pay controls, despite the TUC's call for an end to restrictive incomes policies and a return to 'genuinely free' collective bargaining. The limit of 10.0 per cent on pay increases, set out in the new guidelines, had implications for hours reductions; the Labour Government viewed the shortening of the basic working week with some disfavour. As a member of the General Council explained it:

> The new determination among the unions to press for a cut in working hours is of particular importance, and represents a major difference between the TUC and the Government ... The TUC is now committed to achieving cuts in hours in the present pay round, and is urging trade unions to give priority to this in negotiations ... [and to make it] a central part of their overall bargaining strategy.[25]

The General Council issued a circular to all affiliated unions, containing guidelines and advice on bargaining for shorter working time. There might be scope to win a shorter basic week where an employer sought to introduce new processes, production schedules, and improved plant capacity. A reduction of overtime and higher hourly rates might be negotiated as part of an agreed plan to meet output targets. The objectives, which negotiators were asked to bear in mind, included the four-day working week; an annual holiday of at least four weeks; extended leave or sabbaticals for workers with long service in particular jobs; wider-ranging paid educational leave for workers of all ages, which would also increase their suitability for the job vacancies that might arise; facilities for skill training and time off for skilled workers to update and broaden their skills; and earlier retirement, especially for groups whose work was hazardous and/or arduous. The circular placed particular emphasis on the reduction of overtime working, pointing out that 'at the same time as there are over 1½ million unemployed, over a quarter of all male manual workers do eight or more hours of overtime each week.' It was accepted that overtime might be the only means to cope with certain tasks, and that it might reflect an employer's inability to recruit appropriately skilled workers from the ranks of the locally unemployed. But negotiators were advised to make every effort to reduce or eliminate it where overtime was worked regularly and not periodically as a temporary response to production needs: where overtime hours regularly worked were long – for example, in excess of 20 hours per month; where the local unemployment rate was above the national average; and where there were people unemployed in a local area, who could be recruited to do the kinds of jobs that reduced overtime could create. At the same time, where higher output was needed to meet an increase in market demand, it was essential to ensure that the potential for job creation was not swallowed by overtime working on the part of existing employees. The Labour Research Department had estimated that a 50.0 per cent cut in overtime working nationwide would create a quarter of a million jobs:

> ... if we continue to allow unlimited overtime, if we continue to give priority to claims other than the shorter working week, we will stand condemned of hypocrisy, we will show that our real priority is self-interest ...[26]

The issue of working hours had become a major focus of contention between the TUC and the Labour Government. In principle, the TUC had repudiated the 10.0 per cent limit on pay increases in the last pay round, alhough it was committed to a policy of 'moderate settlements' and had, in fact, refused to support groups seeking to flout the pay guidelines. On the question of working-time the differences between the TUC and the Government were markedly greater. The Government insisted that hours reductions would only be countenanced to the extent that an agreement as a whole complied with pay policy; the TUC was 'equally determined to pursue its demands ... The issue will certainly be at the centre of negotiations over the coming months.'[27]

Len Murray, TUC General Secretary, noted in his speech

introducing the economic debate in 1979 that progress in reducing working hours was very slow. Numerous claims had been pressed in both the public and private sectors, but:

> So far we have not made much progress, and one major reason must be attributed to the 10.0 per cent pay policy. So I believe we must make it clear ... that we will not accept any nationally determined pay limit that can impede our moves to create jobs through the 35-hour week.[28]

It was proposed that the public sector should be targeted, for 'the 35-hour week ... in the public services would cost nothing ... because the extra employment would increase government revenue from income tax ... and reduce public spending through savings on unemployment benefit'.

It was at this stage that the General Council began to advocate negotiation of 'New Technology Agreements' as a means both of stemming the flow of technological displacements and of securing working-time reductions. The *TUC Report on Employment and Technology* noted that the introduction of computerized systems provided negotiators with considerable scope for achieving cuts in the basic working week as a *quid pro quo* for acceptance of changes in working practices and job content, for it opened up the question of working-time patterns and the prospect of greater flexibility in the arrangement of working hours.

The British trade unions were well aware that the unemployment problem was not confined to Britain and that unions in other economically advanced countries were, like themselves, seeking shorter working time to create more job opportunities; but whereas in earlier periods the scope of their concern and hope for action extended over the whole International Labour Organization, the main focus was now on the European dimension and initiatives within the European Economic Community. A resolution, moved by Moss Evans at the 1978 Congress, called for 'united action by the

European Trade Union Confederation to seek a reduction of the working week to 35 hours, without loss of pay, in all countries within the EEC'. The following year the General Council was actively supporting the ETUC's programme of action, which called for a 10.0 per cent reduction in working time without loss of pay, and specific targets including: a basic 35-hour week, an increase in annual paid holidays to six weeks, the right of retirement at age 60 on full pension, an increase in the school leaving age to 16 years throughout the EEC, and the right to paid leave from work for vocational training and further education.

Incomes policy in Britain was in its death throes in 1978, and its unpopularity no doubt contributed to the fall of the Labour Government the following year. The incoming Conservative Government abandoned the idea of crude controls over pay. The forthcoming return to 'free collective bargaining' was broadly welcomed by the unions, but the Conservatives' declared intention to make stringent cuts in government spending brought the alarming prospect of even more job losses. Unemployment, Moss Evans admitted, had risen during the Labour Government's term of office, but that government had 'made some effort to cut the dole queues'; the special programme of the Manpower Services Commission, the regional and industrial subsidies, the National Enterprise Board and the Regional Development Agencies were 'all genuine attempts to get people back to work'. Spending on such projects was now to be slashed, however, for they allegedly perpetuated over-manning by job rescue and job subsidy; the Conservative Government had already cut £42 million from the Temporary Employment Programme, £25 million from the Youth Opportunities Programme, £22 million from training opportunities, and had imposed other cuts on a whole range of regional grants, short-time working funds, and small firms' employment subsidies. The TUC was dismayed. Moss Evans described the wider implications of the Government's policy:

It is not just that an unemployed worker has an endless

> struggle to keep the family afloat; it is not just the nagging worry and uncertainty. On top of that, unemployment breeds depression and neglect in our cities and our towns. When an area is hit by unemployment, the shops close, the services decline, the whole community suffers because, if you are not working, you are not spending; demand for goods throughout the economy is slashed; goods pile up in the warehouses and factories; and that means yet more unemployment.[29]

The TUC now launched a special campaign to reduce working time, that would continue throughout the 1980s and beyond.

Notes

1. Pelling, H. (1992), *A History of British Trade Unionism*, London, Penguin, statistical table, pp.302–5.
2. Statistical analyses in monthly issues of the *Employment Gazette* for the relevant period.
3. Stettner, N. (1969), *Productivity Bargaining and Structural Change*, London, Pergamon; McKersie, R. and Hunter, L. (1973), *Pay, Productivity and Collective Bargaining*, Basingstoke, Macmillan.
4. Parker, S. (1971), *The Future of Work and Leisure*, London, MacGibbon & Kee, and (1983), *Leisure and Work*, London, Allen & Unwin.
5. Roberts, K. (1971), *Leisure*, London, Longman.
6. Millar, R. (1965), *The New Classes*, London, Longman; Turner, G. (1963), *The Car Makers*, London, Eyre & Spottiswoode; Zweig, F. (1961), *The Worker in an Affluent Society*, London, Heinemann; Goldthorpe, J.H. *et al.* (1969), *The Affluent Worker in the Class Structure*, Cambridge, University Press.
7. The dual system of industrial relations is outlined in the Royal Commission on Trade Unions and Employers' Associations (1968), *Report*, Cmnd. 3623.
8. Ineichen, B. (1972), 'Home Ownership and Manual Workers' Lifestyles', *Sociological Review*, No. 20, vol. 3, pp.391–412; Abrams, M. (May 1960), 'New Roots of Working Class Conser-

vatism', *Encounter*, and (1969), *The Changing Pattern of Consumer Spending*, London, Press Exchange.
9. Pollard, S. (1992), *The Development of the British Economy, 1914–1990*, London, Edward Arnold, chs 7 and 8.
10. Trades Union Congress (1960), *Annual Report*, p.345.
11. *Ibid.* p.346.
12. Russell, A. (1991), *The Growth of Occupational Welfare in Britain*, Aldershot, Gower, chs 8 and 14.
13. Trades Union Congress (1961), *Annual Report*, p.416.
14. *Ibid.* (1963), p.454.
15. *Ibid.* p.455.
16. *Ibid.* (1964), p.396.
17. *Ibid.* (1965), p.555.
18. Four of the six holidays referred to were scheduled under the Bank Holidays Act 1871 and the Bank Holidays (Extension) Act 1975; the remaining two, Christmas Day and Good Friday, were generally observed as traditional festivals of the Church calendar.
19. Trades Union Congress (1970), *Annual Report*, p.729.
20. *Ibid.* (1973), p.460.
21. *Ibid.* (1975), p.398.
22. *Ibid.* (1976), p.532.
23. *Ibid.* (1977), p.552.
24. 'TUC Policy on Pay, Hours, and Overtime', *Industrial Relations Review and Report* (October 1978), No. 182, pp.7–9.
25. Quoted *ibid.*
26. Trades Union Congress (1979), *Annual Report*, p.523.
27. 'TUC Outlines Bargaining Priorities for the Coming Year', *Industrial Relations Review and Report* (October 1979), No. 209, pp.9–13.
28. Quoted *ibid.*
29. Trades Union Congress (1979), *Annual Report*, p.522.

6

Working-time Changes, 1939–79

Introduction

The concessions on working time, made by trade unions and workforces during the Second World War, meant acceptance of long working hours and the cancellation or postponement of holiday leave. In the years that followed, the unions won appreciable improvements in the shortening of the basic working week and the lengthening of annual paid holidays. The overtime habit persisted, and it now became something of a problem for employers, for where overtime was systematically contrived by work groups and prolonged, it raised costs and, backed by restrictive practices and demarcations on the shopfloor, it reduced productive efficiency. The general reductions of the basic working week and increases in paid holidays were, for the most part, the outcome of voluntary collective bargaining and claims from the trade unions. Progress, as before, tended to go in fits and starts; and it occurred in the context of government policy and legislation which had an indirect influence on the pace, pattern and direction of advance.

During the war, the Government's highest priorities were national security, production of goods essential to the war effort, and maintenance of strategically important services. Afterwards, there were years of postwar austerity when government policy sought the reconstruction and strengthening of the economy. Before long, recurrent balance of payments crises and 'stop go' economic policy circumscribed bargaining activity in manufacturing industry. Inflation, which soon became problematic, caused governments to introduce a series of policies to control escalating prices and incomes generally throughout the 1960s and up to the end of the 1970s; controls on wage increases were especially stringent in 1967–8 and 1972–4. Wage increases above the norm, whether the norm was statutorily fixed or strongly urged in the interests of national economic competitiveness, were almost invariably permitted where labour productivity increased. The style of productivity bargaining, which the combined effects of incomes policy and rapid price inflation encouraged, focused the attention of negotiators on wage issues; but although pay, as the means to maintaining or improving material living standards, had highest priority at the bargaining table for most of the period, working hours and holiday leave came strongly to the fore at certain times, as the means of improving quality of life.

Governments adopted a role which in many spheres was strongly interventionist in these years, but their attitude towards the general question of working-time was now not directly meddlesome. It was left to negotiators and wage-fixing bodies to reach agreement within the parameters of government policy and legislation for economic growth and financial stability.

Government Intervention and Non-intervention

The outbreak of war in 1939 created the most formidable of challenges both for the British Government and for the British people; and, with the immediate and prospective exigencies of mobilization, industrial production and civil defence, neither the Government nor the TUC acted on the Amulree Committee's recommendations to review in 1940–1 the desirability or otherwise of general legislation on paid holidays. With extensive overtime working to produce essential goods and maintain essential services, the working week for many people extended over six or seven days. Yet the necessity to boost production, as the Ministry of Labour and National Service recognized, had to be balanced against workpeople's need for adequate rest pauses during the day and week to prevent physical exhaustion which might result in falling productivity and risk to national defence.

During the years of greatest peril, the Government cancelled some of the public holidays, for a general shut-down would interrupt the flow of production which was vital to the war effort; likewise, employers were asked to avoid the closure of works premises for annual holidays. It is well-known that, while many workers took their holidays in rotation and outside the popular summer season, some did not take the holiday leave to which they were entitled, others went 'on holiday' to the countryside to help with the harvest, and many had to content themselves with 'holidays at home'.

It is clear that the Government was anxious to avoid stoppages of production, interruptions to transportation of essential goods and personnel, and any slackening in productive effort that might prejudice national efficiency. It is equally clear, however, that the Government did not envisage any abandonment of the principle of paid holidays, and did not act to impede the further extension of entitlement as such. The intention was to avoid general closures and to encourage the spreading of holiday leave over a longer period in the year, and the splitting of the holiday week into two spells. In 1940 employers were asked to cancel their firms' holidays for the time being; in that year also the Government cancelled some of the bank and public holidays.[1]

The Minister of Labour and National Service put out a personal message on 29 May 1940, acknowledging the 'splendid response' to the Government's 'appeal to intensify production', and urging that 'the seven-day week should be continued for a time'.[2]

On 13 June 1940, the Parliamentary Secretary at the Ministry of Labour and National Service stated in reply to a question in the House of Commons:

> The Government have asked for a general cancellation or postponement of holidays during this period of crisis in

order that there may be no interference with the production of munitions and that transport should be left free as far as possible for the needs of evacuation and civil defence.

It was recognized, the statement continued, that seven-day working without adequate rest breaks was not conducive to the maintenance of productive efficiency in the longer term; and employers and workpeople were therefore urged to make arrangements for a weekly rest day as soon as circumstances permitted.

The Hours of Day Work in Factories (Women and Young Persons Order) 1942, made under the Defence (General) Regulations of 1939, freed factories from regulations contained in the 1937 Factory Act relating to working hours and holidays, and permitted hours of work to be increased within the wider limits specified in the schedule attached to the Order.[3]

In May 1942 the Government issued general guidelines for holidays in industry. The 'customary holiday', insofar as it did not exceed one week, might be taken that year, although not necessarily at the 'customary time' or in the 'customary way'; extra facilities for holiday travel could not be made, and the transport services were reminded of their obligation to give priority to 'essential traffic'. The Government considered it undesirable for a general holiday to be observed in a particular town or district; traditional 'wakes weeks' should therefore be abandoned for the time being. The practice of taking holidays by individuals in rotation, it was urged, needed to be more widely adopted, even though in many cases family members might be prevented thereby from having leave of absence at the same time.

Collective agreements and customary practice in relation to annual holidays might be observed, insofar as the holiday period did not exceed one week. Regional Boards of the Ministry of Production, in consultation with employers' organizations and the Regional Transport Commissioners, were asked to take the initiative in arranging for 'staggered holidays'; local authorities were urged to develop further their 'holidays at home' plans of the previous year.[4]

The guidelines issued by the Ministry of Labour and National Service in 1944 were accompanied by the warning that this was going to be an especially difficult year.[5] Meanwhile employers were urged, by agreement with workpeople, to arrange for holiday leave to begin and end on a mid-week day in order to reduce weekend congestion on the railways; they were advised, again, to co-operate in agreeing arrangements for the maximum practicable degree of staggering of holiday leave, both within the firm and between different firms and districts.

Public holidays were cancelled in some years, except insofar as they applied in certain financial institutions as bank holidays under nineteenth-century legislation, in order to avoid a general stoppage of production and congestion of passenger traffic on the railways. The Whitsun and August Monday holidays were cancelled in 1940, and firms engaged in urgent work for the war effort were asked to 'ensure immediate maximum production by working full overtime and weekends'.[6] Also cancelled in 1940 were the Christmas Day holiday in Scotland and Boxing Day in England, Wales and Northern Ireland. In 1941 the Good Friday holiday was cancelled and also the St Patrick's Day holiday in Northern Ireland; and, again, Scotland lost Christmas Day and the rest of the country forfeited Boxing Day. There were fewer cancellations of public holidays in 1943 and 1944; the Government officially endorsed observance of these traditional holidays, in all but 'exceptional' circumstances.

The Ministry of Labour and National Service had issued in March 1942 a notice[7] asking employers to allow 'reasonable' time off from work for married women when their husbands came home on leave from HM Armed Forces and the Mercantile Marine; the recommendation was up to a maximum of 14 unpaid days of holiday for women whose husbands were stationed in this country and a minimum of 14 such days for women whose husbands were serving overseas. In 1945, with the end of the war and the prospect of demobilization in sight, and with the return of servicemen on long leave and of prisoners of war liberated by the Allied Armies, the Minister of Labour and National Service expressed his confidence: 'that employers will, wherever possible, extend the period of special leave of absence from work for wives of men on long leave from overseas, or freed from prison camps, beyond the minimum of fourteen days recommended in 1942.'[8]

In April 1945, although the war with Japan and fighting in the Far East had not yet ended, the Government announced arrangements for a 'cease-fire' holiday to celebrate the conclusion of the war in Europe, as an occasion for 'a general rejoicing that victory has crowned our efforts ...'.[9] In government factories and services the day on which the cease-fire was declared would be treated as a paid holiday from the time of the public announcement, together with the following day; and it would be appropriate, the Government suggested, for all schools to grant holidays likewise. Other employers were asked to give a special day, or days, of holiday, to be determined locally by arrangement with their own workforces. Urgent and necessary work, even so, would have to continue, and those engaged in essential services or maintenance work 'must therefore, in the national interest, be prepared to carry on, as required'. Special arrangements for days in lieu of the cease-fire holiday, or for financial compensation, would be made for those engaged in 'the supply of gas and electricity, the maintenance of important and valuable plant, farm work, vital transport, and food distribution'.

The Government now proposed to discontinue its wartime practice of issuing guidelines for annual and public holidays, but advised that, in view of the growth of entitlement to holidays with pay and the prospectively greater pressure on holiday facilities, industry should continue to plan well ahead for staggered holidays both within the individual firm and between different firms and districts.

Plans, which had been under discussion shortly after the Amulree Committee produced its report, to improve and extend amenities for holiday-makers, had necessarily been shelved during the war. A difficult situation now presented itself with the prospective postwar rush to the seaside. During the war, coastal areas vulnerable to bombing and invasion had been fortified and closed to the public; hotels and other premises at seaside resorts had been commandeered by the forces and government departments, and were not yet fully restored to their normal peacetime functions. At the same time, the Government did not doubt that the inconvenience of transport congestion and shortages of all kinds, which the public had tolerated because of the wartime emergency, would now create dissatisfaction, for none of the difficulties would vanish overnight. Yet it was clear that the peace would bring a vastly increased demand from holiday-makers for a reduced quantity of holiday accommodation, much of which by now was badly in need of refurbishment and some still awaiting reconversion from wartime use.

The Catering Wages Commission, in its 1945 report to the Ministry of Labour on the staggering of holidays,[10] observed that the concentration of holidays in high summer from mid-July to mid-August created difficulties all round, and not least for holiday makers themselves. Congestion was 'the most important and most urgent' of all the matters that needed to be addressed by the catering trades.

The most formidable of the obstacles to spreading holidays over a longer season, members of the Commission believed, was 'inertia and entrenched tradition'; yet there were soundly rational arguments for staggered holidays. There would be greater comfort and convenience in travelling by road and rail, cheaper and less crowded accommodation at hotels and boarding houses outside the peak season, lower prices and shorter queues for entertainment and, contrary to the popular myth, less rain and more hours of sunshine in other summer months. At present, prices at holiday resorts were forced up, partly because demand for holiday catering exceeded supply, and partly also because the resorts had to compensate for the brevity of the holiday season by making very high profits through high prices while the season lasted.

The Catering Wages Commission urged greater publicity as the most likely means of changing holiday habits. The

Ministry of Labour launched a publicity campaign in 1946, with the slogan: 'It's better, remember, in June and September', and published statistics on rainfall, temperature and average daily hours of sunshine to prove the point. The prospect of changing people's holiday preferences was believed to be favourable for, as the Commission argued, 'so many customs are [now] in the melting pot ... when, because of wartime conditions, people have learned to accept a holiday at some time other than July or August ... An opportunity for progress is offered which may never occur again.'[11] In retrospect, it seems naive of the Commission to assume that what was stoically endured under government direction during the wartime emergency would be voluntarily and wholeheartedly embraced when the crisis was over.[12]

The problem of holiday congestion in late July and early August persisted, for not even the most clamorous publicity could resolve the practical impediment of the timing of school holidays, which had to take into account the dates of externally-fixed public examinations. The large number of workpeople with school-age children preferred, and indeed felt duty-bound, to take their annual summer leave in weeks clear of examinations when the schools were closed at the end of the academic year.

The problem was exacerbated by the August Bank Holiday, for the large numbers taking their annual holiday in the first week of August were augmented by the multitudes taking day trips and weekend excursions. A solution to this difficulty, the Commission suggested, might be found if the Government were to declare the August Bank Holiday to be 'movable', so that each district could observe any Monday in August as a public holiday.

The Government, however, was as reluctant to act coercively on these issues as to pass general legislation for a statutory minimum period of annual paid holiday. When the trade unions reminded the Attlee Government of the Amulree Committee's 1938 recommendations, they were informed that legislation on the subject was out of the question, given the country's postwar economic needs and in view of the wide-ranging and costly welfare arrangements already introduced for the benefit of society as a whole. Although the Labour Government was prepared to declare itself strongly in favour of many of the suggestions put forward by the Catering Wages Commission, active intervention was largely confined to publicity, advice and exhortation. The attitude of the incoming Conservative Government of 1951 was not markedly different on these issues.

The problem of holiday congestion, already serious in the later 1940s, was becoming even more acute in the 1950s and 1960s. In Harold Macmillan's 'never had it so good' years of working class affluence and collectively bargained holiday entitlements of two weeks or more for many manual workers, progressively larger numbers were taking one holiday, and sometimes two, away from home each year. The main issues, identified by the Government, the British Institute of Management and other interested parties, were: the persistent concentration of holidays in a short summer season, and the prospect of longer holidays if Britain were to join the EEC.

Holiday congestion and the desirability of staggering were discussed in a Government White Paper issued in July 1963.[13] The type of holiday taken and the means of travel were changing, but the times at which holidays were taken were not. The British Travel and Holidays Association had found in 1962 that 63.0 per cent of all main holidays were taken in July or August, and that nearly three-quarters of all holidays began at the weekend, mostly on Saturdays. The situation was expected to get worse for, with around 20 million people who did not yet go away on holiday, 'the ceiling has by no means been reached', and there was 'no obvious limit to the increase in the number of extra holidays'.

The drawbacks were much the same as those lamented in the later 1940s: packed trains, traffic jams, overcrowded accommodation, poor service at high prices, discomfort for holiday-makers plus the high investment and running cost of providing holiday amenities that would be little used outside the brief and hectic summer season. Again, the main obstacles to the lengthening of the holiday season so as to begin earlier and finish later were said to be entrenched tradition, and school holidays geared to the timing of school-leaving examinations which affected decisions about firms' closures for workpeople's holidays.

If matters were as bad as the Government White Paper claimed, it is surprising that the conclusions reached by its authors were so lacking in imaginative drive:

> It is clear that any cure ... depends mainly on action that only private individuals and bodies can take ... Most of these changes are not themselves matters for direct Government action.[14]

The Government, convinced that direct intervention by central authorities was inappropriate, thus passed the buck; the problems, it believed, must be resolved by individuals and other bodies. There was, of course, a certain logic to the Government's decision; for holiday-makers encountering intolerable travel and accommodation facilities year in year out were more likely to change their holiday habits, and the commercial providers of expensive, inadequate and shoddy holiday services were more likely to undertake improvements when inundated with protests from dissatisfied customers and censured in the national press by investigative journalists. Similarly, when the Industrial Society reviewed the case for staggered holidays in 1963, it did not urge Government intervention: 'A workable solution requires the active co-operation of all sectors of society.'[15]

The prospect in the early 1960s of the three-week standard holiday raised the question of the means by which employers could provide longer periods of leave with maximum administrative efficiency and minimal disruption to production schedules. Clegg, in an occasional paper[16] for the British Institute of Management, did not regard the resolution of the potential problems as the responsibility of the Government; rather, it was a matter of sensible forward planning by employers. The three-week paid holiday was expected to become the norm in Britain in the not too distant future, 'especially with the prospect of the Common Market and the "harmonization" of social benefits before us, for three weeks is standard practice on the continent'.

Past experience suggested that in Britain the third week's holiday would be phased in over a period of years. Several firms had already conceded it, and many more intended to do so shortly; but other employers would 'maintain implacable hostility ... The floodgates will open ... although a tail of backward, less prosperous or just stubborn industries will straggle behind for a while, some of them even for years.' The consequences would be chaotic.

The case for state intervention by an Act of Parliament prescribing the three-week holiday by a specific date in order to ensure an orderly transition was a strong one; but government action of this kind was not a practicable possibility in Britain, for it would be a 'startling breach of the conventions of industrial relations'. Better by far would be an agreement of principle between the Trades Union Congress and the British Employers' Confederation. This would 'disturb tradition less than legislative intervention' as it would be sufficiently flexible for decisions on holiday entitlements to 'remain a voluntary matter, under the control of unions and employers, to be applied, modified or revised as they saw fit'.

Employers in Britain, Clegg advised, had to face up to 'the inevitability of the third week with a little intelligent foresight so as to minimize the inconvenience and expense to the firm'. There was a 'very real danger that British employers will show themselves to be penny-wise and pound-foolish, as they have so often done in recent years'. Postponement of decisions until the last minute would result in 'cumbersome and expensive agreements'. Forethought, early preparation and a bit of common sense from employers would simplify the move to longer holidays: 'There is no rule which obliges us to create problems for ourselves.'[17]

Another issue, and, again, one towards which the Government's attitude was non-interventionist, was average lower holiday entitlement in Britain than in most other developed countries of the western world.[18] The basic annual paid holiday for the average British worker at that time was two weeks or ten working days, although a growing number of agreements provided an extra day or two related to seniority or long service with the same employer. In contrast, as Narasimhan's evidence confirmed in 1963,[19] a basic three-week holiday was already standard for manual workers in Denmark, Norway, Sweden, Finland, France, and parts of Switzerland; and Germany, Belgium, Italy and the Netherlands were moving towards the three-week target. These basic periods were essentially minimum entitlements, which did 'not give a complete and wholly correct picture ...' for holiday leave tended generally to increase with age and/or seniority, so that in France, for example, around 82.0 per cent of wage-earners had at least 18 days and some 11.0 per cent received 24 days or more.

Britain also lagged behind in the matter of public holidays. In comparison with the 6 observed in Britain, the Netherlands had 7, Luxembourg 10, Belgium and West Germany 10 to 12 according to region, and Italy had no less than 16. Taking basic annual holidays and public holidays together, the average British worker received 16 days, while for the bulk of the working populations elsewhere the range was from 21 to 22 days in Luxembourg and the Netherlands, 22 to 24 in Belgium and West Germany, 24 in France, and 24 to 28 in Italy. These periods, Narasimhan noted, did not include additional days related to age, seniority and length of service. Their inclusion in the calculation would leave Britain even further behind.

Regardless of longer basic entitlement reinforced by legislation in many other countries at a comparable stage of economic development, the British Government remained unconvinced of the desirability of intervention by Act of Parliament to improve standards for the working population as a whole.

Weekly Working Hours, 1939–79

The normal working week for large numbers of people in manual employment had been one of 48 hours around the time of the Second World War. Much overtime had been worked during the war years; but with the return to peacetime conditions, characterized though they were for several years by austerity measures deemed necessary by the government of the day, the TUC resumed its campaign to shorten working time, with the objective, adopted in the 1930s, of achieving the 40-hour week.

There were two general movements towards a shorter working week during the decade and a half following the war. The first of these movements occurred in the period 1946 to 1949, when normal weekly hours were reduced from 47 or 48 to 44 or 45, with provision in several cases for the five-day week. The second general reduction occurred between 1959 and 1961, and resulted in a normal working week of 42 or 43 hours.[20] While normal working hours declined during this period, overtime tended to rise, from an average of one hour per week in 1948, to two hours in 1950, and to three hours by 1960. In the case of male manual workers, the average rise in overtime working was more pronounced, amounting to five hours by 1960 (Table 10). A further, and slightly smaller, wave of reductions occurred in 1963–65, so that by 1965 the basic 40-hour week, although not yet general, was widespread.[21]

The further reductions occurring in 1964 and 1965 were mostly the outcome of long-term agreements providing for small annual cuts over a two- or three-year period.[22] In 1963 workers employed in industries operating a 40-hour week, or covered by agreements for its introduction, were estimated to number slightly less than one million or about 7.0 per cent of all workers covered by collective agreements or statutory orders. In 1966 the proportion thus affected had increased to around 50.0 per cent. The rate of change slowed thereafter, with some of the laggards catching up more belatedly. The 40-hour target now became the 40-hour barrier.

With the widespread adoption of the 40-hour week, the 5-day working week became standard. By the end of the 1960s roughly 84.0 per cent of male manual day-workers had a normal 5-day week; only around 10.0 per cent had a 5½-day

TABLE 10
Comparison of Normal and Actual Hours of Work, 1948–76, Manual Workers (United Kingdom)

Year	Normal Weekly Hours			Actual Weekly Hours		
	Men	Women	All	Men	Women	All
1948	44.5	44.6	44.5	46.6	41.5	45.4
1949	44.4	44.5	44.4	46.7	41.6	45.4
1950	44.4	44.5	44.4	47.3	41.7	45.9
1951	44.4	44.5	44.4	49.9	41.6	46.3
1952	44.4	44.5	44.4	47.5	41.2	44.9
1953	44.3	44.5	44.4	47.9	41.8	46.3
1954	44.3	44.4	44.4	48.4	41.8	46.7
1955	44.3	44.4	44.4	48.9	41.7	47.0
1956	44.3	44.4	44.3	48.6	41.3	46.8
1957	44.2	44.4	44.3	48.4	41.2	46.6
1958	44.2	44.3	44.3	47.9	41.0	46.2
1959	44.2	44.3	44.2	48.3	41.4	46.6
1960	43.0	43.4	43.1	48.0	40.7	46.2
1961	42.3	42.3	42.3	47.7	39.8	45.7
1962	42.1	42.2	42.1	47.2	39.5	45.3
1963	42.0	42.1	42.1	47.3	39.6	45.4
1964	41.9	42.1	42.0	47.8	39.7	45.8
1965	41.0	41.2	41.0	47.3	38.9	45.3
1966	40.3	40.5	40.3	46.2	38.3	44.3
1967	40.2	40.4	40.2	46.2	38.2	44.3
1968	40.1	40.2	40.2	46.3	38.4	44.5
1969	40.1	40.1	40.1	46.5	38.1	44.6
1970	40.1	40.0	40.1	45.7	37.9	43.9
1971	40.0	40.0	40.0	44.7	37.7	43.2
1972	40.0	40.0	40.0	45.0	37.9	43.5
1973	40.0	40.0	40.0	45.6	37.7	43.9
1974	40.0	40.0	40.0	45.1	37.4	43.4
1975	40.0	40.0	40.0	43.6	37.0	42.2
1976	40.0	40.0	40.0	44.0	37.4	42.6

The hours quoted are the average hours per week for full-time workers, derived from the annual survey of the earnings and hours of manual workers.

Figures for 1948 to 1968 derived from *British Labour Statistics: Historical Abstract, 1886–1968*, Department of Employment and Productivity, London, HMSO, 1971, Table 84, p.160. Figures for 1969 to 1976 derived from *British Labour Statistics: Year Book 1976*, Table 43, p.109.

week, and as few as 6.0 per cent still had a normal 6-day week.[23]

Britain's move to a basic 40-hour week by and large preceded similar moves in Western Europe, but followed behind emerging trends in other industrialized countries. As Evans and Palmer[24] have shown, the standard 40-hour week had been established in the USA in the 1930s, in Australia in 1947–8, and in Canada in the mid-1950s; the 45-hour week did not become standard in West Germany until the mid-1950s, and the 40-hour week did not become widespread until the early 1970s. The 48-hour week was still standard in Italy at the end of the 1950s; a reduction to 44 or 45 hours did not occur until 1967–9, and, although there were some further reductions, it was not until 1973 that the 40-hour week was established as the norm. In France, given the ineffectiveness of legislation passed in 1936 to establish the 40-hour week, many industries still had a basic week of 45 hours in 1970. Evidence suggests that 'in broad terms, comparable reductions in the [basic] working week in Europe have in the past occurred about ten years behind trends in Britain'.[25]

In Britain, after the hours reductions of the early and mid 1960s, the attention of negotiators in many industries turned more decisively to pay increases permitted, and even unpermitted, under the more stringent incomes policies of the time. Pay increases continued to be the major bargaining priority in the 1970s, particularly during the first half of the decade, with wages chasing and promoting escalating prices. The extraordinary and apparently uncontrollable inflation of both prices and incomes assumed the character of a national crisis. Average wage increases were above 12.0 per cent in 1970, 1971 and 1972, and leapt to around 29.0 per cent in 1974 and 25.0 per cent in 1975, before falling to 11.0 per cent the following year and declining further thereafter.

Even so, there was some movement in basic working-time, where the trade unions and their members were willing to trade part of an increase in real earnings for an increase in leisure time, and to breach the 40-hour barrier in doing so. A basic 37½-hour week was established in the lock, latch and key industry's national agreement of 1972; and the following year an industry-wide agreement covering manual grades in electricity supply established a 38-hour week, with rostered day relief, in exchange for acceptance of flexible deployment of labour. Normal weekly hours were reduced in electrical contracting to 39 in 1974 and to 38 the following year. Most employers, however, including Ford in 1973, resisted any claims for hours cuts. The unions' campaign of the early 1970s to shorten working-time subsided before it could gather any momentum, as a result of the 1974 oil crisis and the inflationary spiral which followed; protection of real incomes became their main priority at the bargaining table.

An investigation conducted by *IRRR* in 1977 found that the working-time question was 'becoming a controversial issue for the first time since the early-1960s'.[26] Under current pay policy, agreements for a shorter basic working week in combination with the adoption of measures to increase productive efficiency, could qualify as self-financing productivity deals, thereby escaping the 10.0 per cent guideline on pay increases and the 12-months rule. A follow-up investigation in 1979[27] disclosed that working-time was a 'common issue' at the forefront in bargaining throughout Western Europe. In Britain, the CBI found that at least half of all the claims reported that year contained the demand for shorter working hours, and there were said to be 'signs that at least some employers are giving ground ...'.[28]

The concessions being made by a few employers were in contravention of official CBI policy, which urged resistance to hours cuts; its 1978 policy statement, *Britain Means Business*, maintained that the cost of hours cuts was 'prohibitive', and that a general move to shorten the working week would result not in job creation but in job destruction: '... the CBI estimates that the introduction of a 35-hour week, with no compensating reduction in pay, would result in perhaps a quarter of a million jobs lost in exporting or import-substituting firms.' Member organizations were reminded in August 1978 that the CBI 'is strongly opposed to any reduction in normal working hours at the present time ... It is essential that all employers stand firm on this issue.'[29]

Regardless of the CBI's warnings to private sector organizations, in the public sector some 125,000 Post Office engineers, after an 11-month dispute and an inquiry headed by Lord McCarthy, won an agreement to cut normal weekly hours from 40 to 37½, on a nil-cost basis, from December 1978. The 1978 pay review covering NHS nurses and midwives produced an undertaking to reduce their basic working week in stages from 40 to 37½ hours by 1981.

In the private sector, despite the CBI's avowed policy, the breaching of the 40-hour barrier was in prospect towards the end of the 1970s. Some agreements to reduce the basic working week to below 40 hours had been reached at both industry and company level; and although none of them covered large numbers, they were sufficient to signal the onset of a new wave of change. An agreement between the Graphic Reproduction Federation and the unions, SLADE and SOGAT, reduced the basic working week of day-workers to 36 in October 1977 and to 35 in October 1978. The Provincial Wholesale Newspaper Distributors' Federation reached a long-term agreement with SOGAT to reduce working hours in stages to give night-workers and day-workers a week of 35 and 37 hours respectively by 1981. The resurgence of negotiation on the working-time question reflects the trade unions' refusal to comply with further stages of the Labour Government's incomes policy.[30]

A survey conducted by the Institute of Administrative Management, covering over 300,000 office staff, found in 1978 that over 80.0 per cent of offices had a working week of between 35 and 37½ hours; that there had been a clear movement towards 35 hours as the norm; and that the great majority of office staff in central London now worked a 35-hour week.[31] The gradual reduction in the working week of these groups had been accompanied by a 'rapid growth in the introduction of arrangements for flexible working hours'. In its 1972 survey the IAM had found that only 9.0 per cent of offices operated flexitime systems, but by 1978 the proportion had risen to 28.0 per cent. *IRRR*'s 1977 survey of 192 organizations disclosed a sharp distinction between the basic weekly working hours of manual and non-manual grades, with only one in eight companies having the same basic working week for both groups.

If the differential in the basic working hours of the two broad occupational categories – all manual and all non-manual – persisted in these years, so also did differentials within these two main groups. In the case of manual workers, while most had a normal 40-hour week, a few had gained reductions to 37, 38 or 39 hours, but a small minority still worked a normal week of 41, 42 or 43 hours. In the case of non-manuals, those employed in the banking, insurance and finance sector tended to have a working week of 35 or 36 hours, compared with the 37 or 38 hours worked by office staffs in industry and manufacturing.

The differential in the actual working week of the two broad groups was much greater, given the persistence of overtime working by male manual workers; and overtime working accentuated the gender differential in working hours. Average weekly overtime worked by male manual workers fluctuated year by year from 1945 to 1979, ranging from one hour in 1947 to over six hours in 1965, 1969 and 1979 (Table 11).

The average figures tend to disguise the very large amounts of overtime worked by some manual workers; in the early 1960s, for example, some groups in electricity supply frequently worked from 10 to 16 hours of overtime.[32] Moreover, the average figures understate the amount of overtime worked per overtime-worker by male operatives in the manufacturing sector (Table 12). In 1977 some manual workers in transport services, civil engineering, the bakeries and milk processing worked more than 10 hours of overtime per week, while less than two hours was worked in retail furnishing; in some cases well over 20.0 per cent of weekly income was composed of overtime earnings, but less than 4.0 per cent in others (Table 13).

TABLE 11
Average Basic and Actual Weekly Working Hours and Average Overtime Hours of Male Manual Workers, 1947–79

Year	Basic Hours	Actual Hours	Overtime Hours
1947	45.3	46.3	1.0
1948	44.6	46.5	1.9
1949	44.4	46.6	2.2
1950	44.4	47.0	2.6
1951	44.4	47.9	3.5
1952	44.4	47.3	2.9
1953	44.3	47.8	3.5
1954	44.3	48.3	4.0
1955	44.3	48.9	4.6
1956	44.3	48.6	4.3
1957	44.3	48.4	4.1
1958	44.2	48.0	3.8
1959	44.2	48.0	3.8
1960	43.3	48.0	4.7
1961	42.5	47.9	5.4
1962	42.1	47.3	5.2
1963	42.0	46.9	4.9
1964	41.9	47.8	5.9
1965	41.2	47.5	6.3
1966	40.3	46.4	6.1
1967	40.2	46.1	5.9
1968	40.1	46.2	6.1
1969	40.1	46.4	6.3
1970	40.1	45.7	5.6
1971	40.0	44.7	4.7
1972	40.0	45.0	5.0
1973	40.0	45.6	5.6
1974	40.0	45.1	5.1
1975	40.0	43.6	3.6
1976	40.0	44.0	4.0
1977	39.9	45.7	5.8
1978	39.9	46.0	6.1
1979	39.9	46.2	6.3

Derived from: *British Labour Statistics: Historical Abstract, 1886–1968*, London, HMSO, 1971, p.160; *Department of Employment Gazette*, London, HMSO, annual; Department of Employment, *New Earnings Survey*, London, HMSO, annual.

TABLE 12
Overtime Working in Manufacturing Industries, 1950–68 (Great Britain): Male Operatives (excluding maintenance staff)

Week Ended	Overtime Workers as % of all Operatives in Work	Average Weekly Overtime Hours per Overtime Worker
1950 December 30	n.a.	6.5
1951 September 22	21.6	8.0
1952 November 29	23.1	7.5
1953 November 28	26.5	8.0
1954 November 27	28.5	8.0
1955 November 26	30.0	8.0
1956 November 24	26.9	8.0
1957 November 30	27.6	8.0
1958 November 22	24.2	7.5
1959 November 21	30.3	7.5
1960 November 26	31.0	8.0
1961 November 25	31.3	8.0
1962 November 17	28.2	8.0
1963 November 16	33.1	8.0
1964 November 14	34.9	8.5
1965 November 13	36.5	8.5
1966 November 19	32.2	8.5
1967 November 18	34.7	8.5
1968 November 16	37.3	8.5

Table relates to establishments with 11 or more employees in all manufacturing industries (except shipbuilding and ship repairing).
Derived from *British Labour Statistics: Historical Abstract 1886–1968*, London, Department of Employment and Productivity, HMSO, 1971, Table 146, pp.279–81.

Arrangement of Working Hours

A marked differentiating feature of manual and non-manual employment was the arrangement of working hours. While shift-working continued to be characteristic for manual workers in certain industries and some public utility services, such as chemical plant operation, machine moulding, transport

TABLE 13

Weekly Working Hours of Male Manual Workers, by Negotiating Group, April 1977: Average Total Hours, Average Overtime Hours, Overtime Earnings as Percentage of Total Earnings

Negotiating Group	Average Total Hours	Average Overtime Hours	Overtime Earnings as % of Total Earnings
Road haulage	53.4	12.1	24.2
Baking (E&W)	53.1	13.0	25.1
Civil engineering	52.9	12.0	20.1
BR conciliation grades	51.6	11.6	27.0
Milk products (E&W)	50.9	10.5	18.8
Company busmen	50.9	10.9	21.0
Municipal busmen	49.4	9.3	20.6
Paper and board	48.6	7.6	18.4
Electrical contracting	48.0	8.9	20.0
LTE busmen	47.9	5.3	12.8
Ship building	47.9	8.0	19.8
Agriculture (E&W)	47.9	7.4	16.8
Electrical cables	47.9	8.2	18.2
Food manufacture	47.8	7.6	18.7
Chemicals	47.2	7.0	15.6
PO manipulative grades	46.3	7.8	17.1
Surface coal miners	46.1	7.8	20.0
Building (Scot)	46.1	6.1	12.3
BR workshops	46.0	6.0	15.2
NHS maintenance	45.9	6.0	14.7
Gas	45.8	5.8	11.4
NHS ancillaries*	45.6	5.6	12.9
Government industrials	45.4	5.5	12.8
Printing (E&W)	45.3	5.7	16.7
Iron and steel	44.9	5.3	13.3
Engineering	44.9	5.0	12.5
Building (E&W)	44.9	4.4	9.0
Local Authority building (Scot)	44.8	4.7	10.2
Local Authority manuals (Scot)	44.7	4.5	10.3
Local Authority manuals (E&W)	44.3	4.3	10.0
Motor retail & repair	44.1	3.7	10.4
Vehicle building	43.9	4.2	10.7
Rubber	43.7	4.4	10.2

TABLE 13 – Continued

Negotiating Group	Average Total Hours	Average Overtime Hours	Overtime Earnings as % of Total Earnings
Spinning & weaving	43.7	4.1	10.4
Retail food*	43.5	3.4	7.8
Furniture	43.4	3.2	7.7
Electricity	43.2	3.2	8.4
Water*	43.2	4.0	9.0
Local authority building (E&W)	43.2	3.0	6.3
PO engineering	42.7	2.7	7.4
Retail furnishing*	41.1	1.6	3.7
Underground coal miners	41.1	4.6	14.6

* Includes some non-manual employees.
Derived from *New Earnings Survey 1977* and *Industrial Relations Review and Report*, No. 174, April 1978, p.14.

services, and electricity supply, it was much less common for non-manual grades where it was confined, by and large, to nurses, telephonists, postmen, security officers and guards, and managers of departmental stores.[33] Conversely, while flexitime systems were beginning to spread in non-manual work in the early 1970s, such arrangements were much less common in manual work. Unlike their counterparts in Europe, British employers were reluctant to experiment with flexitime working on the shopfloor.

The system characteristically involves flexible starting and finishing times, fixed core-hours when all employees are required to be present, a specified number of weekly or monthly contractual hours, and personal choice working-time within a daily 'bandwidth' period. Credit hours – those worked in excess of contractual hours – enable the individual to take a corresponding amount of time off in subsequent weeks; debit hours – the shortfall between hours worked and hours contracted – may be made up by working extra time in subsequent weeks or may be offset by credit hours already accumulated. The efficiency of flexitime arrangements depends on the use of effective and accurate time-recording mechanisms.

There was a surge of interest in the operation of flexitime systems in the early and mid 1970s, following a report on the subject by the Department of Employment and the introduction of schemes in parts of the Civil Service and certain spheres of national and local government. The Inland Revenue was one of the first government departments to move to flexitime working. The system, recommended in the 1971 Kemp-Jones report, *Employment of Women in the Civil Service*, was operated experimentally at a few locations before being extended more widely, and in 1975 a Code of Practice was drawn up by the National Whitley Council for the service. The Code was revised in 1979, following a review of its provisions by representatives of the unions and management, and a new *Guide to Flexible Working Hours* was issued, outlining the main elements to be included in any flexitime scheme operated by a government department. In the private sector, flexitime working spread in financial and insurance services, especially in the London area; outside the London region there was a 'steady trickle' of schemes which, again, were largely confined to white-collar staff.

The initial introduction of flexitime owes more to employers' requirements than the demands of white-collar unions, although NALGO subsequently did much to promote the popularity of such arrangements among its members. The main reasons for employers' willingness to initiate flexitime working during the first half of the 1970s were to attract and retain staff, and to ease rush-hour travelling problems for commuters; it was believed to be particularly attractive to married women for it would be easier for them to reconcile their domestic responsibilities with paid employment outside the home if they were permitted to work flexible hours. Other potential advantages, cited by IDS, included: improved staff morale and job satisfaction, better industrial relations, reduced absence rates and avoidance of the 'late-arrival problem', greater commitment and more responsible attitudes on the part of staff, opportunity for individuals to work to their own natural work rhythms, and fuller utilization of resources over a longer time-span. Such systems were most appropriate in spheres of activity where the efficient performance of the individual's work tasks did not depend on the concurrent presence of others for the entire working day and where there was no impediment from the need to maintain 'customer services' at times when customers expected them to be available. The main costs took the form of expenditure on time-recording equipment and its installation, the administration and monitoring of the scheme, and the additional heating, lighting and security services resulting from keeping business premises open over a longer daily time-span.[34]

The decline of employers' interest in introducing flexitime working in the latter half of the 1970s may reflect the looming spectre of the economic downturn, the increasing uncertainty of markets, gradually rising unemployment and the slackening of labour markets. With a subsiding need for devices to attract and retain staff, the main focus of employers' attention turned to measures to protect the viability of their business enterprises; and that would involve flexibility of a different kind in the 1980s. Alternatively, it may simply be the case that, for the next few years at least, flexitime working did not suit the business requirements of employers who had not already adopted it.

Working-time patterns based on flexitime working, or on shift-working involving anything from two to five shift systems, did not depart from the concept of the basic full-time working week consisting of a standard number of hours; both were adapted and there were often complex versions of it. In contrast, there emerged more conspicuously during this period a segment of the labour force working less than full-time hours. There is a world of difference, of course, between short-time and part-time working. The former is the result of often unanticipated or unavoidable circumstances, such as a temporary shortage of raw materials, or a fall-off of orders, or a trade recession; and it is likely to be welcomed by neither the employer nor the employee, except as an expedient that is preferable to lay-offs. Part-time working, on the other hand, offers advantages both for the employer and the employee. By far the greater proportion of the growing number of part-time workers were married women for whom full-time work was not a realistic option. The advantage of part-time employment was that it enabled them to contribute to family income while leaving time to cope with domestic responsibilities. Employers recognized that women comprised a ready part-time labour supply which was especially suitable for some of their labour needs.

The proportion of women in the total labour force rose from 31.0 per cent in 1951 to 39.0 per cent in 1979; over the same period, while the percentage of all economically active women rose from 35.0 per cent to 47.0 per cent, the proportion of married women taking up paid employment increased from 22.0 per cent to 50.0 per cent.[35] Between 1971 and 1978 there was a negligible increase of less than 1.0 per cent in the number of women in full-time work, but a 33.0 per cent increase (from 2,757,000 to 3,679,000) in the number of women in part-time employment. In 1979, 40.0 per cent of all employed women were engaged on a part-time basis, compared with only 5.0 per cent of all male employees.[36]

There were several reasons underlying employers' decisions to recruit part-time workers. In the financial services sector employers took on part-time secretarial and clerical staff because they were unable to recruit enough full-time staff to meet their requirements. Some took on part-timers as the cheaper option, for their pay rate tended to be lower than for full-time employees and any additional hours worked to oblige the employer were not paid at overtime rates unless they were in excess of the normal full-time working week.

Several employers offered 'housewife shifts' which enabled women to tailor their working hours to fit in with their children's school day and school terms.[37] In the public sector, some regional health authorities had set up arrangements to permit qualified nurses to work part-time in short-staffed hospitals encountering difficulty in recruiting full-time personnel.

Other employers engaged part-timers in order to extend plant utilization or to increase manufacturing hours on the basis of an evening shift. Still others took on part-time staff to gain greater flexibility in manning levels in order to ensure that extra staff were on hand during regular daily or weekly periods when business was especially brisk. This was the main reason for the large and increasing number of part-time shop assistants.[38]

Another working-time issue assuming some prominence in this period was short-time working, which occurred when the employer required workers with full-time jobs for fewer hours than those comprising the normal working week. Short-time working was not an entirely new phenomenon, of course; it had been widespread during, and because of, the interwar recession, and it was far from uncommon in earlier periods. But there were causes other than the state of trade, the most significant of which was widespread strike action, particularly when it occurred in a strategically important industry whose interrupted production had a widespread knock-on effect in many other spheres of employment.

The main cause of short-time working in Britain in 1972 was the miners' strike and the picketing of electricity generating stations to obstruct delivery of coal. The disruption of fuel and energy supplies resulted in a state of emergency and three-day working in many industries and services. There was a recurrence in 1973–4 when the miners again took direct action in their dispute with the Government over their pay claim and in protest about the stringency of current incomes policy. To make matters worse, there was a reduction of oil supply and a four-fold increase in its price, resulting from action taken by the Arab oil producers; and the electricity power workers also introduced an overtime ban when their pay claim was not conceded in full. The Conservative Government thereupon introduced a three-day working week, which contributed to the downfall of the Heath Government in 1974.

Measures to provide some financial protection against the

hazard of short-time working predate the 1970s. The most important precedents were set in 'essential industries' during the Second World War, and these served to familiarize workers with the concept and practice of the guaranteed week. The wartime guarantees applied in industries and services scheduled under the Essential Work (General Provision) Order of 1941, which sought to prevent loss of output resulting from labour turnover by offering security of earnings and/or employment. In effect, persons employed in scheduled undertakings were assured, as a minimum, of payment at the appropriate time-rate for the number of hours comprising the basic working week. In 1945, with the cessation of hostilities, the TUC General Council identified the guaranteed week as one of three features of wartime employment regulation 'worth preserving' in peacetime circumstances.

The guaranteed week agreements which some employers reached with the unions in the 1950s were intended to apply during recurrent short-term interruptions to production, and most contained in-built safeguards to limit the employer's obligation. Characteristically, the weekly wage guaranteed did not amount to the full wage for basic weekly working hours; and agreements invariably contained clauses providing for the suspension of the guarantee in certain situations.[39] An IDS Study[40] published in the early 1970s noted that there were few formal agreements of this kind in the public sector where security of earnings and employment tended to be 'taken for granted'. Most agreements, whether formal or informal and in both the public and private sectors, applied only to persons in permanent full-time work.

Increase in Annual Paid Holidays

Provision for holidays with pay increased during the Second World War and in the years immediately following. By December 1946[41] there had been an increase in the amount of paid holiday allowed under some of the pre-existing agreements, and several more industries had reached settlements or issued orders to introduce paid holidays for the first time. There were now over 1,100 agreements, about 900 of which were industry-wide or district-wide in application. At the same time orders, with statutory force, for paid holiday leave had been issued by the vast majority of Wages Councils,[42] by the Agricultural Wages Boards for England and Wales, Scotland and Northern Ireland, by the Road Haulage Central Wages Board, and by the Wages Board for Industrial and Staff Canteens, which had been set up under the 1943 Catering Wages Act. Of the 52 Wages Councils in Britain and the 18 in Northern Ireland in 1946, all but four had issued confirming orders to pay wages at holiday time. Two of these four – for the jute trade and the flax and hemp trade – had reached collective agreements on the subject; the remaining two – for the drift nets mending trade and the linen and cotton embroidery trade of Northern Ireland – employed mainly outworkers on a piece-rate basis.

Current estimates indicated that between eleven and twelve million manual wage-workers had entitlement to holidays with pay, either by negotiated agreement or statutory order. In addition, large numbers of non-manual employees and the salaried in general received them under other arrangements.

After 1946 there were no further references to the number of agreements and orders providing holidays with pay, nor to the aggregate number of workpeople covered by them. In 1951 'a few additional industries' were reported to have introduced arrangements;[43] by 1959 coverage, by one means or another, seems to have been more or less comprehensive.[44] After 1950 the main focus of investigative interest was not so much the relative proportions of employees with and without paid holidays, but the differing amounts of holiday leave to which they were entitled.

The majority of agreements in operation shortly after the war provided for 12 days of paid holiday: one unbroken week or six consecutive days of annual holiday plus the six public holidays. However, in 'a considerable number of cases' the period was 'not more than six days' and 'nearly as many' provided for 18 days or three weeks. In 1951 nearly three-fifths of the wage-earning workforce had entitlement to 12 days and around one-third received 18 days, inclusive of public holidays. The rate of progress accelerated during the following year, for in 1952 the proportion with an 18-day entitlement had risen to two-thirds; only one-quarter still had 12 days.[45]

Payment for the six public holidays or days in lieu was assumed to be general by 1959. By this time the fortnight was the norm (Table 14). In 1960, 97.0 per cent of manual wage-earners had entitlement to two full weeks, while most of the rest, as in 1951, had more. The lengthening of the paid-holiday period in trades subject to orders issued by the statutory wage-regulating bodies kept pace with, or did not to any significant degree lag behind, advance in industries where entitlement was fixed by voluntary collective bargaining.

The spearheading of moves to annual paid holidays of more than a fortnight was associated with the emergence and hardening of differentials relating to length of service or occupational grade. In the Metropolitan Police Service, for example, constables received 17 days, ordinary sergeants 19 days, and station sergeants 21 days in addition to public holidays or days in lieu. The holiday entitlements of Post Office employees varied according to both job grade and length of service, ranging from 2 weeks and 3 days for postmen with at least one year's service to 4 weeks for Class I technicians with at least five years' service as a technical officer (Table 15).

The proportion of manual workers covered by collective agreements entitling them to extra days of paid holiday according to years of service grew from 4.0 per cent in 1951 to 9.0 per cent in 1955; there was no marked further increase until the mid-1960s (see Table 14).

The qualification for the full basic entitlement, specified most commonly in collective agreements and orders, was 12 months' continuous service at the employing enterprise. In some cases a proportionally shorter holiday or lower holiday pay for the full holiday was permitted for workers with fewer months' service. A few agreements contained penalty clauses

TABLE 14

Basic Holiday Entitlements* in Weeks as set out in National Collective Agreements or Statutory Orders under the Wages Councils Acts and the Agricultural Wages Acts: Manual Workers, 1951–80 (United Kingdom)

Year (end December)	Percentage of workers who have a basic holiday with pay of: 1 week	between 1 & 2 weeks	2 weeks	between 2 & 3 weeks	3 weeks & over	Percentage of workers covered by arrangements providing for extra days of paid holiday dependent on length of service
1951	28	3	66	2	1	4
1955	–	1	96	2	1	9
1960	–	–	97	1	2	9
1962	–	–	97	2	1	10
1963	–	–	97	2	1	10
1964	–	–	92	7	1	20
1965	–	–	75	22	3	22
1966	–	–	63	33	4	27
1967	–	–	60	34	6	27
1968	–	–	56	34	10	27
1969	–	–	50	35	15	30
	2 weeks	between 2 & 3 weeks	3 weeks	between 3 & 4 weeks	4 weeks & over	
1970	41	7	49	3	–	25
1971	28	5	63	4	–	17
1972	8	16	39	33	4	12
1973	1	2	38	52	7	19
1974	1	1	30	40	28	20
1975	1	1	17	51	30	26
1976	–	1	18	47	34	33
1977	–	1	18	47	34	32
1978	–	1	17	47	35	36
1979	–	1	7	42	50	38
1980	–	–	2	24	74	40

*Excluding public and customary holidays

– Less than 0.5 per cent.

Derived from *British Labour Statistics: Historical Abstract 1886–1968*, Department of Employment and Productivity, HMSO, 1971, Table 34, p.91; *Department of Employment Gazette*, 1987, p.132.

TABLE 15
Annual Paid Holidays for Post Office Employees (UK) 1959

Occupational Grade	Holiday Entitlement*	Service Qualification
Manipulative Grades		
Postman	2 weeks 3 days	12 months
	3 weeks	10 years
Postman (higher grade), Telegraphist, Telephonist, Postal and Telegraph Officer	3 weeks	12 months
	3 weeks 3 days	10 years
Engineering Grades		
Labourer	2 weeks 3 days	12 months
Technician Class IIB	2 weeks 3 days	12 months
	3 weeks	10 years
Technician Class IIA	3 weeks	12 months
	3 weeks 3 days	10 years
Technician Class I	3 weeks 3 days	12 months
	4 weeks	5 years (as technical officer)

*In addition to 6 public holidays with pay.
Derived from *Ministry of Labour Gazette*, 1959, p.92

under which a worker would forfeit holiday pay, in full or in part, if he or she had been unjustifiably absent from work on more than a specified number of occasions. Evidently, some employers were still using such penalties as a deterrent to absenteeism. Even as late as 1951 there were agreements, though few in number, according to which payment for the holiday was conditional on good conduct, or satisfactory service, or exemplary time-keeping. Payment for the public holidays did not, as a rule, depend on length of service; the most common requirement was the worker's attendance on the working days immediately preceding and following the day's holiday.

There was minimal progress in the lengthening of the period of paid holiday during the first half of the 1960s. The only marked change was an increase, from 10.0 per cent in 1963 to

20.0 per cent in 1964, in the numbers with entitlement to additional days dependent on years of service. Progress, accelerating in 1965, was maintained throughout the next ten years. It came to a halt in 1975, and there were no further changes until 1979.

The proportion of manual workers whose basic holiday entitlement was confined to two weeks fell to 75.0 per cent in 1965, to 50.0 per cent in 1969 and to 1.0 per cent in 1975. During the same period the proportion entitled to a basic holiday of at least three weeks increased from around 3.0 per cent in 1965 to 15.0 per cent in 1969 and to 63.0 per cent in 1971. By this time, moves towards the four-week holiday were in clear evidence. In 1979 the proportion with four weeks or more leapt to 50.0 per cent, and rose further to 74.0 per cent the following year.[46]

There were concurrent changes in entitlement to additional service-related days of paid holiday. The numbers covered by arrangements of this kind rose from 20.0 per cent in 1964 to 30.0 per cent in 1969. Evidence strongly suggests that the fall to 12.0 thus entitled in 1972 is attributable to phased reductions in the length of service required for the extra days and the ultimate absorption of them into basic entitlements in many cases. After 1972 the numbers covered by arrangements for additional service-related days grew again, with proportional coverage reaching 38.0 per cent by the end of the 1970s and standing at 40.0 per cent at the beginning of the 1980s.

As part of the forward-planning deemed desirable by the British Institute of Management, both the third and fourth weeks tended to be eased in bit by bit over a period of years, on the basis of long-term agreements to that effect. It was relatively rare for the whole week to be introduced all in one go in times when employers were struggling to control production costs and settlements were subject to governments' prices and incomes policies. There were two main approaches to the lengthening of the holiday period in small and graduated stages. One method was to concede the extra week first for manual workers with long service, subsequently to reduce the qualifying period, and finally to permit the additional week to all workpeople with a minimum of 12 months' continuous employment with the company. The main alternative to this method was to introduce the extra week, one or two days at a time, for the entire manual workforce over a specified number of years until the whole week had been phased in.

The intense bargaining activity of the mid 1960s produced the long-term agreements which became characteristic of the period. Also characteristic was provision, contained in many agreements, for the holiday to be split; the *Ministry of Labour Gazette* noted in 1964, and again in 1967, that: 'in nearly all cases the additional days are to be taken during the winter months, or outside the normal holiday period, or at times convenient to the employer.'[47] The trades that lagged behind in the general advance tended to be those in which terms of employment were set by the statutory wage-regulating authorities; progress came more slowly, and the gains were less substantial and introduced more belatedly.

In the 1970s the pattern of advance in holiday entitlements was influenced in some degree by the UK's entry to the EEC, and the rate of progress was affected by further stages of prices and incomes policy imposed by successive governments. The BIM's 1974 survey noted that improvement of fringe benefits in general had been 'effectively slowed down for the time being by the Price and Pay Code', for the cost of such improvements had to be set against the pay limits. The main exceptions to the restrictions were the cost of introducing the New Year's Day holiday, and increase in basic holiday entitlement up to three weeks a year, or the equivalent, where previously they had been lower.[48] The general increase of paid holidays came to a halt in 1975 after the marked slow-down of the previous year. Retrospective comment in *Social Trends* noted that: 'the trend continued to 1975 when incomes policy then directed attention to other aspects of pay and work incentives.' It was not until mid 1979 that the rise began to accelerate again.[49] The TUC was already providing affiliated unions with comparative information on holiday entitlements and basic working hours in 1973, with a view to negotiation for aligning British practice with the higher standards prevailing in the EEC. Murlis found in 1974 that 'British managers, employees and unions are interested in European benefits practice and concerned that its more generous policies, such as longer holidays ... should be adopted here as soon as possible'.[50] Given the counter-influence of incomes policy, any such interests and concerns remained pipe-dreams until 1979.[51]

Changing Differentials in Holiday Entitlements

Differentials in entitlements, within the trend of a general increase in paid holidays, were still stark in the 1960s, despite the Industrial Society's claim that manual workers had 'benefited most' from recent change in that area. Of the 171 companies covered by the IS's 1966 survey, a basic holiday of 3 weeks or more was granted to manual workers in only 17.0 per cent of organizations, to non-manual employees in 30.0 per cent, to manual supervisory grades in 49.0 per cent, and to non-manual supervisory staffs in 62.0 per cent.[52] Differentials in maximum entitlements (basic plus service-related days) were also strikingly evident; a maximum entitlement of 3 weeks or more was available to manual workers in only 52.0 per cent of companies, but to non-manual employees in 88.0 per cent of them, to manual supervisory staffs in 90.5 per cent and to non-manual supervisors in 98.0 per cent of them (Table 16). Of the twelve companies submitting information about the holiday leave of senior managers, executives, directors and heads of branches, only two allowed as little as 3 weeks; all the rest permitted at least 4 weeks, and two provided 6 weeks or more. Some employing enterprises had taken steps, by introducing staff status arrangements for manual workers, for example, 'to reduce or remove existing differentials between employee grades'. At present, however, such arrangements 'cannot ... be regarded as widespread'.

There was wider acknowledgment in the early 1970s that differentials were a nuisance. Murlis's questionnaire survey disclosed in 1974 that 'status differentials in benefits' were

TABLE 16
Percentage of Companies Providing Basic and Maximum* Holiday Entitlements for Different Occupational Classes, 1966

	Percentage of companies providing holidays for:							
	Manual		Manual Supervisory		Non-Manual		Non-Manual Supervisory	
Number of days**	basic	max	basic	max	basic	max	basic	max
10	44.0	21.0	25.0	4.0	35.0	3.0	22.0	1.0
11–14	39.0	27.0	26.0	5.5	27.0	9.0	16.0	1.0
15	15.0	34.0	38.0	42.0	32.0	53.0	50.0	40.0
16–19	2.0	8.0	8.0	17.0	5.0	16.0	9.0	12.5
20	–	10.0	3.0	25.0	1.0	14.0	2.5	35.5
21–24	–	–	–	6.5	–	5.0	0.5	5.0
25	–	–	–	–	–	–	–	2.5
26+	–	–	–	–	–	–	–	2.5

* Basic holiday entitlements plus additional days dependent on length of service and/or other criteria.
** 5 days = one working week.
Derived from Industrial Society, *Holidays: Current Practices and Trends, 1966*, Industrial Society, London, 1967, pp.16, 17.

regarded by about a third of managers and most shopfloor workers as a source of discontent; they were said to 'cause ill-feeling' and to be 'a divisive influence which adversely affects efficiency'. Their retention continued to be favoured by many of the privileged as an incentive or as a reward for long service, acceptance of greater responsibility, or achievement of high occupational status. Attitudes were changing, however. Certain benefits such as annual paid holidays, were no longer regarded as 'fringe' or 'luxury' items, but as basic 'rights' which ought to be equally available to everyone who worked in paid employment; and this view was 'bound to become even more strongly held as the European practice of staff status for all categories of employees is extended to Britain'.[53]

Differentials, analysed by occupational status, were substan-

TABLE 17
Analysis of Annual Paid Holiday Entitlements*, by Occupation, April 1970: Male Full-time Employees Aged 21 and over (Great Britain)

Occupation Group	Percentage of Employees with Entitlements* of:					
	2 weeks or under	Over 2, up to 3 weeks	Over 3, up to 4 weeks	Over 4, up to 5 weeks	Over 5, up to 6 weeks	Over 6 weeks
1. Managers	4.3	34.4	33.7	18.0	4.6	5.0
2. Supervisors & foremen	6.8	38.2	34.3	14.4	3.5	2.8
3. Engineers, scientists, technologists	2.6	25.3	43.4	19.4	4.6	4.6
4. Technicians	2.5	29.0	46.0	15.6	3.6	3.3
5. Academic & teaching	0.4	2.5	4.8	3.3	4.1	84.4
6. Medical, dental, nursing & welfare	8.8	16.8	10.6	19.6	18.1	18.0
7. Other professional & technical	2.3	27.9	30.6	22.7	7.5	8.8
8. Office & communications	3.3	32.7	45.8	16.0	1.1	0.5
9. Sales	13.0	54.0	24.8	7.2	0.3	0.1
10. Security	7.1	36.5	34.2	17.8	2.6	1.5
11. Catering, domestic & other services	18.6	60.9	13.0	3.6	0.7	2.7
12. Farming, forestry, horticultural	20.5	62.8	13.3	2.9	0.1	0.1
13. Transport	19.4	60.2	16.7	1.7	0.2	1.4
14. Building, engineering etc.	17.7	70.3	9.6	1.7	0.4	0.2
15. Textile, clothing & footwear	4.2	79.1	13.9	2.5	0.2	0.1
16. Other occupations	11.3	64.3	21.6	2.4	0.2	0.1
Summary of groups 14–16						
Skilled manual	13.8	62.0	20.9	2.5	0.5	0.2
Semi-skilled manual	10.0	78.3	9.7	1.8	0.1	–
Unskilled manual	22.4	68.7	7.4	1.1	0.1	–
All manual occupations	14.8	64.2	17.2	2.8	0.3	0.4
All non-manual occupations	3.8	30.2	35.1	16.8	4.3	9.6
All occupations	11.2	53.2	23.1	7.4	1.6	3.5

* Excluding bank or public holidays but including additional entitlements for seniority, etc.
– means less than 0.05 percent.
Derived from *New Earnings Survey, 1970*, part F.

TABLE 18

Analysis of Annual Paid Holiday Entitlements*, by Occupation, April 1970: Female Full-time Employees Aged 18 and Over (Great Britain)

Occupation Group	Percentage of employees with entitlements* of:					
	2 weeks or under	Over 2, up to 3 weeks	Over 3, up to 4 weeks	Over 4, up to 5 weeks	Over 5, up to 6 weeks	Over 6
1. Managers	8.8	44.7	25.9	12.5	3.0	4.8
2. Supervisors & forewomen	6.2	41.0	33.0	11.0	4.7	3.9
3. Technicians	5.0	49.9	34.2	8.4	1.9	0.6
4. Academic & teaching	0.6	0.9	1.2	0.6	0.9	94.9
5. Medical, dental, nursing & welfare	3.9	14.6	17.4	27.7	21.5	14.7
6. Other professional & technical	5.4	34.3	29.6	21.7	5.4	3.2
7. Office & communications	9.3	48.6	34.5	6.3	0.6	0.2
8. Sales	19.2	55.9	19.0	5.5	0.1	–
9. Catering, domestic & other services	24.4	58.8	11.9	2.3	0.8	1.3
10. Farming, forestry, horticultural	33.8	56.6	6.9	0.7	–	–
11. Transport	27.9	46.9	22.4	2.8	–	–
12. Building, engineering, etc.	6.5	85.3	7.2	0.9	–	–
13. Textile, clothing & footwear	6.9	76.4	14.8	1.6	0.1	–
14. Other occupations	15.8	71.2	10.8	2.0	–	–
Summary of groups 12–14						
Skilled manual	8.5	71.1	15.2	2.0	–	–
Semi-skilled manual	8.0	80.0	10.3	1.5	–	–
Unskilled manual	17.0	71.8	9.4	1.6	–	–
All manual occupations	15.0	69.5	12.4	2.1	0.3	0.4
All non-manual occupations	8.6	39.9	27.3	9.0	3.6	11.0
All occupations	11.1	51.4	21.5	6.3	2.3	6.9

* Excluding bank or public holidays but including additional entitlements for seniority, etc.
– means less than 0.05 per cent.
Derived from *New Earnings Survey, 1970*, Part F.

tial in 1970. Non-manual classes were more privileged than manual grades, and skilled manual workers were more advantaged than both the semi-skilled and the unskilled. The most advantaged of all, in terms of holiday entitlements, were those in professional occupations (Tables 17 and 18).

The disparity was declining by 1974. In that year it was noted in the *Employment Gazette* that 'manual workers have, to some extent, been catching up with the non-manual workers'.[54] The manual workers most likely to be catching up

TABLE 19
Annual Holiday Entitlements* of Manual and Non-manual Male Full-time Employees Aged 21 and Over: 1970, 1974 and 1981

Percentage of employees with annual holiday entitlements, in weeks, of:	1970 Manual	1970 Non-manual	1974 Manual	1974 Non-manual	1981 Manual	1981 Non-manual
Zero	0.2	0.2	0.9	0.9	0.8	1.2
Up to & including 2	14.8	3.8	3.5	1.7	1.2	0.8
Between 2 & 3	13.9	5.7	1.5	0.5	0.7	0.3
3 weeks	50.3	24.5	39.7	22.4	4.9	4.3
Between 3 & 4	14.1	17.2	31.3	14.2	5.4	3.4
4 weeks	3.1	17.9	13.2	27.5	25.5	21.5
Between 4 & 5	2.8 (Between 4 & 5 and 5 weeks)	16.8 (Between 4 & 5 and 5 weeks)	8.5	15.4	43.4	27.4
5 weeks			0.6	4.0	7.3	13.7
Between 5 & 6	0.3 (Between 5 & 6 and 6 weeks)	4.3 (Between 5 & 6 and 6 weeks)	0.4	2.7	9.4	12.7
6 weeks			0.1	3.2	0.5	3.7
Over 6	0.4	9.6	0.4	7.6**	1.0	11.1

* Annual paid holidays, excluding public holidays (6 in 1970, 7 in 1974, 8 in 1981), but including additional entitlement for seniority and any local (floating) days additional to the public holidays.

** The under-representation of local authority and National Health Service employees in the 1974 *New Earnings Survey* would particularly affect these figures. The percentages in these groups were probably about the same in 1974 as in 1970.

Derived from *New Earnings Survey* for 1970, 1974 and 1981; results as summarised in the *Employment Gazette*, December 1981, pp.534–5.

were those employed in large companies. The differentials, though still in evidence, had been further reduced by 1981. (Tables 19 and 20)

The surveys, conducted by *IRRR* in 1977 and 1979, disclosed that 'most employees now get a basic annual holiday entitlement of four weeks a year', and that 'the move towards five weeks' leave a year is definitely underway for employees with long service'. Also characteristic was the trend to harmo-

TABLE 20
Annual Holiday Entitlements* of Manual and Non-manual Female Full-time Employees Aged 18 and over: 1970, 1974 and 1981

Percentage of employees with annual holiday entitlements, in weeks, of:	1970 Manual	1970 Non-manual	1974 Manual	1974 Non-manual	1981 Manual	1981 Non-manual
Zero	0.3	0.5	1.2	1.4	1.1	0.9
Up to & including 2	15.0	8.6	5.9	3.6	2.0	1.0
Between 2 & 3	17.4	11.2	2.1	1.0	1.2	0.4
3 weeks	52.1	28.8	39.9	34.8	6.1	5.4
Between 3 & 4	10.7	19.7	38.8	17.1	12.3	4.3
4 weeks	1.7	7.7	8.9	18.9	28.7	30.3
Between 4 & 5	2.1 (Between 4 & 5 and 5 weeks)	9.0 (Between 4 & 5 and 5 weeks)	2.0	7.9	35.2	26.8
5 weeks			0.2	2.2	7.0	10.2
Between 5 & 6	0.3 (Between 5 & 6 and 6 weeks)	3.6 (Between 5 & 6 and 6 weeks)	0.1	1.9	4.8	7.9
6 weeks			0.1	1.2	0.4	1.1
Over 6	0.4	11.0	0.9	10.0**	1.2	11.6

* Annual paid holidays, excluding public holidays (6 in 1970, 7 in 1974, 8 in 1981), but including additional entitlement for seniority and any local (floating) days additional to the public holidays.

** The under-representation of local authority and National Health Service employees in the 1974 *New Earnings Survey* would particularly affect these figures. The percentages in these groups were probably about the same in 1974 as in 1970.

Derived from *New Earnings Survey* for 1970, 1974 and 1981; results as summarized in the *Employment Gazette*, December 1981, pp.534–5.

nize entitlements. Of the companies submitting evidence, two out of three provided the same entitlement for all employees, irrespective of job grade, occupational status and collar colour. The organizations covered by the surveys were not necessarily a representative sample of companies in general; it seems likely that they were among the most advanced in terms of their personnel policies and the total remuneration packages they offered. Even so, developments at the 'leading edge' were signposts of the direction of change; the path taken by the leaders would soon be followed by others.

Notes

1. *Ministry of Labour Gazette* (1940), January p.11, February pp.40–1, 47, May p.132, July pp.186, 206.
2. This, and the following two extracts, *ibid.* June p.157.
3. *Ibid.* (May 1940), p.107; (June 1940), p.123
4. *Ibid.* (March 1943), p.36
5. *Ibid.* (March 1944), p.48
6. *Ibid.* (July 1940), pp.186, 206
7. *Ibid.* (April 1942), p.84
8. *Ibid.* (May 1945), p.79
9. *Ibid.* (April 1945), p.62
10. *The Staggering of Holidays*, Report to the Minister of Labour and National Service by the Catering Wages Commission, under Section 2 of the Catering Wages Act, 1943, (1945), London, HMSO.
11. *Ibid.* p.8
12. Pimlott, J.A.R. (1976) *The Englishman's Holiday: A Social History*, 2nd Edn., Sussex, Harvester, 1976, p.228.
13. Board of Trade (July 1963), *Staggered Holidays*, Cmnd. 2105, London, HMSO.
14. *Ibid.* p.2
15. Industrial Society (1963), *The Case for Staggered Holidays*, London, IS.
16. Clegg, H. and Narasimhan, P.S. (1963) *The Implications for Management of Longer Standard Holidays*, BIM Occasional Paper No. 9, London, British Institute of Management.
17. *Ibid.* p.11

18. *Ministry of Labour Gazette* (1962), February p.88, March p.106.
19. Clegg, H. and Narasimhan, P.S., *op. cit.* p.12.
20. *Ministry of Labour Gazette*, (November 1961), p.445
21. Jenkins, C. and Sherman, B. (1981), *The Leisure Shock*, London, Eyre Methuen, p.12.
22. *Ministry of Labour Gazette* (January 1964), p.2.
23. National Board for Prices and Incomes (1970), *Hours of Work, Overtime and Shiftworking*, Report No. 161, London, HMSO, p.7.
24. Evans, A. and Palmer, S. (1985), *Negotiating Shorter Working Hours*, Basingstoke, Macmillan, p.10.
25. *Ibid.*
26. 'Pay and Benefits Bulletin', *Industrial Relations Review and Report*, No. 164 (November 1977), pp.2–5.
27. 'Towards a Shorter Working Week: The Bargaining Record', *Industrial Relations Review and Report*, No. 204 (July 1979) pp. 2–4.
28. *Ibid.*
29. Quoted *ibid.*
30. *Ibid.*
31. Institute of Administrative Management (1979), *Office Hours, Turnover, and Payment Practice*, Beckenham, IAM.
32. Edwards, R.S. and Roberts, R.D.V. (1971) *Status, Productivity and Pay, A Major Experiment: A Study of the Electricity Supply Industry's Agreements and their Outcomes, 1961–71*, Basingstoke, Macmillan, introduction, ch.1.
33. Evans, A. and Palmer, S., *op. cit.* pp. 139–209.
34. Incomes Data Services (1983), *Flexible Working Hours*, Study No. 301, London, IDS, covers the main developments and issues.
35. *Social Trends 11* (1980), London, HMSO, Table (with comment) 5.2.
36. *Employment Gazette* (February 1981), p.61.
37. Many examples cited in 'Part-Time Employment', *Industrial Relations Review and Report*, No. 172, (March 1978), pp.2–7.
38. *Ibid.*
39. 'Guaranteed Week Agreements', *Ministry of Labour Gazette* (1956), pp.393–6.
40. Incomes Data Services (1972), *The Guaranteed Week: Part 1*, Study No. 20, London, IDS; (1973), *The Guaranteed Week: Part 2*, Study No. 22, London, IDS; (1981), *The Guaranteed Week:*

Part 3, Study No. 81, London, IDS; see also Industrial Society (1973), *Security of Earnings and Employment,* Survey and Report Series, No. 183, London, IS; Fincham, R. (18 July 1974), 'Inequality and the Three-Day Week', *New Society*, pp.135–7.

41. *Ministry of Labour Gazette* (December 1946), pp.344–8; see also issues for September 1944, pp.144–7, and for August 1947, pp.201–4.
42. The trade board system was replaced by a structure of wages councils under an Act of 1945.
43. *Ministry of Labour Gazette* (April 1951), pp.135–9.
44. *Ibid.* (March 1959), pp.89–93.
45. *Ibid.* (May 1952), p.157.
46. 'Holiday Entitlements: An IRRR Survey', *Industrial Relations Review and Report*, No. 166. (December 1977), pp.10–13.
47. Many such details in *Ministry of Labour Gazette;* see especially issues for 1964 and 1967.
48. Murlis, H. (1975), *Employee Benefits Today: A Survey of Attitudes and Company Practice*, Management Survey Report No. 19, London, British Institute of Management, p.6.
49. *Social Trends 12* (1982), London, HMSO, p.71.
50. Murlis, H., *op. cit.* p.3.
51. 'Holiday Entitlements in 30 Top British Organizations: An IRRR Study', *Industrial Relations Review and Report*, No. 202 (June 1979) pp.2–14.
52. Industrial Society (1966), *Holidays: Current Practices and Trends*, Information Survey and Report Series, No. 134, London, IS, pp.1, 16–17.
53. Murlis, H., *op. cit.* p.7.
54. *Employment Gazette* (December 1974), p.1118.

PART III
1979–99

7

The TUC's Working-time Campaign, from 1979

Introduction

Economic circumstances in this period were markedly different from those that characterized each of the stages through which the British economy had passed since the Second World War. Following hard on the heels of the incipient downturn, evident towards the end of the 1970s, came the rolling recession of the 1980s, when any recovery tended to be partial and short-lived. The already diminishing industrial and manufacturing sector contracted even further, resulting in fewer jobs for men, particularly in unskilled or semi-skilled work; and British exporters struggled against ever keener competition for shrinking global markets for manufactured goods. Conversely, the service sector expanded and provided increasing employment opportunities for women.

The recession was accompanied by a substantial rise in unemployment and its persistence at a relatively high level to the end of the 1980s. After increasing slowly from around 3.0 per cent in 1970 to 5.4 per cent in 1979, the unemployment rate leapt to 10.6 per cent in 1981 and to 13.1 per cent in 1983; thereafter, it remained in double figures until 1988 when it fell to 8.5 per cent and then to 6.9 per cent the following year.[1] Unemployment displaced inflation as the main social ill and became a main focus of TUC policy. Unemployment contributed to the decline in the numerical strength of trade unionism; membership fell from a historical peak of around 13¼ million in 1979 to less than 10¼ million in 1989, and then to just under 7 million in 1996. With proliferating redundancies in manufacturing industry – the traditional strongholds of powerfully organized male-dominated manual trade unions – and generally slack external labour markets, the balance of power in industrial relations shifted in favour of employers. The trade unions, with reduced bargaining clout, became more circumspect, adopting what has been termed a 'new realism' in their stance at the bargaining table.

In years when the recession, change in the structure of the economy and in the organization of the firm, and the onward rush of new technology were combining both to reduce and change employers' labour requirements, the trade unions became cautious of using the now time-worn strategies of the go-slow, work-to-rule, withdrawal of goodwill, and the strike. Days lost annually through strikes were far fewer in most years than in the preceding decade. Apart from the exceptional occasions of the 'winter of discontent' in 1978–9 and the miners' national strike in 1984, when nearly 29½ million and over 27 million working days were lost, respectively, the whole decade was markedly less strike-torn than the one which preceded it.[2]

At the same time, after the fluctuations and uncertainties of both domestic and export markets in the 1970s, employers were now beginning to adopt business strategies and manning practices which would give them sufficient flexibility to respond readily and rapidly to changing market demands of a kind that were difficult to predict with any degree of confidence. Their need was for functional and numerical flexibility of labour.[3] Flexibility in labour utilization and deployment was one of the main causes of the proportional decline in permanent full-time jobs and the steady rise of jobs that were part-time and/or short-term. According to Hakim, the latter two categories plus the increased numbers of self-employed people, accounted for around 38.0 per cent of all employment in Britain in 1987.[4] This is another part of the explanation for falling trade union membership in the period.

The trade unions, chastened by plant closures and employment insecurity, were the more disposed to co-operate in measures proposed by employers for the rescue and longer-term survival of firms; job and skill demarcations, shopfloor restrictive practices, job rights and trade boundaries were relaxed or dismantled in negotiated agreements, which at the same time offered opportunities for retraining, the acquisition of new skills, and career advancement where employment could reasonably be expected to be permanent and full-time.

There were also changes in the structure and style of collective bargaining. The importance of industry-wide bargaining to negotiate national agreements, which had been waning since the days of Donovan, now fell into steep decline; collective bargaining became progressively more decentralized as employers withdrew from multi-employer bargaining units to negotiate with their own workforces at the level of the company, the division or the plant. Notable also in this period was employers' abandonment of their traditional practice of recognizing, and negotiating with, several different unions representing separate groups, each with its own annual settlement date. The arrangement was cumbersome and time-consuming, encouraged leap-frogging claims, reflected trade boundaries, and impeded flexible utilization and deployment of labour. Now, employers setting up on greenfield sites either recognized no trade union or granted bargaining rights to a single union to represent all manual grades or all employees below managerial level; in established companies where two or more unions already had recognized bargaining rights, employers tended to move to single-table bargaining in which all the unions in question negotiated as a single body with a single annual settlement date.

It was in this context that the TUC mounted its campaign for shorter working-time in an attempt to stem the flood of redundancies, to ameliorate unemployment, and to relieve the stress and strain suffered by the employed. The European Trade Union Confederation, the central agency containing representation of the national trade union bodies of the European Community's several member states, had adopted a programme in April 1977 to reduce unemployment in the EC by shortening total working life; the initial objective was to shorten the working year by increasing annual paid holidays and reducing the basic working week towards an intended 35-hour norm. After many months of resistance, the European Council of Ministers gave the go-ahead in November 1979 for the European Commission, jointly with workpeople's and employers' representatives, to develop a policy on working time and the ways and means of reducing it. Since then, the ETUC has pressed for action and urged constituent unions in each member state to pursue the programme through collective bargaining.[5] The TUC's campaign in Britain was thus part of a wider European initiative.

The Confederation of British Industry also shifted its stance. In August 1978 the CBI was urging its members to oppose unions' claims for cuts in basic working hours; but in a document, *Jobs: Facing the Future*, published in January 1980, the CBI had apparently accepted the inevitability of making concessions; employers, it was suggested, should develop a joint approach with the unions, for it was preferable to plan ahead to avoid being 'forced into conceding damaging unplanned cuts at the bargaining table'. It made sense to 'look at ways of minimizing the impact of reduced working time, instead of simply opposing it'. Without preparation, 'the real danger is that, sooner or later, bargaining pressures will force through reductions in hours – perhaps after damaging industrial disputes – which will make British trade and industry less competitive and thus in time make the unemployment situation worse.'[6]

The TUC's Campaign: Early Successes

Reduced working time was one of the most important of all the unions' objectives in the 1980s. A major campaign had been launched by the TUC in the summer of 1978. The Post Office Engineering Union's success that year in reducing its members' basic 40-hour week to 37½ hours was a breakthrough, but the most influential of the early agreements to breach the 40-hour barrier was the engineering industry's 1979 agreement between the Engineering Employers' Federation and the Amalgamated Engineering Union for the move to a 39-hour week in November 1981. Elsewhere, in 1980, some hours reductions had been agreed, discussions were underway in many other firms and industries, and in some cases joint working parties had been set up to examine the possibilities without commitment.

Meanwhile, given the employment implications of new information technology for office staffs, the larger white-collar unions, including APEX and ASTMS, had adopted a 30-hour target. Although non-manual employees generally had a basic week of less than 40 hours, most had standard hours of more than 35. Forceful claims were being pressed by the manual trade unions, but any reductions they secured would have a knock-on effect upon office staffs, and the white-collar unions were prepared to demand the maintenance of their hours differential *vis à vis* manual grades at an overall lower level, or cash compensation for surrendering their time-honoured advantage.

The General Council's *Progress Report*, issued in December 1980, disclosed that since mid-1978 union negotiators had won hours reductions for almost five million manual workers in full-time employment. The 35-hour week was still a distant objective, but 'the TUC can certainly claim to have overcome initial resistance to any change in the pattern of hours which has prevailed since the mid-1960s'.[7] Most of the agreements reached so far had shortened the basic week without loss of pay; the majority had made modest reductions of only one hour, with commitment to further cuts to be phased in sometime in the future; and, characteristically, they contained clauses to offset the cost by workforces' acceptance of changes in working practices to raise productivity. The style of agreement embodying 'forward commitment', with an interval of two or more years between its negotiation and its implementation, was set by the engineering industry. In a circular to member firms, the Engineering Employers' Federation made the point that a major advantage of an hours reduction planned two full years ahead was to provide management with a breathing space to make preparations for the minimization of any cost increase. Managements in other companies, particularly those with continuous-process production and shift-working, also sought an interim period to prepare; the chemical and allied industries' agreement, for example, was formally reached in January 1981, but would not take effect until May 1983.[8]

As the recession began to deepen at the beginning of the decade, the TUC leadership called for strenuous efforts to secure longer standard holidays and a shorter working week, emphasizing the need for action to contain, reduce, and wherever possible to eliminate, overtime working. Advance was being monitored by the General Council, and information was regularly circulated to affiliated unions in a series of *Progress Reports*. In their deliberations on ways and means of intensifying the campaign, members of the Council drew up a consultative document containing 'proposals for a firmer TUC programme of action', and raised the possibility of some legal underpinning of collectively bargained gains.[9]

The TUC held a special Conference on Unemployment and Working-Time, on 9 April 1981, which was attended by the president of the ETUC. It was acknowledged that the main solution to Britain's mounting unemployment problem lay in an effective economic policy – which did not seem to be forthcoming from the Conservative Government; but, by general consent, trade unions' action to reduce working time could play an important part in preventing further redundancies, and could ensure that future economic recovery produced jobs and leisure for all, rather than long hours and high earnings for some and a life of unemployment and dependence on state benefits for the rest. It was decided that the General Council should continue to co-ordinate action, by issuing guidelines for negotiators and disseminating information on progress. There was no consensus on the question of legislation, however; while some union leaders believed collective bargaining to be the single most effective means of shortening the working week and felt that there had already been too much government interference in trade union activities, others argued that legislation could provide legal security for concessions won at the bargaining table.

The guidelines,[10] issued by the General Council in July 1981, were detailed and comprehensive, and their publication marked an important stage in the TUC's campaign. The document began with a warning statement: 'The recession continues, redundancies occur daily, registered unemployment moves towards the 3 million mark, and millions more jobs are increasingly at risk.' The central part of the unions' policy to combat unemployment consisted of measures for reflation and growth of the economy, as outlined in the TUC's 1981 *Economic Review*. The shortening of working-time could play an important supporting role in the preservation and generation of jobs, but reductions in the basic working week would have little effect without a drastic pruning of overtime; they could not ignore the fact that: 'even in the depths of the recession ... overtime per overtime worker continues to average at around 10 hours per week, even in sectors where unemployment is considerable.'[11]

The spread of new information technology and microelectronics in general, which reduced employers' labour requirements, made action to shorten working-time all the more urgent. The TUC's 1979 *Employment and Technology Report* had urged negotiators to make hours reductions a central feature of bargaining and agreement on the introduction of new technology, and specifically to seek the 35-hour week, six weeks of annual paid holiday, voluntary early retirement on adequate pensions, and cuts in overtime working.

Each union was expected to demonstrate, in 12 months' time, that progress had been made, especially in sectors with persistently long working hours; the General Council expressed its willingness, on request, to convene informal meetings of unions negotiating in sectors where both basic and actual hours of work were especially long. As part of the campaign, the General Council would be bringing increased pressure to bear on both the Government and the CBI, drawing attention to the part that reduced working-time could play in protecting existing jobs, creating more employment in the future, and improving the quality of life.

Negotiators were advised, before advancing a claim, to

ensure that they were fully informed of the working-time patterns of those they represented, and at the bargaining table to bear in mind: TUC policy and targets; their own members' preferences about how working-time should be reduced; the need to co-ordinate claims with other unions with recognized bargaining rights in the firm or industry; and the need to resist any employers' attempts to 'buy out' demands for shorter working hours: 'Tell your members that, unlike pay, hours reductions cannot be eroded by inflation.'

Affiliated unions were reminded that 'cutting overtime is a major TUC priority'. It was essential to negotiate much tighter initial limits on overtime and total working hours, and to ensure that decisions on overtime were under joint control. Wherever possible, overtime was to be completely eliminated – over a period of years, perhaps, by progressively tightening the overtime limit or reducing it bit by bit with annually negotiated increases in basic pay. Joint procedures for dealing with exemptions should be set up, to allow them 'only where absolutely necessary to meet special needs and emergencies'. Hours worked in excess of the overtime limits should be compensated by time off in lieu, so that average hours worked during the week or month remained within the agreed limits. Negotiators were also reminded of the importance of 'maintaining premium payments for unsocial hours, even if time off in lieu is given' and of 'ensuring that such premia are high enough to discourage employers from using overtime as a form of cheap labour'.

These measures could not be fully effective, it was admitted, unless the underlying causes of overtime were tackled. Suggested ways of removing the need for overtime hours included:

- higher manning levels, plus improved training and retraining schemes, which could reduce overtime resulting from *skill shortages*;
- higher manning levels plus improvements in health and safety at work, which could reduce the use of overtime to *fill gaps in production schedules*, caused by sickness, absenteeism and labour turnover;

- higher basic rates, which would prevent overtime from being used to provide a reasonable and competitive *level of earnings*;
- special regional rates or allowances, or locally determined rates or bonuses, which could replace the use of overtime to top up *low industry-wide rates.*[12]

Another area, identified in the consultative document as in need of bargaining attention, was working-time in shift-work and continuous-process production. TUC guidelines here included negotiation to abolish the practice, which was widespread among such groups, of working on their scheduled rest days and putting in extra hours on other days including weekends and public holidays. Negotiators were advised to 'ensure that, in addition to appropriate premium payments, unsocial-hours work at nights, weekends and holidays is fully compensated by rest days or time-in-lieu, so that overall hours do not exceed basic levels'. The introduction of additional shift crews, including a relief crew, would help to 'increase employment, spread the burden of shift-work, reduce overall hours, and lengthen the gap between shifts.' It might be possible also, it was suggested, to discriminate positively in favour of those working unsocial hours, by making special provision for them for a shorter basic week, longer holidays and earlier retirement.

Unions were reminded that better ways of arranging working hours might be found, which would improve the quality of life. A reduction in weekly hours of work could provide the occasion to 'experiment with shorter, more flexible daily patterns' which might be more convenient for people with family commitments. Alternatively, employees might prefer to take the reduction in the form of larger blocks of time; they might find that a whole day off per month, a half-day Friday, a four-day week, or a nine-day fortnight 'more useful for leisure or educational purposes'. Other suggestions included 'job and finish', personal paid holidays, and sabbaticals of up to a full year.

Negotiators, it was acknowledged, would need to counter

employers' objections about the costs of reducing working-time; they might effectively argue that shorter hours could:

- produce a fairer and more stable pay structure;
- focus on the need for a better use of resources with basic hours, including new work schedules and patterns of work organization;
- reduce costs resulting from boredom, strain, sickness, absenteeism and labour turnover, and improve morale and performance;
- provide a basis for a more flexible response to fluctuations in demand than was possible where long working hours and high overtime levels were systematic and institutionalized;
- focus on a need for a more fundamental approach to skill shortages, involving higher manning, additional crew shifts, and training schemes to provide a more skilled and adaptable workforce;
- help to stop employers relying on the extensive use of outdated machinery, and encourage investment in efficient new processes and technology.[13]

The main objectives of the campaign were to help to save existing jobs and to create new ones for the future. To those ends, joint committees might be set up to ensure that any cost savings made by employers were translated into new full-time jobs wherever possible. Where job losses threatened, negotiators might cut overtime in exchange for an agreement for no involuntary redundancy; and they could draw employers' attention to the negative impact of shake-out: 'Insecurity makes workers hostile to change, and, once dispersed, a skilled production team can be very difficult to re-establish.' Early retirement of older workers would release jobs to younger people. Unions should therefore 'negotiate occupational pension schemes to a level that will allow older workers a real choice of earlier retirement without financial loss'. In conjunction with this, they might consider schemes for approaching retirement, by progressively reducing hours and increasing holidays for those nearing the end of their working lives, so as to ease the transition from work to retirement.

There was no denying that technological advance was inevitable; indeed, it was vital to economic regeneration and competitive business performance. Negotiators were reminded that:

> Only a positive approach to hours, employment, job security, manpower development and the quality of working life can produce a climate in which technological change is welcomed rather than seen as a threat to be avoided at all costs.

Discussion at the 1981 Congress was dominated by the unemployment problem; in Dave Basnett's words: 'Its shadow darkens every part of the country; it is part of a national economic disaster; and it is a personal tragedy for millions.' The unions, he asserted, must do whatever they could to deal with the scourge of lost jobs: 'It is sheer lunacy that this country, with the fastest growing rate of unemployment in the Common Market, should force its shrinking labour force to work just about the longest hours in Europe.'

The unions had made remarkable progress, despite a bargaining background of deepening recession. The two great barriers – the 40-hour week and the four-week holiday – had already been breached in several industries. The economic situation was worsening, however; unemployment had doubled in the last two years, and further job losses were being caused by 'an entirely unplanned and unregulated technological revolution'.

There was general support for Mr Basnett's call to 'turn the campaign into an all-out offensive.' It was not just a matter of reducing the basic working week and increasing holidays:

> We all know the time bomb which ticks away beneath any campaign to deal with working hours, and that is overtime ... the continuing curse of British industrial life, which divides worker from worker, and workers from

their families, which elevates greed into a principle, and which ... actually keeps wage rates down ... Overtime is stolen time, time stolen by employers to avoid employing more of our people, time which blights the hopes of young people desperate for a job ...[14]

The campaign, he asserted, would be a failure unless overtime could be drastically reduced where it was grossly excessive and systematic; much of it was avoidable: 'Any employer who cannot run his business without huge dollops of overtime does not know how to run a business at all.'

There were, Mr Basnett acknowledged, deep feelings within Congress about the incursion of the law into industrial relations: 'We are aware of what the judges think of us ... but we should not forget that enlightened parliamentary action has in the past given us what we could not achieve through collective bargaining.' The General Council had therefore been giving thoughtful consideration to the possibilities of legislation. They had acquired information about arrangements in other countries, and had sought the views of affiliated unions on the issue: 'We are not satisfied, however, that we have come up with all the answers. Before we commit ourselves ... we want to be satisfied that we have got it right.' The future possibilities of legislation on working-time did not diminish the need to pursue the TUC's objectives by means of collective bargaining. Employers' responses to the unions' claims for reduced working hours would be closely monitored, for 'what happens at the bargaining table must help to determine the final attitude that we take on legal limits'.

The effect of new technology on employment also needed to be carefully monitored. The TUC, Mr Basnett maintained, had never assumed that microelectronic technology was an automatic threat to jobs, but it would 'act as a haphazard job killer so long as we continue allowing it to be introduced in an unplanned way'. A year before, the TUC and CBI had jointly issued a *Statement on Technological Change*, stating unequivocally that the introduction of new technology must be by joint agreement. That document had contained a declaration that a joint approach 'is clearly the best way to develop ... an understanding, so that fears and suspicions ... can be allayed and opportunities grasped'. The CBI Grand Council had subsequently changed its mind, and had withdrawn support for the idea of new technology agreements. Even so, agreements of this kind were still part of the TUC's policy on unemployment.

A long and detailed resolution was moved at Congress that year by Clive Jenkins, who reminded delegates of the 'legislative provisions in a number of EEC countries, restricting by law the number of hours worked per year, and the superior holiday provisions existing in many of these countries'. The motion called for action to 'limit the number of hours worked annually, reduce the working week by statute to a maximum of 35 hours, provide for a minimum holiday entitlement of six weeks per annum, plus sabbatical leave after a stipulated number of years ... and reduce the qualifying age for retirement pensions to 60 years'. Any legislation to impose legal limits on working hours 'must specifically include small employers, unlike some Tory statutes that permit their exclusion'. There had been relatively little progress on new technology agreements; and much concern was voiced at the CBI's refusal to encourage them in the private sector and the failure of the Government to give a helpful lead.[15]

The General Council was urged to initiate discussions within the TUC/Labour Party Liaison Committee to formulate a common policy for an incoming Labour government, based on the TUC's 1979 policy document, *Employment and Technology*, and the Labour Party's discussion paper, *Microelectronics*. They would have to make a fresh examination of possible means of bolstering collective bargaining with new laws to establish a new plateau from which the unions could work. This was the more urgent, for 'the great organizations, the multi-nationals and the publicly-owned enterprises will pour money into a round-the-clock global flow of information'. The result would be job losses in Britain and throughout the developed world. Legislation, of the kind which limited working hours in the main countries of Western Europe, was essential in Britain, to provide a base for trade union action industry by industry and company by company: 'We are top of the European league for long working hours.' The unions, Mr Jenkins believed, ought to think in terms of the four-day working week and the three-day weekend, and, like Sweden, Belgium and Germany, of annual rather than weekly working hours.[16]

More assiduous and strenuous efforts from negotiators were urged by some of the delegates who remained unconvinced that legislation was the best way forward. As Mr Kitson observed: 'Minimum standards laid down in legislation tend to become maximum standards. That has already been demonstrated in the Wages Councils.' His union, the TGWU, would 'not beg any government to do things that we should be doing ourselves'. A delegate representing the AUEW-TASS objected to rigidly fixed targets, in view of the widely varying working patterns and traditions in the public and private sectors, in industry, commerce and services, in manual and non-manual work, and for men and women. The TUC's working-time campaign should seek reductions from whatever levels currently obtained in the different spheres of employment to the lowest possible levels obtainable in negotiation. Information technology was beginning to spread rapidly in office work; and white-collar workers already on a 35-hour week would need their hours further, and substantially, reduced if jobs were to be preserved. There was nothing to be gained if those who had already achieved the target simply stood still. Moves to an even shorter working week, spearheaded by the stronger unions, made it easier for others to follow their example.

The idea of the 'harmonization' of employment conditions, which had been recently discussed, had been misunderstood by some delegates. Harmonization of terms and benefits, including working hours and holidays, meant equalization by improvement of the worst towards the best standards; but 'best' was a moving target, not a fixed one. 'In some parts of our Movement,' the AUEW-TASS speaker continued, 'there is a misguided view that harmonization means that those who have achieved better working conditions ... should stand still while others catch up.' But in the past, when women doing the same work as men were to receive equal pay with their male colleagues, no-one, and least of all women trade unionists, had expected men to stand still until women's pay rates caught up: 'Male workers, supported by female workers, decisively and correctly rejected that idea, on the basis that the only people to benefit would be the employers.' Similarly, on the question of working-time, policy should neither deter nor prevent the pace-makers from winning better terms than the suggested targets: 'No-one is asking those on 35 hours per week to stand still'; they: 'should be fighting to reduce their weekly hours to 30.'

Collective bargaining produced some progress, but the amount pruned from the working week and the numbers affected by the relevant agreements were something of a disappointment to the TUC. That experience, coupled with further increase in unemployment, caused the TUC's Economic Committee to issue a discussion document in 1982 outlining the case in favour of legislation to limit working hours.[17]

Legislation, it was stressed, should reinforce, not replace, collective bargaining efforts. The schedule proposed in the discussion paper included: a major government statement on working-time, setting target reductions; a Code of Practice from the Department of Employment, on working hours and employment; provision by ACAS of advice and information for bargaining groups; an Act of Parliament on Working-Time and Employment; the introduction of a scheme for state-financed incentives linking employment subsidies to recruitment of labour. The TUC envisaged 'a two-pronged approach – state subsidies coupled with legislation – as a "carrot" and "stick" scheme which, together with collective bargaining, offers the prospect of real progress.'[18] In France, it was noted, the Mitterrand Government, in collaboration with the unions, had introduced an effective strategy, combining 'an ordinance on working-time with ordinances on solidarity contracts – that is, measures using state subsidies to speed up larger reductions in working hours and to encourage recruitment'.[19] In Britain, the TUC favoured legislation which would allow and encourage collective bargaining to improve on the minimum standards and targets set statutorily, and which would stimulate wider collective bargaining on the issue.

It was, perhaps, unrealistic of the TUC to expect its proposals to carry much weight with a Conservative government wedded to 'free enterprise' and committed to the imposition of legal constraints seeking to curb trade union influence and effectiveness. The document, it is true, was essentially a discussion paper,[20] and its contents might receive greater favour from the TUC/Labour Party Liaison Committee and be taken on board by a future Labour government; but, as the unions admitted, the unemployment situation was deteriorating and they could not afford to sit back and wait for the next general election on the off-chance that a Labour government, if elected, would pass legislation about which there was no consensus among the unions.

If delegates at Congress were not in full agreement about legislation, no-one dissented from the idea of reducing working-time as a means to job creation. The rank and file union members did not always see eye to eye with their elected union officers on the overtime issue, however; it was noted that, as recently as two months before, the average amount of overtime being worked per overtime worker in manufacturing industry was eight hours per man per week, compared with two hours in West Germany. There were formidable practical difficulties in reducing overtime in Britain:

> Sadly, many trade union members are dependent on overtime to supplement meagre basic rates. Also, many of our members are hooked on overtime ... In other instances members are pressurized to work voluntary overtime ... We must recognize that the level of overtime which was acceptable to us in the fat years of the 1950s and 1960s cannot be acceptable to the Trade Union Movement in the lean years of the present.[21]

Another explanation for the persistence of overtime was

given by Mrs Travis of APEX. Many employers were currently facing major cash-flow problems 'resulting from the Government's ill-advised policies', and they were consequently shedding labour and resorting to the cheaper alternative of working fewer people for longer hours by imposing overtime on those still employed. But 'the captains of industry are guilty of muddled thinking... The effect will be to depress market demand even further ... for every man and every woman that is made unemployed is one less person that is able to purchase cars, televisions, radios or ... even food.' Some members actively sought overtime out of sheer greed, she continued; and it was deceitful, insincere and quite unprincipled of unions to allow their members to work a 60-hour week, while at the same time calling for a united effort for a week of 35 hours.

Employers were not entirely to blame; starved of investment funds, many had little alternative but to close plants, cut costs, and curtail their business operations:

> Industry is bleeding to death. I say to the captains of industry that it is equally ... their obligation to join us and to say to this present Government that, if their cash-flow problems cannot be resolved, it is up to the Government to put more investment into industry to give it the right to survive.[22]

The Government, however, intent on cuts in public expenditure and convinced of the efficacy of competitive market forces, was disinclined to act upon the TUC's policy proposals to rescue industry.

When, in December 1982, members of the General Council reviewed progress to date, they concluded that the campaign for shorter working-time continued to meet with some success. Virtually all of the unions had won concessions; average basic weekly hours were falling below 40 for more and more workers, basic holiday entitlements continued to rise towards five weeks, and several recent agreements provided for a second or third round of reductions to the basic working week. Such advance was encouraging, but sectors badly hit by the recession, and low-paid groups in some regions, continued to lag behind; and for many, retirement pensions were too low to allow early retirement to be an attractive option. Overtime, even in sectors facing extensive redundancies, had recently shown signs of rising to pre-recession levels; and very few agreements explicitly tied hours cuts and acceptance of new technology to a positive policy of job creation. By general consent, the momentum of the campaign had to be maintained.

At its meeting in May 1983, the General Council considered the form that legislation on working hours might take, without pre-judging the outcome of discussion on the subject with 'a future sympathetic government'.

A resolution moved at Congress that year, when the rate of registered unemployment was above 13.0 per cent, called upon the unions to give highest priority to the shortening of the working year and a drastic reduction of overtime, and asked the TUC/Labour Party Liaison Committee to draw up a policy for legislation to limit hours of employment.[23] The speaker's comments echoed the General Council's earlier observations. The TUC's campaign had had some effect, for during the last 18 months, on average, 'normal weekly hours for manual workers have fallen from 39.8 to 39.3', and the proportion with a basic working week of less than 40 hours 'has risen from 41.0 per cent to nearly 66.0 per cent'.

This was not the whole picture, however, for hours reductions of one, two, three and even four hours for some groups had coincided with an increase in numbers unemployed to over 3½ million. At the same time, the speaker noted, other changes had occurred over which the trade unions had no control; these changes had contributed to the reduction of average hours worked, but were not necessarily welcome in all respects. Employers had reacted to the recession by cutting hours and pay for the most vulnerable groups, many of whom were in low-paid employment in retail distribution, catering, and the public services; but the greatest contributor to the fall in average hours had been 'the shift of employment from manual to non-manual, from manufacturing to services, the growth in part-time work ... and in some cases ... a return to casual employment'. Decisions to reduce hours of work had been taken unilaterally by employers, as a response to the recession and technological advance in the context of ongoing structural change in the economy as a whole. The TUC should beware of making simplistic assumptions in interpreting the statistics on working hours.

Overtime working persisted; there were now fewer male manual workers in the shrinking manufacturing sector and 'the upturn this year has seen an increase in overtime working on their part'. In the services sector, low basic pay rates caused a willingness to work overtime to earn a 'living wage'; but, conversely, overtime kept the basic rate low. The continued acceptance, often at the employer's insistence, of long overtime hours by some groups served to disadvantage others in the same sphere of employment for whom there was no overtime option. As one delegate observed: 'We know that a reduction of overtime can be divisive. A buy-out of overtime helps some workers but ... not others.' Its uneven incidence 'means that there is not a clear incentive to put cuts in overtime at the top of the bargaining agenda'. Negotiators needed a 'clearer strategy from the top' in order to reduce 'resistance from the shopfloor' and discourage employers from 'using overtime to avoid adequate manning levels'.[24]

The TUC's campaign for shorter working-time was inextricably linked with its campaign against low pay. Low pay, defined as earnings below £90 per week, affected some seven million workpeople, it was noted, including over half of all female workers; it was endemic in hairdressing and the hotel, catering and distributive trades. In such circumstances, people 'will work overtime whenever they can get it; they will not heed our exhortations that they should not do it because of the high level of unemployment'. To make matters worse, the Government was intent on dismantling what little legal protection the low-paid worker had, including the Fair Wages Resolution, the Wages Councils, and the Wages Inspectorate. The prospect of even lower pay brought with it the prospect of even greater willingness to work overtime.

During 1983 there had been 'a considerable slow-down in moves to shorter hours', and in February 1984, in an attempt to regain the momentum, the TUC held a conference on the subject, at which a revised version of the 1981 guidelines and checklist was discussed.[25] Those in attendance endorsed proposals that the conditions of manual and non-manual groups should be brought into greater harmony, and that the links with the unions seeking hours reductions in continental Europe should be strengthened.

In response to the first of these proposals, the Confederation of Shipbuilding and Engineering Unions, at its 1984 conference, resolved upon harmonization not only of the basic working hours of manual and non-manual grades but of all employment terms and benefits; also adopted were resolutions for increased pressure to reduce working-time, as a major objective, the limitation of overtime working, and the negotiation of 'no-strike deals'. The CSEU was, again, seeking a national agreement with the Engineering Employers' Federation for a 35-hour week and a six-week annual holiday. A year earlier the EEF and the CSEU had set up a joint working party to discuss issues of general importance in all sections of the shipbuilding and engineering industry. Alex Ferry, the CSEU's general secretary, noted, in his report of the six working party meetings held so far, that the employers were seeking 'revolutionary changes' in working practices in return for 'as yet entirely unspecified hours concessions'.[26] It was decided that the joint working party should continue with its discussions, 'subject to the employers taking a more positive line on reduced working hours and modifying some of their proposals for change'. Jim Fairly, of the AUEW, in reporting with regret the recent increase in overtime working in the engineering trades at a time of continuing job losses, pressed for the imposition of a limit of 10 overtime hours per worker per month, and strongly argued the case for legislation to eliminate systematic and institutionalized overtime working. Some dissent was voiced by a TGWU spokesman, however; the union favoured a general reduction of overtime, but was opposed in principle to statutory regulation of it.

When the TUC held its annual conference in 1984, it was reported that union representatives had pressed for the shortening of working hours at a series of meetings held during the year by the European Community's Economic and Social Committee, and that a Recommendation had been adopted, against opposition from employers, for a reduction and reorganization of working-time; ways and means of effecting reductions would be left to joint decision by employers and unions, so as to facilitate radical but necessary structural change. A Recommendation, however, had no legally binding force in any EC member state. In May and June of 1984, the TUC General Council had met delegates from West Germany's national trade union body, the DGB, who confirmed that their country's trade unions were united in their campaign for a 35-hour week, earlier retirement, and legislation requiring overtime to be compensated by time off in lieu, as the projected rate of economic growth would be insufficient to have much effect in reducing unemployment in Germany in the foreseeable future in the absence of measures to shorten working time. The DGB estimated that its proposals would reduce unemployment in the Federal Republic by almost two million, and that initially higher unit labour costs would be offset by the consequent cost-savings on unemployment benefits and greater income-tax revenue from the increased numbers in employment. It was agreed that the TUC and DGB should maintain their close co-operation in the ETUC, and that they should jointly campaign for substantial working-time reductions throughout the EC. During the year, the TUC's General Secretary attended a special meeting of the Austrian Federation of Trade Unions, the OGB, on the theme of 'Work for All'; the conference adopted a resolution calling for a progressive reduction of the working week from 40 hours to 35, 'in order to create jobs and to express solidarity with the unemployed'.[27] The British Government, unconvinced that reductions in working hours throughout Britain would have much effect in lessening unemployment, remained unenthusiastic about EC Recommendations on the matter.

A motion for a shorter working life, carried by Congress in

1984, noted that, unlike Britain, other EC member states had shown far greater willingness to tackle unemployment by reducing working-time. In Belgium the 38-hour week was 'almost universal'. In France the Government had imposed a statutory maximum of 39 hours and there were many agreements for less. In West Germany the DGB had won some major concessions. Britain lagged behind: 'In Thatcher's Britain ... we work on average more hours and suffer higher unemployment than almost any other country in the western industrialized world ...' It was also 'normal' in continental Europe for manual and non-manual grades to have the same basic working hours, whereas in Britain the majority of manual workers had a longer basic week than their non-manual colleagues: 'There is no justification for that.' Unions affiliated to the TUC 'must therefore unite and create a harmonized demand for 35 hours for all workers – blue-collar, white-collar, male or female.' Overtime was still unacceptably high in Britain; it affected roughly half of all male manual workers, amounted on average to 9½ hours per week, and was worked even in sectors of industry that had not yet won the 40-hour basic week.

So far, the unions had focused their best efforts on shortening the basic working week but, at the 1984 Congress, the scope of the campaign was widened to include more decisive action to increase holiday entitlements. Here too, Britain lagged behind. In Belgium, France, West Germany, Spain and Luxembourg, an annual holiday of at least five weeks was standard, while in Britain there were some sectors which had not yet achieved the fourth week. Longer holidays would 'make a major and real contribution to shorter working-time, year by year, and that is part of our claim that is not to be overlooked'.[28] Earlier retirement, by shortening working life, would also help to reduce unemployment. There were currently around 1½ million workpeople over the age of 60; the time had surely come to harmonize the retirement age for all at 60, and in the longer term to reduce it to 55: 'Whether we like it or not, new technology makes this absolutely imperative.'

The Government had recently claimed that new enterprises in the new growth industries would provide more jobs. A POEU delegate disagreed; telecommunications and information technology generally were popularly regarded as 'new industry', but 'our experience is not of new industry creating jobs, but of new technology devouring jobs, and at an ever-increasing rate'. Thousands were becoming redundant, 'even though telecommunications is a rapidly expanding growth industry'. The same effect was rippling through other sectors, wherever microelectronic technology and computerized processes were spreading. Technological advance would continue, whether the government in office was Labour or Conservative; and it ought not to be obstructed by the unions – 'We are not Luddites' – but it had to be controlled and 'used to enable workpeople to enjoy better, happier lives' with more leisure at their disposal:

> We must look to the new challenge of technology as an opportunity to create more leisure, earned after a period of productive and fulfilling working life, not the creation of unemployment and the leisure of the dole queue ...[29]

Again, negotiation of better occupational pensions would make early retirement a practicable possibility for more people, and would release jobs for the young.

The General Council's review of progress to mid-1985 indicated that although negotiation of a shorter basic week had continued during the preceding 12 months, with 'well over half a million workers receiving reductions', the main focus was now shifting towards agreements for longer holidays, a 'record number' of which had been reached during the past year. Some agreements made preparation for retirement by progressively reducing working hours for those approaching retirement age; and others made improved provision for paid paternity and bereavement leave. There was other evidence which was less encouraging, however; overtime working had continued to rise, and very few agreements explicitly tied hours reductions to job creation or job preservation – 'as particularly recommended in the TUC guidelines'.

By the mid 1980s the campaign seemed to be running out of steam; the task now facing the General Council was to revitalize it.

Reinvigorating the Campaign

Unemployment was still a major problem in the mid 1980s. The prospects of first jobs for school leavers and of re-employment for older workers, who had borne much of the brunt of redundancy, were bleak. For these people, unemployment was prolonged and the job search disheartening. Registered unemployment of 3,037,000 persons and an official unemployment rate of 11.2 per cent in 1985[30] probably understated the extent of the problem; the TUC estimated that 'well over 4 million' were without jobs. A delegate at that year's Congress noted that the 'TUC campaign for reduced working-time has been in existence for some years, but what it needs now is new vigour'.[31] The avowed policy was for a working life shortened by means of the reduced basic week, less overtime, longer holidays, sabbaticals, earlier retirement, and more paternity/maternity leave; but many workpeople preferred other things: 'We have to face it ... that when it has come to the crunch we have dropped that part of the claim, because workers see the main issue as wages.' Progress in securing hours cuts had slowed down: 'We will never get any movement ... unless we begin to campaign in a more vigorous way.' Year in year out, delegates had 'paid lip service' to the idea that the amount of overtime being worked in the midst of mass unemployment was 'an absolute scandal'. The truth of the matter was that 'we have not campaigned as we ought' by convincing the rank and file union membership of the need to eliminate it.

A resolution carried in 1985 called for 'renewed emphasis' on the TUC's working-time objectives, and a 'broader strategy' by approaching the target from every conceivable angle. Negotiators were reminded of the aims: a basic 32-hour week, a minimum holiday entitlement of six weeks, sabbaticals, longer paternity and maternity leave, elimination of all 'contractual overtime', a lowering of the retirement age 'in ways which maximize employment', and acceptance of new technology only if it was linked to full job protection for existing employees; at the same time, the TUC was pressing for legislation, as in most Western European countries, to limit permissible amounts of overtime in any one week.

The recent and prospective job losses caused by new telecommunications technology were alarmingly high. That industry's employees could 'hardly be opposed to new technology', but the result was insecurity of employment 'in a competitive and now privatized environment'. The industry had already shed 16,000 jobs in three years; and there were further projected cuts: 'a 90.0 per cent job reduction ... in electronic exchanges, a 50.0 per cent job reduction in the transmission network, a 26.0 per cent cut in customer services ...' There were many other industries similarly affected, including printing and 'the car industry where robotics abound'.

The following year, the TUC's Economic Committee noted the General Council's reservations, that the 35-hour, rather than a 32-hour, week would remain the more immediate objective for most bargaining groups; and that the call for legislation on overtime should be interpreted in terms of discussion of the subject 'with a future sympathetic government'.

The 1987 *Progress Report* outlined the main features of the legislation desired by the TUC, without prejudging the outcome of future discussions with a Labour government. The unions would face greater challenges in the immediate future, as a result of actions taken by the Conservative Government to weaken existing legislation on working-time: the repeal of restrictions on night-work in bakeries and of the powers of Wages Councils to set maximum hours and minimum holidays, and changes to the legislation on women's retirement age. This last ran counter to the TUC's policy to reduce men's retirement age to 60. Most unions, it was regretted, had 'only chopped an hour off the working week since 1979'; and overtime, far from declining, had in fact been rising. There had been a little progress on maternity and paternity leave, but virtually none on sabbaticals. Unemployment, at 2.9 million, was still unacceptably high.

The campaign, so far, had sought shorter working-time mainly as a means to ameliorate the unemployment problem, but in 1987 the main focus was on workpeople's need for more leisure to improve the quality of family life. Ms McWilliams, of the TGWU, reminded Congress of the large number of married women now in paid employment outside the home. Where both partners had full-time jobs, there was little free time for them to care for their families and to enjoy life; and where the male partner was the sole breadwinner, he surely needed time to spend with his family and to help his wife with domestic and childcare tasks. The Coram Institute's research into family life had disclosed that fathers working overtime often did not arrive home before their children were put to bed. Women with babies and young children frequently had to cope all day, and sometimes all night, without the support of their partners. Research showed that many marriages tended to 'break down ... over rows about who is not pulling their weight, who is never at home when they are needed most'. Congress, she urged, must remember the needs of family life in campaigning to reduce working-time, the more so in view of the escalating divorce rate, with one in three marriages breaking up. By general consent, a living wage was essential, but essential also was sufficient free time to enable men to take their fair share of domestic responsibilities: 'The realities of the labour market must be adapted to the realities of family life.'

The General Council that year had considered proposals from the ETUC on reduced working-time under the Single European Act. The TUC intended to hold further consultations with the Labour Party but, as the General Council noted, previous European-wide initiatives to legislate on working-time had been opposed. In Britain, the trend towards longer holidays 'remained healthy', but the slow-down of progress in shortening basic working hours continued, and overtime working in 1988 was found to be higher than at any time since 1950.

The CSEU, in line with ETUC proposals, had embarked upon 'a massive campaign for the 35-hour week'. It was a campaign uniting all the blue-collar and white-collar workers of the CSEU's constituent unions, in pursuit of the harmonization of working hours at 35 per basic week. The industry could afford the concession, for 'since 1980 both productivity and profits have soared'. The objective of harmonizing working hours was contained in a long and complex resolution carrying the general heading of 'Europe 1992: Trade Union Strategy'. The relevant clause stated:

> Trade unions should consider adopting collective bargaining objectives aimed at moving towards an upward harmonization of terms and conditions within the Community; those objectives should include a common minimum wage, the ETUC goal of a 35-hour normal basic working week, and the right of all workers to an occupational pension scheme.[32]

The CSEU's campaign was based on a commitment that any settlement would provide shorter hours for both staff and manual groups, with ultimate convergence on the 35-hour week for all. In 1990, the CSEU succeeded in securing a 37-hour week as a first step towards its goal; some 600 agreements covering around three million workers had been reached, providing for an immediate or phased reduction of the standard working week to 37 hours. Engineering workers in West Germany, it was reported, had won an agreement to establish the 35-hour week as the norm in the key North Wurtenburg area by 1995. This would be of considerable assistance to British unions, 'particularly when employers begin, yet again, to express concern about possible loss of international competitiveness'.[33]

Shorter hours, it was asserted, had been earned by the engineering industry's workers, for they had 'delivered the record output, productivity and profitability, that Mrs

Thatcher continually boasts about'. Facts demolished the lie that shorter hours damaged the economy, for those countries that had seen the greatest reductions in working hours topped Europe's productivity league: 'The truth is ... that when British workers work long hours, they collaborate with inefficiency and mismanagement ...'

There were echoes of the latter idea in a resolution at the 1990 Congress, linking long working hours to stress-related illness. The effects of stress, Ms McGrath explained, took many forms. The short-term effects included headaches, migraine, backache, tension, muscle cramp, poor sleep, tiredness, low morale, skin rashes, and impaired vision. In the longer term, stress could cause high blood pressure, stomach ulcers, asthma, dermatitis and heart disease. It also contributed to behavioural problems, such as difficulty with relationships, and also to heavy smoking, excessive drinking, dependence on tranquillizers, drug abuse, depression, and feelings of alienation and isolation. The CBI's recent estimate of the annual financial cost of stress-induced absenteeism, lowered efficiency, increased accidents, poor time-keeping, and premature retirement, amounted to £1,300 million. That was a formidable financial burden for employers; but the CBI's investigation completely overlooked the heavy costs of a different kind for workpeople and their families.

A speaker, supporting the motion, acknowledged that excessive working-time was not the only cause of stress, but admitted that it was 'certainly a very significant one'. Company culture often induced employees, especially those in non-manual, professional and managerial jobs, to spend a great deal of time at work. It was believed to be the means to promotion as demonstrating loyalty to the company; and 'in these days of performance-related pay, these pressures are even stronger'. The employee's health, social life, and family relationships were all adversely affected: 'If the job cannot be done in the normal working week, then it is badly designed or overloaded ...'[34]

The General Council's 1995 report, noted that, despite the very real working-time gains made in some sectors, some 5.7

million full-time manual workers, about one in three, 'had to work 45 hours a week or more'. That represented an increase of nearly 25.0 per cent since 1984. In 1992, 20.0 per cent of all men in full-time employment worked over 48 hours per week, compared with less than 10.0 per cent in the rest of the EU. Research, commissioned by the TUC, showed that a major cause of stress at work was a combination of job insecurity and an ever-increasing workload; stress was one of the main factors leading to absenteeism and staff turnover, which cost British employers an estimated £1.3 billion per annum. The Department of Health estimated the cost of sickness absence for stress and mental disorder at over £5 billion per annum.[35]

Trade union membership, amounting to 7 million in 1996, had nearly halved since 1979; membership was particularly low among part-time workers and young workers below the age of 25. The General Council was unconvinced by the Government's claim that lower unemployment and significantly better economic and labour market performance in Britain than in the other major economies of Europe in 1995 and 1996 were attributable to its policy of deregulation – the removal and weakening of employment protections, curbs on the trade unions, and 'attacks on the unemployed'. The more likely explanation for Britain's lower unemployment rate was that the British workforce was shrinking with more people dropping out of the active labour market, while the reverse was the case in most other EU countries.[36]

The decline of industry-wide multi-employer bargaining and national agreements made the unions' targeted working-time standards the more difficult to attain. Their efforts to realize them would be maintained into the future.

Notes

1. Pollard, S. (1992), *The Development of the British Economy, 1914–1990*, London, Edward Arnold, p.417; annual average statistics in the *Employment Gazette* and *Social Trends*.
2. Pelling, H. (1992), *A History of British Trade Unionism*, London,

Penguin, pp. 277, 283–4, 287–92, 305; for industrial relations in the 1970s see Wrigley, C. (1996), 'Trade Unions, Strikes and the Government', in Coopey, R. and Woodward, N., eds, *Britain in the 1970s: The Troubled Economy*, London, UCL Press.

3. Atkinson, J. (1984), *Manning for Uncertainty: Some Emerging Workplace Patterns*, IMS Research Paper, Brighton, Institute of Manpower Studies, University of Sussex; Incomes Data Services (1984), *Craft Flexibility*, Study No. 322, London, IDS; 'Flexible Employment Strategies', *Industrial Relations Review and Report*, No. 325 (August 1984), pp.13–16.
4. Hakim, C. (1987), 'Trends in the Flexible Workforce', *Employment Gazette*, November, pp.549–59.
5. 'The Union Campaign for Reduced Working Time: An *IRRR* Review', *Industrial Relations Review and Report*, No. 217 (February 1980), pp.2–6.
6. Quoted *ibid.* p.3.
7. 'Reductions in Working Time: A Round-Up of National Agreements', *Industrial Relations Review and Report*, No. 242 (February 1981), p.2.
8. *Ibid.*
9. Trades Union Congress (1981), *Annual Report*, p.264.
10. Full text of the document is given *ibid.* pp.265–8.
11. *Ibid.* p.516.
12. *Ibid.* p.266.
13. *Ibid.* p.267.
14. *Ibid.* p.517.
15. *Ibid.* pp.518–9.
16. Annual working hours for engineering workers are given as 1500 in Sweden, 1600 in Belgium, 1700 in West Germany, and 1900 in Britain.
17. 'Overtime: Restricting its Level', *Industrial Relations Review and Report*, No. 270 (April 1982), p.2.
18. 'TUC Proposals for Legislation on Working Time', *Industrial Relations Review and Report*, No. 279 (September 1982), pp.13–15.
19. *Ibid.* p.13.
20. Trades Union Congress (1982), *Annual Report*, p.546.
21. *Ibid.* p.547.
22. *Ibid.* p.550.
23. *Ibid.* (1983), p.481.
24. *Ibid.* p.482.

25. 'The Shorter Working Week: An IRRR Review' and 'Extract from TUC Discussion Paper on Reduced Working Time', *Industrial Relations Review and Report*, No. 312 (January 1984), pp.2,3.
26. 'CSEU Pushes for Shorter Working Hours', *Ibid.* No. 324 (July 1984), p.16.
27. Trades Union Congress (1984), *Annual Report*, pp.288–9.
28. *Ibid.* p.500.
29. *Ibid.* p.502.
30. OECD, *Annual Abstract of Statistics.*
31. Trades Union Congress (1985), *Annual Report*, p.523.
32. *Ibid.* (1988), p.575.
33. *Ibid.* (1990), p.195.
34. *Ibid.* p.517; Labour Research Department (1994), *Stress at Work: A Trade Union Response*, London, LRD.
35. Trades Union Congress (1995), *General Council Report*, pp. 38–9.
36. *Ibid.* (1996), pp.10, 22.

8

Changes in Working-time Since 1979

Introduction

In 1979 the newly elected Conservative Government, which would be followed by an unbroken succession of others until 1997, abandoned prices and incomes policy as an interventionist instrument to be used nationwide to control inflation across the whole economy. Government policy now focused on the freedom of market forces, the creation of an enterprise culture, measures to encourage small businesses and self-employment, and the pruning of the public sector. Among the main objectives were privatization of nationalized industries and public utility services, deregulation of the labour market, and decentralization of pay determination and bargaining over terms and conditions of employment. All of this was calculated to produce economic regeneration by unfettering business enterprise and giving employers greater scope and flexibility to devise business strategies suited to their own particular developmental needs to grow, prosper, compete and survive in both domestic and overseas markets in the context of economic globalization. The backdrop to these initiatives was the long-run recession of the 1980s during which promising upturns proved to be discouragingly short-lived, until after the mid-1990s, when Britain could compare favourably with other major European states in terms of economic growth and unemployment level.

Employers encountering progressively keener competition in the 1980s came to recognize the need for flexibility in order to permit them to respond readily and effectively to the fluctuations and uncertainties of markets, changes in consumer tastes and preferences, and the challenging potential of new and information technology that offered opportunities to boost productivity but which changed skill and labour requirements. Employers needed to streamline their operations, and to devise flexible business strategies which called for flexible manning; numerical and functional flexibility of labour would enable a company to utilize and deploy its human resources more effectively and more cost-efficiently. The firm best placed to cope with the recession and market volatility was 'fast, flat, flexible and down-sized'.[1]

Numerical flexibility of labour would permit the employer readily to adjust headcount, and the associated costs, to the needs of business, and could be accomplished by employing people in temporary, part-time, and seasonal capacities and on short-term contracts. Functional flexibility, requiring individual versatility, re-skilling and multi-skilling, in combination with the eradication of the traditional demarcations, restrictive practices, job rights and trade boundaries of yesteryear, would remove institutionalized impediments to effective labour utilization and deployment. The move from national industry-wide multi-employer bargaining, likewise, would relax the constraints and rigidities imposed on employers by national agreements which were felt to hold back the most progressive, to inflict undue strain on others, and to produce the 'lowest common denominator effect'. Government policy and legislation aimed to create an environment conducive to employers' quest for flexibility and business competitiveness.

The Government's Role

The Donovan Commission's 1968 report[2] had disclosed the tension between the formal institutionalized system of collective bargaining at national industry-wide level and the informal system operating at the level of the company, the division and the plant. A decade later Brown[3] argued the rising importance of company-specific and site-level bargaining, following withdrawal by progressively more employers from national multi-employer negotiating structures. This trend persisted into and beyond the 1980s, and it marked the declining influence and importance of national agreements and the system of national joint industrial councils which had been chivvied into existence by the Government subsequent to the Whitley report of 1917.

The trend to decentralized bargaining was most in evidence in the private sector in the mid 1980s, but with accelerating privatization and the breakup of the monolithic public utility services into a number of separate autonomous units, the advance of decentralized bargaining proceeded apace into the 1990s, encouraged by exhortations from the Government for pay levels and pay increases that would reflect regional labour markets and local unemployment rates. To assist the restructuring of collective bargaining, the Government abolished the Fair Wages Resolution. Multi-employer bargaining in the private sector was disparaged as having created rigid wage-rate systems which restricted the downward adjustability of pay, deemed necessary to promote jobs regionally where unemployment was especially high.[4] To the same end, the Government curtailed the powers of the Wages Councils in 1986. A White Paper, issued in 1988, urged the need to change traditional ways of determining pay in order to achieve the flexibility essential to growth of the economy and of employment. Industry-wide settlement of wages by the Wages Councils fell into decay with the Trade Union Reform and Employment Rights Act of 1993, under which employers were relieved of the statutory obligation to pay minimum wage rates formerly set by the councils. As *IRRR* observed that year: 'The impact of government policy on multi-employer bargaining in the private sector can be seen directly with the recent abolition of the Wages Councils and its privatization programme, which have been linked to the ending of long-standing national bargaining arrangements.'[5]

An important part of the Conservatives' economic policy for greater responsiveness to market forces took the form of measures to curb trade union rights and immunities, to restrain their activities, and to weaken collective forms of bargaining. Legislation to tame Britain's allegedly overpowerful unions is widely acknowledged to be 'the most impressive and permanent of the Conservative Government's achievements between 1979 and 1990'.[6] Contemporary comment drew sharp contrasts between the relatively calm industrial relations since 1985 and the turbulence of the two preceding decades when trade union power was said to be at its height. A 1991 White Paper observed retrospectively that:

> Britain's poor industrial relations were generally acknowledged to be a fundamental cause of the weakening of the British economy. British industry's record of strikes, restrictive practices, and overmanning seriously and persistently damaged its ability to compete in the markets of the world ... In many cases union leaders were seen to be both irresponsible and undemocratic in exercising their industrial power. British industrial relations were increasingly disfigured by scenes of intimidating picketing and by strikes directly aimed at the community ... Direct intervention in collective bargaining through various forms of incomes policy had failed to tackle the problem of rising earnings unmatched by improvements in productivity. By the end of the 1970s, incomes policies were discredited in both theory and practice.[7]

The consequence of employment legislation in the chastening context of long-run recession and persistently high unemployment in the 1980s was that the 'trade union issue' no longer loomed large as a political problem by 1990. Intent on marginalizing the unions, Prime Minister Margaret Thatcher rarely received TUC delegations to discuss the economy, industrial relations or any other policy matters. The most that the unions could do was to exercise a very limited influence through their nominees on tripartite bodies such as ACAS, HSC, the EOC, and NEDC.

No less than six pieces of legislation were passed between 1980 and 1993 to bring the unions to heel. Together, these measures effected the most fundamental transformation of Britain's labour laws since the passage of the Trade Disputes Act of 1906. The Government's policy, from 1983 onward, to privatize state-owned industry, was partly motivated by its determination to weaken the unions' muscle to exert monopolistic and highly politicized bargaining power in the public sector.

The Government's White Paper, *Employment: The Challenge for the Nation*, explicitly repudiated the postwar commitment to the principle of state responsibility to maintain or achieve full employment. The role to be adopted now was that of 'guiding and supporting the national effort for jobs' by three inter-related initiatives: to contain inflation; to remove impediments to employment and to encourage skill training; and to assist the long-term unemployed by direct state schemes.[8]

As early as July 1979, following the 'winter of discontent', the Employment Secretary issued a consultative document with proposals seeking to redress the power imbalance between unions and employers. The Employment Act, which followed in 1980, outlawed secondary picketing, allowed new closed shops only if over 80.0 per cent of those eligible to vote were in favour, and reserved the worker's right on grounds of conscience not to join a closed shop. The 1982 Employment Act allowed unions to be sued for damages, made them liable for any 'unlawful actions' authorized or endorsed by a union officer, and further circumscribed the operation of the closed shop. Additional curbs were imposed by the 1984 Trade Union Act which legally obligated trade unions to hold secret ballots for direct election of executive committees at least every five years; a secret ballot was also legally required before a union called workers out on strike, and a strike without majority consent would remove the union's immunity from civil action in the courts.

These provisions were in various ways reinforced in further pieces of legislation in 1986, 1988, 1989, 1990 and 1993. Taken together, these abolished remaining legal protections for the post-entry closed shop, removed the right of a union to discipline a member for refusing to take part in a 'lawful strike', and gave all union members the right to a postal vote in all union elections and strike ballots. Trade union officials were now made legally liable for unofficial strikes by their members. Employers were given the right to dismiss employees taking unofficial strike action; and sympathetic strikes and all remaining forms of secondary action were outlawed. The 1993 Trade Union Reform and Employment Rights Act further weakened trade union autonomy, and protected an employer's right to offer financial inducements to workers to leave the unions. The functions of ACAS were changed so that it was no longer to promote collective bargaining. All pre-strike ballots were to be postal and subject to independent scrutiny.[9]

The Government's assault on collectivist systems of bargaining was paralleled by its encouragement of performance-related pay and personal employment contracts, which were deemed to be more appropriate to a deregulated labour market. A 1992 White Paper, *People, Jobs and Opportunity*, stated that:

> There is every reason to be confident that by the end of the 1990s we will have moved decisively away from the collectivist pay arrangements, which restricted individual choice and damaged employment growth, to a situation where the pay of the great majority will reflect their individual contributions at work ... There is a growing trend to individually negotiated reward packages which reflect the individual's personal skills, experience, efforts and performance.[10]

By 1993, Taylor observes, Britain had the most restrictive industrial relations laws of any Western European market economy, yet there is little evidence that the majority of employers actively sought to derecognize the trade unions. Where relatively large numbers were employed, it was still administratively simpler and made more cost-efficient use of management's time to have some form of collectivist representation of the workforce. Changes there were, but the move tended to be from multi-employer industry-wide bargaining to negotiation at the level of the company, the division or the site, and to single unionism or single-table bargaining and the creation of company councils. At the same time, there were moves to integrated pay and grading structures, as part of an employer's policy for harmonized employment conditions, which disregarded collar colour and provided opportunities for career development through skill acquisition in a salary structure which usually covered all grades below management level; integrated structures of this kind cleared the way for more flexible labour utilization and deployment. Faced with the realities of the labour market, the unions were increasingly disposed to co-operate in employers' measures to improve business performance. Whether for better or for worse in its effect on the unions' ability to improve employment terms, Taylor claims that the Government's industrial relations strategy worked 'in harmony with the more fundamental structural changes that were going on inside the labour market'.[11] In the run-up to the 1997 general election, the leadership of the Labour Party made it explicitly clear that the policy of an elected Labour Government would not include the reversal of the industrial relations legislation passed by the Conservatives since 1979.

The Conservative Government's policy for free enterprise and flexibility in the British economy is equally well illustrated in its attitude to the European Community's initiatives to impose restrictions on working-time. The Community proposed in 1992 to lay down regulations on maximum working hours and minimum rest periods in all EC member states. Most European states, Wareing notes, already had comprehensive statutory regulations on working-time, but the UK, and to a lesser extent Denmark and Ireland, preserved scope for voluntary arrangements, because their industrial relations traditions had tended to favour voluntary rather than legislative regulation of employment conditions: 'The EC proposals are thus at odds with the belief of successive UK governments that working hours, like most other terms and conditions of employment, should be determined not by governments but by employers and their employees.'[12]

The Draft EC Directive of 1992 formed part of the Community's Action Programme to implement the Social Charter agreed in 1989 by all member states except the UK. The draft, first proposed in August 1990, had been much amended in its turbulent passage through the complex decision-making machinery of the EC, and the UK, with no general legislation to restrict working-time, had been at the forefront of opposition and the initiator of many of the amendments subsequently made. The British Government withdrew from absolute opposition, in return for certain concessions which would enable British employers to evade the strictures of maximum hours regulation.

The main EC proposals were for a maximum 48-hour week including overtime, averaged over a specific reference period, a minimum daily rest period of 11 consecutive hours, a minimum of two rest periods of 35 hours per fortnight, a minimum annual holiday entitlement of four weeks, and a daily rest break for all employees working over six hours per day. The main amendment causing the British Government to withdraw from its former stance of outright opposition was the provision that, although workpeople had the right to insist on observance of the 48-hour maximum, they retained the right to work in excess of that maximum if they so wished.

The effect of this important concession, won by the British Government, was to preserve freedom and flexibility for firms which already had, or might need in the future, a longer actual working week in a highly competitive globalized economy. It did nothing to assist the TUC's efforts to cajole British workers out of their overtime habit; but it gave workpeople some control over their earnings by preserving their right to work whatever hours they wanted to increase their take-home pay. In the absence of, and the Conservative Government's hostility to, a statutory minimum hourly wage rate, however, the cost-of-living pressures on the low paid, including many women heading single-parent households, 'voluntarily' to work long hours intensified and added to the stress and strain of those worst placed to improve their lot.

Hours of Work

A basic working week of 40 hours had become the norm in Britain in the 1960s, and it remained characteristic until the end of the following decade, when a few agreements began to breach the 40-hour barrier. The most significant of these was the 1979 national engineering agreement, which provided a 39-hour week for over two million workers, with effect from 1981. The abandonment of prices and incomes policy by the Government had removed one of the most obstructive impediments to negotiation of the shorter basic week, and with the trend now set by a major industry, other such agreements followed in other sectors. More workers had their hours reduced in 1981 than in any single year since 1966.[13] Whereas in the five-year period, 1975–9, only slightly more than half a million workpeople had gained a reduction of the basic working week, in the following period, 1980–5, over 8¼ million had their working hours shortened.

If the return to free collective bargaining helped to open the floodgates to the number of agreements reached and the number of workpeople affected by them, the actual reductions secured were relatively modest; in 1980 average basic hours per week stood at 39.8, and were still as high as 39.0 at the end of 1984.[14] The scant reductions following in the next few years produced little further change overall, for in 1989 basic weekly hours averaged at just below 39. In that year an estimated 28.0 per cent of workpeople covered by national agreements had a standard working week of 39 hours or less. The 1995 *New Earnings Survey* disclosed that 17.7 per cent of men in full-time manual employment and 47.5 per cent in full-time non-manual work had a basic week of 37 hours or less; for women in full-time manual and non-manual employment the corresponding proportions were 77.8 and 89.7 respectively. Relatively small proportions of workpeople had a basic week of over 42 hours: 9.0 per cent and 5.7 per cent of manual and non-manual men respectively, and 3.2 and 1.3 of manual and non-manual women.

All of the national agreements on working-time, which were

reached at the beginning of the 1980s, reduced weekly hours without loss of pay, often took the form of a 'future commitment', mostly made a reduction of only one hour with any larger reductions to be phased in gradually, and often included productivity or other provisions to offset the cost.[15] Agreed delays of two or more years before implementation were not uncommon. National agreements covering major industries, including gas, water, building and chemicals, pruned only one hour from the manual worker's standard week; but, unusually, the plumbing industry cut the basic week by two hours to 38 all in one go in 1980, and under agreements covering the exhibition industry the 40-hour week which had obtained in 1979 was to be reduced by two hours in 1980, and by one hour in each of the years 1981, 1984 and 1985, to produce a basic 35-hour week. The exhibition industry appears to have been the first national bargaining group to achieve the TUC's target. Under national agreements in the public sector, by 1984 basic hours had been cut to 38¾ in British Gas, to 38 in London Transport and the Water Authorities, and to 37 in British Nuclear Fuels and Electricity Supply.

The very modest reductions, evident in national average figures, disguise the more substantial improvements won by certain groups and in several individual companies; indeed in the later 1980s and the 1990s, with deregulation of the labour market, decentralization of pay determination, and the associated decay of industry-wide bargaining at national level, the working hours fixed in national agreements became progressively less useful as a guide to working-time changes. There were some early company agreements and other group-specific arrangements for a basic week of less than 40 hours for manual grades. In the electrical contracting branch of the construction industry the 38-hour week, already achieved in 1975–6, was further reduced to 37½ in 1981. Manual grades at Ronson were granted a 35-hour week, to be phased in by 1982. At Barker & Dobson a three-hour cut produced a 37-hour four-day week; and at ICI a 37½-hour week, resulting from a cut of two and a half hours, was introduced for shift-workers in one move in 1983. Reed Decorative Products introduced a 37½ hour week in line with many other companies in the printing industry. In 1984 Metal Box moved to a 35-hour week, Reed Corrugated Cases to a week of 37½ hours, and in the same year Petrofina agreed a 37½ hour week for tanker drivers and related distribution workers in line with provision made at Esso two years earlier.

Reductions in working-time during the later 1980s tended to be small and affected fewer workpeople, but the momentum of change picked up again in the early 1990s. The most significant development occurred in the engineering industry, which consolidated its move to the 37-hour week. The industry's national bargaining structure had fallen apart, but in 1990 the CSEU claimed to have finalized, or outlined, agreements to shorten the working week in around 60 engineering companies.[16] In most cases the two-hour reduction from 39 to 37 hours would be made in stages. Incoform Bramah and Crabtree of Gateshead would each make four half-hour cuts over a two-year period, while at both Mitchell Shackleton and Marshall Engineering the reduction would be implemented in three stages; in contrast, several companies, including Rolls Royce, Vickers-Mitchell Bearings and Vickers Precision Components, would accomplish the move by two one-hour cuts.

Some significance may be attached to the fact that engineering companies were moving to a 37-hour week in the early 1990s, and that many chemical companies, having moved to a 38-hour week some years before, were now contemplating a further round of cuts. In the past, both of these industries had been in the van of progress, setting precedents for others to follow. *IRRR* observed in 1994 that: 'Historically, reductions in UK working hours have not occurred gradually; rather, they have been concentrated in periods of rapid change, often triggered by one pacesetting agreement.'[17] The engineering unions had pioneered the 40-hour week in 1965 and the 39-hour standard in 1979. Other industries had followed their lead. The CSEU, which consisted of 19 unions, including influential bodies such as the AEEU,

GMB, UCATT, and TGWU, took the initiative again in 1989, reinforcing their claims by selective strikes. When the first phase of the campaign ended in April 1991, the CSEU claimed to have concluded 1,666 agreements affecting over half a million workers, which established a 37-hour norm in the engineering industry. These reductions were said to have 'precipitated a shorter working week in other sectors of the economy ... [with] about 50 agreements, signed between January 1990 and June 1994, shortening the basic working week for over 1½ million workpeople'. In effect, 'the 37-hour week is slowly becoming the new norm'.[18]

The more substantial reductions down to 37 hours, or even less, often occurred in companies with policies to harmonize the conditions of manual and white-collar staff and where an industry had expressed a general commitment to the principle of harmonization. Some of the agreements reached in the early 1980s harmonized the working hours of manual and staff grades. The Independent Broadcasting Authority, for example, moved to a basic 35-hour week for all of its full-time employees in July 1982 'as part of its harmonization policy'; Berger Paints reduced manual workers' hours to 37½ in December 1983, which was the deadline for 'the final part of its harmonization programme'; and May and Baker cut manual grades' basic week to 37½ hours in July 1982 to bring them 'into line with staff hours'. Similarly, the Atomic Energy Authority implemented the 37-hour week during that same year, so as to 'bring manuals into line with non-industrial staff'.[19] In the mid 1980s Imperial Tobacco agreed a major cut in working-time as part of its policy to harmonize the basic hours of staff and manual grades; manual workers moved to a 36¼-hour week 1984, 'in line with office staff', and the following year the working week for all grades of employees was reduced to a standard 35 hours.[20] *IRRR* observed towards the end of the 1980s that cuts in working hours were a 'frequent element of harmonization programmes'.[21] Recent developments of this kind had occurred at James Howden, Kodak, and British Telecommunications, for example. The engineering industry's commitment to the principle of harmonization, dating from 1979, goes some way in explaining the working-time reductions for manual workers in many companies in that industry, and accounts for employers' resistance to corresponding reductions for white-collar staff. Claims from the staff unions for a reduction from 37½ hours to 36 were resisted by the EEF on the grounds that in the rest of Europe manual and staff employees had the same basic hours, and that no discussions were being held outside the UK to reduce staff and manual hours separately.

In the mid-1990s 'harmonization across sites and across grades' was said to be 'a major motive for cutting hours', for, as in engineering, 'many companies have cut basic hours for both manual and staff employees to bring them into line with each other.'[22] Goodyear, for example, had recently reduced the basic week of its manual and staff grades by 1½ and 1 hour, respectively, to align the working week for both at 37 hours. A similar pattern of change occurred at C. & J. Clark in footwear. Harmonization was also a main motive in hours reductions at Jacob's Bakery, J. & B., PLM Redfearn, Tamrands, and the NAAFI. In the water industry the equalization of the basic hours of manual and staff grades had been 'a major development in the industrial relations policies adopted by the newly privatized water companies'. Harmonization of hours had been accomplished by both Northumbria and Welsh Water 'as part of a move towards single status', and with that same longer-term objective, the basic weekly hours of industrial and craft grades had been cut by the Anglian, North West, Severn Trent, Wessex, and Yorkshire water companies.

Industry-wide bargaining and national agreements had had an important influence in spreading the shorter working week throughout the British economy in times past. That situation still obtained in the early 1980s. Since then, however, collective bargaining has become progressively more decentralized, and the Wages Councils were disbanded in 1993. The erosion of traditional bargaining structures in the latter half of the 1980s and into the 1990s carried with it the implication that the speed and coverage of hours reductions would be affected. In seeking improved conditions for employees, the trade unions in progressively more cases had to bargain company by company and plant by plant.

There were, as in earlier periods, some sectors which lagged behind in shortening basic working hours. In 1983 a standard week of 40 hours or more was still worked in agriculture, the building and construction industry, some personal services, parts of the NHS, and much of the food and drink and the textiles and clothing trades. It was not until the end of 1985 that agreements for the 39-hour week were reached in the clothing, hosiery, cotton and allied textiles, textile finishing, and carpet manufacturing sectors. Still in the process of catching up, with discussions underway, were multiple bakeries, flour milling, the building brick and allied trades, licensed residential establishments, and licensed restaurants. These laggards were left behind again when moves to establish the 37-hour norm occurred in the 1990s.

Overtime working persisted throughout the 1980s and into the 1990s, despite the TUC's avowed intention to reduce it. It tended to rise and fall in line with the trade cycle, but the trend showed no marked overall decline. The limitation of overtime, and its elimination whenever possible, as we have seen, formed an important part of the TUC's policy on working-time. Similarly, the CBI, in its 1980 publication, *Jobs: Facing the Future*, saw scope for reducing overtime working and urged a voluntary approach by employers and unions, linked to improvements in efficiency and flexibility. As both of these national organizations found, however, although policy might exist on paper, implementing it at the local level was all but impossible, and sometimes impracticable; and the issue tended to be among the first to be dropped at the bargaining table in favour of earnings.

In the depths of the recession in the early 1980s, there were very few national or company agreements to limit overtime working; insofar as they existed at national level, they consisted of general exhortations to minimize it or placed relatively high limits on permitted amounts, and they contained often numerous exemptions. In 1984 the TUC described as 'staggering' the 10.1 hours of weekly overtime averaged by the 56.8 per cent of the male manual workforce engaged in overtime working. The longest weekly overtime hours were worked by prison officers (19.3), railway workers (16.4), HGV drivers (14.0), and crane drivers (14.0).[23] *IRRR* found that, with a few exceptions, national agreements to curtail overtime had had only marginal impact on the actual levels worked:

> National-level exhortation is one thing, concrete results locally another. The impact of overtime on earnings, plus, from the employer's point of view, the relatively low-cost flexibility it offers in the production process, make it difficult to bridge the gap between national aspirations and actual practice.[24]

With employers progressively more intent on flexibility and rapid reaction to changing market demands, existing and new agreements to curb overtime had had no profound and lasting impact on the amounts worked up to the mid 1990s.[25]

The increases in holiday entitlements and reductions in the basic working week without loss of pay, which the unions had won at the bargaining table, were not without strings, for employers required reciprocal concessions from their workforces. Employers sought flexibility to improve efficiency to enable them to prosper or even just survive in progressively keener competition for markets in years when new and information technology was spreading rapidly in all sectors of the economy and bringing with it the requirement of new skills, or new combinations of skills, or different working methods, or changes in job content. Their business strategies involved not only training and retraining of workforces, but also the latter's relaxation of restrictive practices, skill demarcations, job rights and trade boundaries. The objective was to increase productivity and quality. Agreements on the shortening of working-time were almost always conditional upon the containment of production costs, and were intended to be partly, largely, or wholly self-financing.

National agreements tended to link reduced working hours to 'some fairly unspecific clauses pledging trade unions' co-operation in measures to improve efficiency and to minimize the cost of the hours cuts'.[26] The 1979 national engineering agreement, for example, simply states that: 'the parties ... are committed to giving maximum co-operation at all levels ... to ensure that productivity is increased so that there are no increases in manufacturing costs as a result of the reduction in working hours.' Similarly, the national agreement covering the paint, varnish and lacquer industry contained the statement that 'in agreeing to reduce the standard working week ... both sides accept that it is essential to achieve changes in operational arrangements in order to minimize consequential cost increases and to maintain a competitive position in national and international markets'. The Chemical Industries Association in 1982 produced guidelines, on measures to increase hourly productivity, for member companies implementing the 38-hour week; the measures included: greater job mobility, more flexibility in manpower usage, economies in manning, increased tempo of work, elimination of unproductive time, more roster/shift work, changes in existing working patterns, new measures of providing relief cover, reductions in overtime, and changes in the wages structure.[27] Likewise, the agreement of the pharmaceuticals and fine chemicals industry identified as measures for consideration in association with working time cuts: employees to learn and take turns on other jobs, expansion of job content with a view to economy of manning and provision of reliefs, greater mobility and flexibility between jobs, economy in the use of manpower, changes in the patterns of shift/day work, more roster/shift work, and minimization of non-productive time. General commitments contained in national agreements had the advantage, from the employers' viewpoint, of enabling them to make whatever changes in working practices each and any of them deemed to be necessary in their own interests. Workforces, on the other hand, found themselves committed to the unspecific and the unknown.

Company and plant level agreements, in contrast, tended to

itemize the particular concessions required from workpeople in exchange for reduced working-time. An agreement reached in 1990 at NEI Parsons contained a long and detailed clause of this kind:

Changes in Working Practices at NEI Parsons

Arrangements for interchangeability to deal with departmental load fluctuations and a limited degree of multiskill working have previously been established and embodied in recent agreements between management and unions at NEI Parsons.

The following additional changes will be subject to early implementation and progressively developed to increase the degree of interchangeability available throughout the factory. Training will be made available as necessary.

(a) Interchangeability of work between union groups, or between skilled trades and between semi-skilled trades respectively within a department ...
(b) Interchangeability of work and/or people between departments. It is expected that the majority of transfers will be effected to utilize existing skills or skill overlap.
(c) The scope of semi-skilled activities will be broadened to increase the degree of overlap ... following appropriate training ...
(d) Action will be taken within the requirements of safe working practices to fully utilize skills and equipment to progress work in the most effective manner and to avoid production delay. On occasion this may involve skilled workers carrying out semi-skilled functions ...
(e) Where appropriate, 'manufacturing cell' operations will be progressively developed, i.e., team responsibility for an identifiable sequence of operations. This also implies interchangeability by individuals within the team to complete all necessary operations.
(f) Multi-machine manning will apply where it is reason-

able and practicable. For example, where one operator can reasonably attend to two or more machines operating at the same time, owing to their close proximity and periods of automatic operation which leave sufficient time for setting up and all necessary checks on alternate machines.

(g) Apprentices and/or those who have recently achieved the adult rate will undertake further training on additional (mixed) modules. By this means, for example, multi-skilled maintenance operators will gradually reinforce the existing millwrights and electricians on plant maintenance ...

(h) Action will be taken to address and remove any inefficiencies or unnecessary delays in placing subcontract work, which have occurred particularly in 'service' areas.

(i) Three-shift working will continue in accordance with the agreed arrangements and shift patterns without further negotiations until April 1992 when a review will be conducted.

(j) A high level of union encouragement matched by company counselling will be applied to the task of replacing cash with cashless pay. If this is not achieved by April 1990 management will exercise the right to introduce it contractually.

(k) A review of shop stewards will be conducted annually to ensure the company's needs are correctly met.

(l) A fundamental change in attitudes will be jointly and vigorously promoted to avoid delays and to increase productivity levels without detriment to product quality. Commitment to full utilization of available time will be an essential part of this process.

The implementation of all changes listed will be subject to monitoring by the existing Management/Union Resources Meeting.[28]

Cost-offsets were common in the 1990s. Most agreements

for hours reductions, in the engineering industry[29] and other sectors, contained provisions to offset any adverse costs as a consequence of the reductions. The provisions took three main forms. First, there was the reallocation of time, which involved the abolition of 'non-productive time' such as paid breaks and washing time and the introduction of bell-to-bell working. Second, there were changes in working practices, most obviously focused on greater functional flexibility including multi-skilling and increased multi-machine manning of multi-machine operations. Third, there were savings that did not affect working hours or working practices as such; these cost-pruning measures included moves to cashless pay, changes of sick pay arrangements, penalties for lateness, and a closer monitoring of absenteeism.

There are obvious implications here for the creation of jobs to ameliorate the unemployment problem. The extent to which the fall in the unemployment rate in the late 1980s and 1990s can be attributed to longer holidays and the shorter basic working week is highly questionable. It may be fairly argued that shorter working-time served to preserve existing jobs and to prevent even greater numbers of redundancies than those which occurred; and it must be remembered that moves to higher productivity, per person and per hour, would certainly have been made in these years, regardless of any working-time reductions. Hours cuts seem to have provided the occasion, rather than the main cause, of measures implemented by employers to raise productive efficiency. Surveys, commissioned by the Department of Employment in the early 1980s, disclosed that reductions in working-time did not generate significant increases in employment opportunities for those without jobs: 'Increased productivity, and to a lesser extent increased overtime, is usually sufficient to compensate for reductions in basic working-time.'[30] Evidence suggested that firms hardly ever recruited more people as a consequence of reducing the working week.[31] Firms in the printing and engineering industries, for example, had reduced hours of labour without adversely affecting levels of output, for they had counterbalanced shorter hours with gains in labour efficiency, so that 'the net employment effect was insignificant'. In these two industries employment declined in 1981 and 1982, even though output increased and the working week was shortened: 'The underlying tendency, therefore, was not merely to reduce total hours in line with the shorter week, but also to reduce the actual numbers employed.'[32] This is unsurprising, in years when both of these industries were being profoundly affected by the spread of new and information technology which permitted markedly higher productivity per hour. Intermittent upturns in demand produced more overtime rather than more recruits to the labour force. Investigations undertaken in the early 1990s led to similar conclusions. There was some evidence that reduced working-time produced higher employment levels in the short to medium term, but 'increased employment took the form of greater job retention and fewer redundancies than would otherwise have been the case in a period of recession'. However, where hours cuts were not offset by productivity gains or wage reductions, the result was an increase in costs. The implication was that 'if these higher costs persist ... the longer-term effect will be to reduce employment'.[33]

The other main changes in working hours, apart from those occasioned by further increases in the numbers employed in less than permanent and less than full-time capacities, affected the arrangement of the time worked. Interest began to focus on the idea of annual hours, committed hours, and the compressed working week.

The renewed interest in the concept of annualized hours, dating from the paper and board industry's 1982 agreement, had increased markedly by the late 1980s, for such arrangements offered flexibility and optimal use of working time, especially in continuous process production and in industries and services with pronounced seasonal peaks in market demand. The shortening of the basic working week in the context of market pressures of this kind was cited as 'by far the most common reason for moving to annual hours'.[34]

An annual hours arrangement gave Crosslea,[35] manufacturer of tumble dryers, a flexible working year to accommodate seasonal peaks and troughs in sales, thereby avoiding stock-piling and its associated costs in the slack season. With the reduction to a basic week of 39 hours, employees agreed to a 32-hour week in the four summer months and a 43-hour week in the remaining eight months, giving them an average working week of 39 hours over the whole year. By 1994, in the context of cuts to the basic working week, hours had been annualized at Zeneca Pharmaceuticals, British Sugar, Rockware Glass, Electrolux, and Komatsu (UK), to identify but a few. The 1993 Labour Force Survey disclosed that 9.0 per cent, or around two million employees in the UK worked some form of annualized hours.

Committed hours were often based on the concept of annualized working time; these, too, provided flexibility to enable a company to respond quickly to surges in consumer demand and unexpected problems. Such arrangements enabled companies to 'make the most efficient use of hours by providing management with a commitment from employees to work the hours necessary for the effective functions of the business'.[36] By the late 1980s they had spread in distribution and continuous-process manufacturing, having been introduced at Esso, at BP's chemical plant at Grangemouth, at Whitbread's Romsey and Portsmouth distribution depots, at CBL Cellophane's Barrow site, and for Shell's distribution workers. Shell's 1987 agreement with the TGWU, for example, enabled the company to cope efficiently when airliners with massive fuel requirements were unexpectedly diverted to airports other than their scheduled destinations. Under the terms of the agreement, drivers opted for a standard contract with a basic 37½-hour week and no guarantee of overtime, or for a committed hours contract entitling them to a higher annual salary but committing them to acceptance of up to an additional 390 hours per annum within weekly and monthly limits. The committed hours would be used on a regular and planned basis but, more importantly, they provided the company with flexibility to meet short-term fluctuations in business and to improve the reliability of deliveries.

Committed hours arrangements did not provide a simple all-purpose solution to the need for flexible working hours, whether for absence cover, variable workloads, production peaks, or planned maintenance, but they eased the task of adjusting working hours to companies' business requirements, and they usually formed part of a broader policy encompassing pay structures, productivity, absence monitoring, manning levels, and the full range of employment terms.

Another variation in the arrangement of working, which became more widely adopted in these years, was the compressed working week. This was a spin-off from the shortening of basic hours worked weekly. In essence, basic hours were worked over fewer days than the five conventionally comprising the working week. The idea was neither entirely new nor entirely unknown, but it had 'taken on a fresh significance in the present climate of pressure for shorter hours'.[37] Whatever the particular variant – the four-day or four-and-a-half-day week or the nine-day fortnight – the effect was to lengthen the workfree weekend rather than to shorten each of the five working weekdays by a few minutes. Many employers claimed that the compressed week had improved recruitment, retention and absence rates. The prospect of greater leisure has an appeal in itself, and employees may well feel less inclined to 'take days off when the working week contains fewer days and each day's earnings are proportionately higher'.[38] A compressed week meant that an extra day or half-day could be worked to meet emergencies without disrupting the traditional two-day weekend. However, there would be no cost-saving for employers or increased leisure for workpeople if regular daily overtime was simply translated into entire days of overtime every week. Compressed working was not appropriate in all spheres of business activity, such as those requiring full-time cover or high customer contact; but elsewhere it contributed to greater variety in working patterns.[39]

Paid Holidays

There had been relatively little improvement in holiday entitlements between 1975 and 1979, probably as a result of incomes policy; thereafter, growth was resumed. In 1979, around half of all manual workers covered by collective agreements or wages orders had a basic entitlement of less than four weeks; by 1983, the proportion with at least four weeks had risen to 94.0 per cent. There was also a marked increase in the numbers with five weeks or more: from 1.0 per cent in 1981 to 23.0 per cent by 1986 (Table 21).

Agreements reached in 1979, covering 1¼ million workers, provided for increases of one or two days per year to reach

TABLE 21

Basic Holiday Entitlements* in Weeks as set out in National Collective Agreements or Statutory Orders under the Wages Councils Acts and the Agricultural Wages Acts: Manual Workers, 1979–86 (United Kingdom)

	Percentage of workers who have a basic holiday with pay of:						Percentage of workers covered by arrangements providing
Year (end December)	less than 3 weeks	3 weeks	between 3 & 4 weeks	4 weeks	between 4 & 5 weeks	5 weeks and over	for extra days of paid holiday dependent on length of service
1979	1	7	42	50**	–	–	38
1980	–	2	24	19	55	–	40
1981	–	2	11	25	61	1	37+
1982	–	2	5	21	53	10	35+
1983	–	–	6	17	60	18	36+
1984	–	–	5	15	61	19	35+
1985	–	–	1	16	63	20	32+
1986	–	–	–	14	63	23	32+

* Minimum entitlements as laid down in national collective agreements and wages regulation orders, excluding bank and public holidays and additional service-related days.

** Includes some employees with entitlements of more than four weeks.

\+ The fall since 1980 is mainly attributable to the deletion from Wages Council orders and agreements of references to service-related entitlements. This does not necessarily imply that previous arrangements would not continue on a voluntary basis.

– Denotes less than 0.5 per cent.

Note: Under the 1986 Wages Act the Wages Councils were no longer required to specify minimum holiday entitlements.

Derived from *Employment Gazette*, London, HMSO, 1987, p.132.

five weeks by 1982. The 1981 *New Earnings Survey* showed a distinct narrowing of the traditional manual/non-manual differential in holiday entitlement; by that year, 87.0 per cent of manual men and 90.0 per cent of their non-manual counterparts were entitled to a paid holiday of at least four weeks. The trend was similar in the case of manual and non-manual women; and the former gender differential in holiday entitlement was also significantly reduced. In the case of manual and non-manual women, the proportions were 77.0 per cent and 88.0 per cent respectively.

The most marked differentials in 1981 were at the higher levels of entitlement. In the case of men, 41.2 per cent of non-manuals but only 18.2 per cent of manuals had five weeks or more; the comparable proportions of women were 30.7 per cent and 13.2 per cent. By far the most advantaged were professional and related groups in education, welfare and health services and similar grades in the fields of science, engineering and technology. Among the least advantaged, with basic holiday entitlements of less than four weeks, were workers in agriculture, forestry and fishing, in the clothing and footwear trades, and in textiles.

The rate of change slowed in the mid-1980s and did not accelerate to any marked degree thereafter. Slow but steady increases continued, so that, in the early 1990s, nine out of ten people in full-time work had more than four weeks, and three out of ten had at least five weeks.[40]

The 1979 national engineering agreement set the pace in pursuit of the fifth week; this agreement, covering around two million manual workers, provided for increases of one or two days per year, to produce a basic entitlement of five weeks in 1982–3.[41] In addition, there was provision for the five-week holiday in several agreements reached in the private sector at the level of the company: Cadbury Schweppes, Cadbury Typhoo, H.J. Heinz, Crown Cork, Dunlop, Glaxo, United Biscuits, National Cash Register, and Yorkshire Imperial and Distillers, for example.[42] In the later 1980s and the 1990s, with deregulation of the labour market, decentralization of pay determination, and privatization of parts of the public sector, company agreements and local bargaining became the main means to improvements in holiday entitlements. In 1986 company agreements for the five-week holiday had been reached at ICI, Crown Paints, Mobil Oil and Octel, among others.[43] The CBI's 1989 survey disclosed that, of the 282 manufacturing companies covered by its investigation, 56.9 per cent and 59.0 per cent gave a basic 25-day entitlement for manual and non-manual grades respectively; in the 203 service-sector organizations, basic entitlements were very much lower, but there was generous provision for service-related days.[44]

These were basic entitlements, but in some cases, extra service-related holidays gave maximum entitlements of over 5 weeks or 25 days. At the Talbot Motor Company, for example, maximum entitlement amounted to 27 days: after 4 years for white-collar staff but after 20 years for manual grades. At Mercedes Benz the achievable maximum was 30 days after 20 years' service.[45]

In general, the pattern of advance was similar to the style of the 1960s and early 1970s: small annual additions to the basic period over several years, or a gradual reduction of the qualifying period of service for extra days and ultimate consolidation of some or all of them into a new higher basic entitlement. The contrast between the manufacturing and service sectors, noted by the CBI in 1981, may be explained by the different approaches they adopted or by the different stages they had reached in the implementation of similar policies.

After 1979 some employers and some of the trade unions began to take progressively greater interest in the reduction of the traditional manual/non-manual differential in holiday entitlement, with the longer-term objective of harmonizing the period of paid holiday for both of the broad occupational groups. The Engineering Employers' Federation adopted such a policy as early as 1979; the engineering industry's agreement had 'set the pattern, for white-collar and management as well as for manual employees, in terms of holidays',[46] and several companies in that industry were planning to absorb the service-related holidays of white-collar and managerial staff within the 25-day basic entitlement scheduled for 1982–3 under the EEF-CSEU national agreement. *IRRR*'s 1981 survey[47] found that: 'Harmonized holiday entitlement for all levels of employee was the most common theme ... in private sector organizations.' The survey covered only 32 private-sector companies, and these were probably among the most progressive in terms of their personnel policies; but 19 of them had harmonized the holiday period for all grades, and eight others had partial harmonization in that the entitlements of manual grades and white-collar office staffs had been equalized but higher entitlements had been retained for management. Full harmonization was found, for example, at Mars, Metal Box, E.R. Squibb, British Sugar, Colgate-Palmolive, and Continental Can; partial harmonization had occurred at Imperial Tobacco, United Biscuits, Birds Eye Walls, and Westland Helicopters, among others. The public sector lagged behind in the trend to harmonize periods of paid holiday; here in the early 1980s 'the accent is still on holiday entitlement related to seniority and service, reflecting the fact that people often spend their whole career in one organization'.[48] Only in electricity supply and Local Authority services did 'anything resembling harmonization apply' in 1981.

The trend to harmonize, or partly harmonize, holiday entitlements was more pronounced in 1982 and 1984.[49] *IRRR*'s small-scale surveys of these years showed that some of the companies with such arrangements provided a standard holiday period for all, with no service-related days; others provided extra days for long service, and entitlement and progression were the same for all groups. These tended to be 'single status' companies; at Hoechst, for example, the basic 23-day holiday increased to 25 days after 10 years' service and to 30 days after 20 years, while at Honeywell the basic entitlement of 25 days increased to 30 days after 10 years' service. More companies had now moved to partial harmonization. Some of these had common entitlements for white-collar groups and management but lower entitlements for manual grades; others had identical provision for white-collar and manual workers but higher entitlements for management. In still others, both basic and maximum entitlements were identical, but length of service required to achieve the maximum differed according to occupational status; the service qualification for non-manual groups might be five or ten years, but it might amount to fifteen or twenty years for manual workers. Many recently established foreign-owned companies, such as Toshiba and National Semiconductor, had common holiday entitlements from the outset as part of an overall package of single-status terms and conditions; in longer-established companies 'harmonization has frequently been achieved by a combination of a progressive rise in manual workers' entitlements ... and employers' resistance to compensatory increases for staff grades'.[50]

Increases in holiday leave during the next few years came slowly but persistently, to produce 'the five-week norm' in the early 1990s. In 1992, *IRRR* found that 'the trend towards a basic five-week holiday (25 days per year) is very strong',[51] and that, as in 1989, 'harmonization [of white-collar/blue collar and production/non-production workers' conditions] remains ... an important factor in improvements to holiday entitlements'. The main reasons given by companies for improving holiday leave were the general trend to harmonized conditions, the need for comparability with other companies in the industry or region in the context of market pressure, and claims from trade unions at the bargaining table.

Two aspects of provision for annual holiday leave, which were the focus of closer scrutiny at the end of the 1980s, were choice of holiday weeks and calculation of holiday pay. Formal rules and restrictions, governing the times in the year when holiday leave was to be taken, applied in around three-quarters of the 200 companies surveyed by *IRRR* in 1989. Employers imposed restrictions on choice, because of the nature of the production processes they operated or of the services they provided for their clients and customers; but very often the holiday pattern was determined by the employee's job function. A general shutdown for a couple of weeks in summer and over the Christmas to New Year period was common in manufacturing industry; elsewhere, there was some choice outside the 'prohibited periods' of peak trading; in some cases there were rota systems or 'spreading' arrangements. The tightest control, in manufacturing industry, was for operational reasons which made it 'convenient or essential' for the employer to apply the shutdown imposing obligatory holiday periods, or conversely, as in the retail and leisure trades, holiday absence was prohibited at times in the year when business was most brisk. It seems possible that the absence of major protest from workforces about constraints of this kind owes a great deal to well-established holiday habits, local tradition, and satisfaction with the improved holiday entitlements won for them by their negotiating representatives. The constraints were most restrictive for manual workers, but there were large numbers of non-manual employees who did not have complete freedom of choice in deciding when to take their holiday leave; and there is little to suggest that this differential between the two broad groups was deeply resented by manual grades.

Dissatisfaction over the traditional differential in holiday pay calculation was much more keenly felt by manual workforces. Non-manual workers generally received normal salary during the holiday weeks, so that there was little or no difference in their level of income when at work and when on holiday. In contrast, manual workers usually received their basic rate for the standard working week; as overtime earnings and certain other pay supplements did not count for purposes of calculating holiday pay, the manual worker's income for holiday weeks tended to be lower than take-home pay when he or she was at work.

Practice had begun to change during the 1970s, when there was evidence of 'a gradual improvement in the level of holiday pay for manual workers in line with greater harmonization of conditions for all employees.'[52] There had been some moves from paying basic rates to payment of basic rate plus a set supplement and to basic plus regular shift premium or other regular allowances. By 1980 some agreements were providing for holiday pay at average P60 earnings. During the next few years it became more common for firms to pay 'average earnings', calculated over the preceding year or half-year, for holiday weeks, 'average earnings' being based on a formula that took into account regular pay components but which excluded overtime earnings. At the end of the decade the two main factors determining the employer's approach to holiday pay calculation were identified by *IRRR* as the nature of the payment system which applied to the normal working week, and the distinction made for pay purposes between salaried staff and wages-grade employees.[53]

Many of the employers who had adopted policies to harmonize the terms, benefits and employment conditions of manual and non-manual staffs had introduced integrated pay and grading structures as fundamental to such policies. In effect, manual groups covered by arrangements of this kind became salaried, and their holiday pay was determined according to criteria applying to all the grades to which the integrated pay structure applied. Elsewhere, there were other approaches whose effect was to raise the manual worker's holiday pay so as to bring it closer to average earnings; some firms paid a holiday bonus or gave enhanced holiday pay rates.

There were, of course, some workpeople who were not covered by these arrangements to increase holiday entitlement and holiday pay, and others lagged behind. By the mid 1990s over a third of all employed people had jobs that were less than permanent or less than full-time. While some, but by no means all, part-time workers received paid holidays on a *pro-rata* basis, many of those who worked in a temporary, seasonal or casual capacity gained little or nothing; and for the rising numbers of mainly men in self-employment the improvements won by the trade unions at the bargaining table were an irrelevance.

It seems that, despite their weakened bargaining position since 1979, the unions succeeded in winning improvements in working-time, with moves to a norm of a 37-hour basic week, and a 5-week holiday. As the TUC General Council noted in 1996, however, around 5.7 million employees 'had to work' 45 hours or more per week. At the same time, the prolonged working day is no longer confined to manual grades, as in times past. Some of the longest hours actually worked, and without overtime pay, are endured by middle management and some professional grades in educational and medical services.

The main focus of the unions' interest in working-time during this period, as before, was on the amount of it. The employers' attention, in contrast, was as much concerned with the arrangement of working hours as with their number. The revision of shift-working patterns with the shortening of the basic week, flexitime working, hours commitment schemes, annualized hours arrangements, along with bell-to-bell working and other methods of cutting out unproductive time, have all stemmed from employers' initiative.[54] The overall effect has been an intensification of employees' work effort for the hours spent in performance of their work tasks and for which they are paid.

Notes

1. Atkinson, J. (1984), *Manning for Uncertainty: Some Emerging UK Work Patterns*, IMS Research Paper, Sussex, Institute of Manpower Studies; NEDO (1986), *Changing Working Patterns: How Companies Achieve Flexibility to Meet New Needs*, London, National Economic Development Office; 'Flexible Employment Strategies', *Industrial Relations Review and Report*, No. 325, August 1984, pp.13–16; McGregor, A. and Sproull, A. (1992), 'Employers and the Flexible Workforce', *Employment Gazette*, May, pp.225–34; Hunter, L. and MacInnes, J. (1992), 'Employers and Labour Flexibility: The Evidence from Case Studies', *Employment Gazette*, June, pp.307–15; Institute of Management and Manpower (1994), *Survey of Long-Term Employment Strategies*, London, IMM; Kirosingh, M. (1989), 'Changed Working Practices', *Employment Gazette*, August, pp.422–9.
2. Royal Commission on Trade Unions and Employers' Associations (1968), *Report*, Cmnd. 3623.
3. Brown, W. (1981), *The Changing Contours of Industrial Relations in Britain*, Oxford, Blackwell.

4. Brown, W. and Walsh, J. (1991), 'Pay Determination in Britain in the 1980s: The Anatomy of Decentralization', *Oxford Review of Economic Policy*, Vol. 7, No. 1, pp.44–58.
5. 'Decline in Multi-Employer Bargaining Charted', *Industrial Relations Review and Report*, No. 544 (September 1993), pp.7–11.
6. Taylor, R. (1993), *The Trade Union Question in British Politics: Government and Unions since 1945*, Oxford, Blackwell, p.265.
7. White Paper (1991), *Industrial Relations in the 1990s*, Cm. 1602, p.8.
8. White Paper (1985), *Employment: Challenge for the Nation*, Department of Employment, Cmnd. 9474, p.6.
9. Main provisions of labour legislation, 1980 to 1993 in Taylor, R., *op. cit.* pp.321–5.
10. White Paper (1992), *People, Jobs and Opportunity*, Cm. 1810, p.39.
11. Taylor, R., *op. cit.* p.314.
12. Wareing, A. (1992), 'Working Arrangements and Patterns of Working Hours in Britain', *Employment Gazette,* March, pp.88–100.
13. *Employment Gazette* (April 1982), p.165.
14. Figures given monthly and annually in *Employment Gazette.*
15. 'Reductions in Working Hours: A Round-Up of National Agreements', *Industrial Relations Review and Report*, No. 242 (February 1981), pp.2–6.
16. 'Engineering Industry Consolidates Moves to 37-Hour Week', *Industrial Relations Review and Report*, No. 461 (April 1990), pp.8–10.
17. 'Whatever Happened to the Shorter Working Week?', *ibid.* No. 572 (November 1994), pp.10–16.
18. *Ibid.*
19. 'Shorter Working Week: An *IRRR* Review', *ibid.* No. 312 (January 1984), pp.2–7.
20. 'Shorter Working Week: An *IRRR* Review', *ibid.* No. 336 (January 1985), pp.2–5.
21. 'Reductions in Working Time: Running Out of Steam?', *ibid.* No. 407 (January 1988), pp.2–6.
22. 'Holidays and Hours Survey 2: Recent Changes and Trends', *ibid.* No. 524 (November 1992), pp.4–10.
23. TUC (1984), 'Review of Working Time in Britain and Western Europe', cited in 'Shorter Hours Drive Slows', *ibid.* No. 433 (February 1989), p.2.
24. 'Overtime: Restricting its Level', *ibid.* No. 270 (April 1982), p.2.

25. 'After Hours: A Survey of Overtime Working', *ibid.* No. 468 (July 1990), pp.11–14
26. 'Reductions in Working Hours: A Round-Up of National Agreements', *ibid.* No. 242 (February 1981), p.3.
27. 'Shorter Hours in Chemicals: CIA Guidance', *ibid.* No. 289 (September 1982), pp.11–13.
28. Document extract given in 'Productivity Offsets for Shorter Hours in Engineering', *ibid.* No. 464 (May 1990), pp.6–10.
29. Richardson, R. and Rubin, M. (1994), *The Economic Effects of Reductions in Working Hours: The UK Engineering Industry*, Research Series, Paper No. 34, Department of Employment, and by the same authors (1992), *The 1989/91 Shorter Working Week Campaign in Engineering: A Pyrrhic Defeat?*, Centre for Economic Performance, London, LSE.
30. 'Shorter Hours through National Agreements', *Employment Gazette* (October 1983), pp.432–6.
31. 'Shorter Hours in Practice', *Industrial Relations Review and Report,* No. 330 (October 1984), p.10; 'Implementing the Shorter Working Week in the Engineering Industry', *ibid.* No. 262 (December 1981), pp.2–7.
32. *Employment Gazette* (October 1983), p.432.
33. 'Whatever Happened to the Shorter Working Week?', *Industrial Relations Review and Report*, No 572 (November 1994), pp.2–7.
34. Desmons, G. and Vidal-Hall, T. (1987), *Annual Hours: A Study of Annual Hours Arrangements in the UK*, London, Industrial Society; Incomes Data Services (1991), *Annual Hours*, Study No. 486, London, IDS; Blyton, R. (1985), *Changes in Working Time*, London, Croom Helm.
35. 'Flexible Working Year at Crosslea', *Industrial Relations Review and Report*, No. 386 (February 1987), pp.2–4.
36. 'Hours Commitment Schemes Becoming More Popular', *ibid.* No. 385 (February 1987), pp.2–7.
37. 'The Compressed Working Week: An *IRRR* Study', *ibid.* No. 223 (May 1980), pp.2–6.
38. *Ibid.* pp.2–3.
39. *Ibid.*
40. *Social Trends 22* (1992) and *Social Trends 23* (1993), London, HMSO.
41. '*IRRR* Holiday Survey', *Industrial Relations Review and Report*, No. 220 (March 1980), pp.2–10, and No. 245 (April 1981), pp.2–15.

42. 'Holidays for Manual Workers', *ibid.* No. 274 (June 1982), pp.12–19, and No. 296 (May 1983), pp.2–7; 'Holiday Entitlements I: Industry Analysis', *ibid.* No. 323 (July 1984), pp.2–6.
43. 'Holidays: 1986 Annual Survey', *ibid.* No. 376 (September 1986), pp.2–10.
44. CBI (1989), *Holiday Arrangements in British Industry*, cited and quoted in 'Holiday Survey I: How Much Leave?', *ibid.* No. 444 (July 1989), pp.6–12.
45. 'Holidays I: Basic and Service Entitlement', *ibid.* No. 347 (July 1985), pp.9–17.
46. '*IRRR* Holiday Survey: Part 2', *ibid.* No. 249 (June 1981), pp.8–15.
47. *Ibid.*
48. *Ibid.*
49. 'Survey of Staff Holidays', *ibid.* No. 283 (November 1982), pp.7–12; 'Holiday Entitlement 2: Company Provision', *ibid.* No. 327 (September 1984), pp.2–11.
50. *Ibid.*
51. 'Holidays and Hours Survey 2: Recent Changes and Trends', *ibid.* No. 524 (November 1992), pp.4–10; 'Holiday Survey 3: Absence Rules and Pay', *ibid.* No. 540 (October 1989), pp.10–14.
52. '*IRRR* Holiday Survey', *ibid.* No. 220 (March 1980), p.9.
53. 'Holiday Survey 3: Absence Rules and Pay', *ibid.* No. 540 (October 1989), pp.10–14.
54. Blyton, P. (1994), 'Working Hours' in Sisson, K. (ed), *Personnel Management: A Comprehensive Guide to Theory and Practice in Britain*, Oxford, Blackwell.

AFTERWORD

Disraeli said, long ago, that 'increased means and increased leisure are the two civilizers of man'.[1] In Britain the extent to which these functions have been served owes more than is generally acknowledged to the work of the trade unions, both past and present.

The TUC's efforts, during the twentieth century, to reduce working-time while also protecting and improving pay, have met with measurable success. In the absence of general legislation in Britain to impose an upper limit on basic weekly hours and overtime working, to fix a minimum holiday entitlement, and to obligate employers to pay wages and salaries for time spent on holiday leave by their employees, the advances made on all of these fronts have been won almost entirely by union negotiators in the process of collective bargaining.

Employees in Britain still work longer hours today than most of their counterparts in EU member states and other economically advanced countries, however. Wareing has argued that there is little to suggest discomposing truculence and seething discontent among British workpeople as a result of long working hours; his survey found in 1990 that over 90.0 per cent of the people covered by his survey claimed to be satisfied with their current working-time patterns;[2] and a marked willingness to accept and even seek overtime, in defiance of official TUC policy, leads to the same conclusion. The so-called 'lazy British worker' would seem to be an elusive figure today.

The implications of overtime for employment creation, as the TUC has repeatedly urged, are real enough; but the persistence of the overtime habit cannot be attributed wholly to the cupidity of the relatively well-remunerated and the financial desperation of the low-paid, for as Rifkin succinctly puts it:

> Many companies prefer to employ a smaller workforce at longer hours, rather than a larger one at shorter hours, to save the cost of providing additional benefits, including health care and pensions. Even with payment at time and a half for overtime, companies still pay out less than they would if they had to pay for benefit packages for a larger workforce.[3]

By the same argument, employers also save on national insurance costs and similar financial obligations relative to headcount.

The unions have identified many causes underlying their quest for shorter working-time during the course of the twentieth century. The focus in the recent past upon hours reductions in order to ameliorate unemployment has tended to divert attention from other fundamentally important reasons. The TUC, it is true, has campaigned for its working-time objectives most vigorously during periods of high and persistent unemployment with the aim of preserving and generating jobs; and Bienefeld[4] has claimed that, even when unemployment was not a major social problem, the fear of its return sometime in the future was a main motivating cause of the unions' claims for cuts to the working week.

The real effect on employment of the hours reductions won by the unions is difficult to gauge, but it seems highly probable that job losses in the 1980s would have been even higher without them. That Britain's unemployment rate was the lowest in Europe in 1997 is attributable to economic recovery and withdrawals from the active labour market rather than to hours cuts and the more equitable distribution of the available work, which the TUC sought.

Some observers have warned that, with the inexorable advance of microelectronics, robotics, and information and telecommunications technology, global unemployment will continue to rise in the foreseeable future, and that the marked inequalities, evident in earnings and between those with and those without jobs, will become wider still. The complacent satisfaction with working hours and working patterns, disclosed by Wareing's investigation in the early 1990s, may not last long. Angell cautions that 'the signs are clear: the future is inequality'. He predicts mass unemployment for the unskilled, and a slow death for the nation state; for 'as markets become global and the traditional workplace gives way to cyberspace, only the élite will have anything to offer the world's economies'.[5]

In 1995 Rifkin and others cogently argued the need for a working week of 30 or even 20 hours to bring labour requirements into line with the enhanced productive capacity of new technology. In 1996 Barratt Brown and Coates[6] claimed retrospectively of the preceding decade that some two million more people could have been employed in Britain if all full-time employees had worked a week of 40 hours instead of 44 or 48. The same year, Stephen Byers, drawing on Labour Force Survey statistics, noted that in Britain some 4.5 million people worked more than 48 hours per week, including 1.8 million working over 55 hours and 1.1 million working over 60 hours; Britain's average working week of 43.3 hours was three hours longer than the European average. Lucy Daniels, director of Parents at Work, identified 'long working hours' as injurious to family life: 'People are working on average two hours a week longer than they did ten years ago. Some people, particularly those in middle management, are working exceptionally long hours.' Byers's observation, that 'with such a dramatic increase in working hours, people will now be questioning whether we have got the right balance between employers and employees', gives pause for serious thought.[7]

Unemployment has been one of the most important reasons, and during the two major recessions of the present century *the* most strenuously pressed reason, given by the unions for hours reductions. However, they have mounted other cogent lines of argument. One of these is shorter working-time as workpeople's rightful share of the fruits of higher productivity, the improving profit performance of the employing enterprise, and the rising prosperity of the economy as a whole. Certainly, the main general reductions have occurred during or shortly following marked productivity improvements flowing from technological and other innovations which have increased productive efficiency,[8] but part of the worker's share has taken the forms of higher pay and more or better fringe benefits. Gains in these areas, like working-time, have occurred in periods of rising productivity and economic prosperity.[9] The question that needs to be addressed is whether workpeople are receiving their fair and rightful share overall. A larger slice of the cake might allow more of the worker's portion to be taken in the form of leisure.

The need to protect employees' physical health and mental well-being has also featured prominently in the TUC's arguments in support of shorter working-time. It has been an ongoing theme, regardless of the state of the economy, but the argument has been strongly pressed at times of greater intensification of both the work pace and the work effort. The economic case was calculated to appeal to employers' business sense; for the company, the effect of reduced working hours would be a workforce that was physically more efficient, mentally more alert, less disposed to lateness and absenteeism, and less likely to make mistakes, disregard safety regulations and produce poor quality or faulty goods as a result of fatigue; at the same time, morale would be higher, labour turnover lower, and industrial relations more harmonious. But the TUC is equally and profoundly concerned with the socially beneficial effect of shorter working hours on employees' lives outside the workplace, for people would have more time for their families, for their home life, for their domestic duties, for new interests and recreations, for travel to broaden the mind, and for personal and social development.

From the TUC's viewpoint, a higher material living standard for workpeople is an important objective, but so also is an improvement in the quality of life both within and without the workplace. The increasingly frequent references in the TUC's recent annual reports to the need to reduce stress at work, especially ‘long hour stress’, and the itemization of the debilities and illnesses, both physical and mental, caused by overworking, make sobering reading.[10] Workpeople who were overworked suffered lowered vitality and demoralization; and the situation was undesirable for the country, in terms of working days lost through sickness absence, and avoidable costs to the state social insurance scheme.

There is also the more general consideration that the unpaid work of duties and obligations to family, friends, neighbours and the community at large, which can be burdensome and perhaps grudgingly undertaken when people are short of free time, may be performed the more willingly, cheerfully and self-gratifyingly if they can be done in a more leisurely fashion. Such tasks require spare energy as well as spare time, and performance of them contributes in no small measure to a sense of individual worth and personal fulfilment. Without interaction of this kind, society loses its cohesion and sense of community. The very fabric of society becomes threadbare. The enterprise culture, much beloved by the main political parties in Britain, has its advantages, but the focus on the individual means that we forget that individuals and groups are interdependent and, ideally, mutually supportive.

The TUC’s line of reasoning based on the principle of parity and/or equality has also been an ongoing one. Parity for manual workers, by aligning their employment terms, benefits and conditions with those of non-manual grades, seems to have have been most strongly pressed in relation to paid holidays earlier in the twentieth century, in class-conscious language which conveyed a sense of injustice, unfairness and resentment about the manual worker’s inferior treatment as a second-class citizen. Although the idea of ‘staff status’ for manual workers has never generated much enthusiasm from the TUC, the more recent concept of ‘harmonized’ conditions for the two broad occupational groups has found favour and has been strongly pressed by some of the unions in negotiation of both hours and holidays. The argument seems to have carried some weight; the socio-cultural values of the ‘classless society’,[11] favoured by the last Conservative Government, are conducive to a wider recognition of the need to abandon the outdated class distinctions observed in the workplace of times past; such collar-colour distinctions are anachronistic today. During the last two decades progressively more employers have adopted harmonization policies, as much for their own essentially practical purposes as for philosophical reasons.

Moves to harmonized conditions suggest a narrowing of the working-time differential, but, in point of fact, the disparity in hours worked is greater in Britain than in the rest of Europe. There is greater alignment in the basic working week and holiday entitlement of employees in manual occupations and the more routine kinds of non-manual work, but in middle management and for some professional grades in the educational, medical and legal services, an actual working week of 50 or more hours is not uncommon. Some of the longest hours tend to be in spheres of employment where the work is task-orientated, rather than hours-based with overtime reckoned at premium rates of pay. In task-focused work, people put in the hours needed to complete, by a given deadline, the tasks assigned to them. It has been argued that the long hours put in by some of these people reflects inefficient time-management, incompetence, or personal unsuitability for the work in question; but there is evidence to suggest that, with the restructuring of a company or a public service, the work tasks and job content of some employees have become more onerous, more demanding, and extended to include additional responsibilities and functions. In other words, long hours can, and do, reflect job overload, and expose the employee to work-induced stress and burn-out.[12] The Labour Research Department reported in 1994 that only a minority of organizations had preventive policies addressing the problem of occupational stress.

Parity in working time between Britain and other developed economies has proved to be equally, and possibly more, contentious. A degree of similarity may flow from globalization, but British governments have been generally resistant to the unions' argument that working hours and paid holidays in Britain ought by interventionist measures to be aligned with standards in the most advanced of the developed economies. In the past, successive governments, including the Attlee-led postwar Labour Government, turned a deaf ear to the TUC's proposals for general legislation to regulate working time, of the kind enacted by the governments of several leading European states.

Both the Commission of the European Union and the European Parliament, many years ago, were explicitly in favour of a general shortening of the working week as a means to relieve Europe's unemployment problem. A memorandum, issued by the Commission in 1982, noted the importance of avoiding 'the hardening of two distinct groups in society – those with stable employment and those without – a development which would have disruptive social consequences and would endanger the very foundations of all democratic societies in the longer term'. Governments and industries had a duty to 'maintain and create jobs through the reduction of working-time, in order to achieve greater equity at a time of very high and rising unemployment'.[13] The European Parliament likewise pronounced in favour of measures to 'guarantee ... a significant reduction in daily, weekly, and/or yearly working hours and in working life, in order to significantly slow down and subsequently halt the trend towards growing unemployment'.[14]

The British Conservative Government led the opposition to European Directives on working-time during the 1980s, and in the 1990s secured a clause to the 48-hour week Directive, which effectively freed employers from any obligation to observe that upper limit to the working week. The TUC was deeply disappointed but not altogether surprised. Whether the election of a New Labour Government in 1997 will result in a markedly different stance seems doubtful, given its attitude to the issue in September 1998. It is ironic that, while British Government ministers intervened to remove legal impediments to longer working hours in factories during the crises of the two world wars and were prepared to impose a three-day week during the energy crisis of the early 1970s, they have been adamant in refusing to intervene to limit working hours during the unemployment crisis of the 1980s. In Britain, general legislation to curtail working hours as a means to generating employment has never been put to the test, even as a temporary and experimental measure which might become permanent if the results proved favourable to employment.

There are, of course, as the TUC fully recognizes, other means to job creation, most obviously by government policy which encourages economic growth and provides skill training to enable job seekers to fill the kinds of job vacancies that arise. But the main growth areas of the present and the recent past have been in the service sector in work that tends to be low-paid, or less than permanent or less than full-time, thereby widening the gulf between high and low incomes and between the 'insiders' with relatively stable employment and the 'outsiders' exposed to job insecurity and the risk of unemployment.

It can be argued that government policy which has encouraged a substantial amount of inward investment has caused manufacturing jobs to be created in the many subsidiaries set up in Britain by foreign-owned companies. Britain had some obvious attractions in the recent past for companies seeking global expansion and a European base: generous government grant-aid, an absence of minimum wage and maximum hours legislation and certain other legal constraints, such as existed in many other European countries, upon business activities, and the imposition of curbs on the trade unions to prevent collectively organized obstruction.[15] A return to the days of turbulent industrial relations when certain unions were apparently able to hold management to ransom, intimidate their own members into compliance, and disrupt essential services, would benefit no-one. But the controls on excess and irresponsibility, which are attractive to inward investors as an acknowledgement of managers' 'right to manage', are also restraints upon the trade unions' ability to protect and improve workpeople's welfare, their standard of living, and their quality of life. This is the most profoundly important function of sensible and responsible trade unionism. If in the past the balance of industrial relations was too much on to the side of 'over-mighty trade unions', the scales seem now to have swung too much on to the side of employers. Some, though by no means all, of the latter have both the scope and the disposition to act with the same kind of blinkered self-interest that the unions were accused of a generation ago. The Conservative Government's inclination to frown upon and actively discourage union membership and collective bargaining systems to determine pay, hours and other employment terms has had the most dire of implications for workpeople's standard of living and quality of life. Wareing's 'satisfied workers' have reaped the benefits of past trade union efforts; future trade union efforts may produce less satisfaction, given the recent lengthening of actual working hours for some people and the declining ability of numerically and strategically weakened trade unions to counteract the tendency.

There are now widespread claims about the administrative, organizational and financial impracticalities involved in predominantly state-provided social welfare, and the possibilities of 're-privatizing' welfare services have been under active consideration for some time.[16] The prospect of further moves to dismantle the postwar welfare state widens the outlook and scope for the private welfare agencies. The main alternatives are the individual acting alone on his or her own behalf for social insurance purposes, and the trade unions acting in collaboration with employers to produce better company welfare arrangements. These are not mutually exclusive means; rather, they are mutually supportive and reinforcing. But the company-wide or plant-wide significance of matters such as working hours, holiday leave and payment systems argues the importance of the union-management collaborative role in these essential dimensions of workplace welfare. Union negotiators, via the TUC, are better informed and experienced about such issues than are individual employees or the company councils favoured by non-union companies. A prospective pruning of the state's responsibility for social welfare suggests the need for numerical growth of union membership and recognition of trade unions by employers for joint problem-solving purposes in the welfare sphere.

Taylor[17] takes the view that the 'old Labour Movement', with its 'collectivist convictions and an ethos of social justice and fraternity' has passed away, and that 'nothing coherent or settled looks set to take its place'. Laybourn,[18] less pessimistically, notes a 'remarkable resilience', even though the unions are 'in a turmoil' and the 'trade union movement as a whole has been weakened'. On either view, the unions' capability to reduce working-time, or to improve any other working condition, is circumscribed. Workpeople might pause to ponder who would look out for their interests if the unions were to wither away completely.

Finally, the globalized economy has come to be dominated by globalized companies whose activities affect employment stability, employees' earnings and hours worked, wherever the operations of international big business have spread. Without the counterbalance of a globalized structure of influence from trade unions and governments, the power of these ever-growing giants is awesome. In defence of the giants of 'world-class manufacturing', however, whether from the USA, Japan or elsewhere, it must be noted that the British subsidiaries of some of them were among the first to reduce and equalize the basic week and holiday entitlements as part of their personnel policies to harmonize conditions. The same can be said of some of Britain's own large globalized companies, such as ICI and Pilkington. Most of them have collective systems of one kind or another to determine employment conditions. It seems highly probable that the recent lengthening of the hours that some people 'have to work', noted by the TUC General Council in 1996, is associated with the marked growth since 1980 in the number of small- and medium-sized firms, especially in the service sector. These are less likely to recognize trade unions and to have harmonized conditions;[19] and growth and expansion of their business operations will be initially, and perhaps for some time, accomplished by a lengthening of the hours worked by existing employees rather than an increase in the numbers employed. Storey[20] pointed out in 1994 that, in the European economy as a whole, over 95.0 per cent of firms can be officially classed as small, and that they provide over half of all jobs. In Europe, firms with more than 100 employees are the exception rather than the rule. The unions must effectively focus their efforts to reduce working-time upon small- and medium-sized firms if their hard-won gains of the past are not to be lost.

Past governments justified their refusal to pass general legislation to regulate working-time mainly on the grounds that Britain had well-established institutional structures and systems of collective bargaining for voluntary settlement of employment conditions. Between 1979 and 1997 successive Conservative governments presided over the drastic weakening of collective bargaining arrangements and the associated institutional structures, while at the same time demonstrating implacable hostility to the idea of legislation for maximum working hours and minimum wages. At present, working-time in Britain is subject neither to comprehensive collectively bargained controls nor to generally effective legal constraints. Hours of work are not responsive, in the same way and to the same extent as pay rates, to unfettered labour market forces – the supply of and demand for labour. Unless the Labour Government, elected in 1997, takes action to reconstruct the voluntary system or to establish effective legal restrictions, Britain's working-time future cannot be other than bleak.

Statistical information on working-time in the later 1990s, produced by the Office of National Statistics, is not reassuring. In 1998 more than 5 million people, about one-fifth of all persons in full-time employment in the United Kingdom usually worked more than 48 hours per week in their main job. This affected around 30 per cent of men and some 7 per cent of women. The percentage of full-time employees with a usual working week of over 40 hours rose from 56 per cent of men and 19 per cent of women in 1992 to 59 per cent of men and 20 per cent of women in 1997. As large a proportion as 20 per cent of men worked over 50 hours per week, with 7 per cent working at least 60 hours.

The 45.8 average weekly hours usually worked by men in full-time jobs in the United Kingdom in 1996 were distinctly longer than the EU average of 41.3 hours, comparing unfavourably with usual working weeks of less than 40 hours in Belgium, Italy, Finland, Denmark, and the Netherlands, and with the 40.5 hours in France and Germany.

The EU Working Time Regulations, which came into force in October 1998, require employers to take 'all reasonable steps' to ensure that their employees do not work, against their will, more than 48 hours per week averaged over the given reference period. Those regulations did not apply to certain important sectors and groups, such as transport, sea fishing, other work at sea, and junior hospital doctors; and in 1999 there was evidence that in the United Kingdom some employees covered by the regulations were being pressurized to sign opt-out agreements against their wishes. In February 1999 the GMB brought the first of these cases before the courts; but it seems likely that many employees will prefer to work the longer hours reluctantly rather than to risk resistance in the context of employment insecurity. Many jobs today are short-term or temporary, and dismissal of unco-operative workers is not difficult for an employer to accomplish. Redundancy is no longer front-page news week in and week out. Yet the unemployment problem, although not as large as it was in the 1980s, has not gone away. Around 1.8 million people in the United Kingdom were without jobs in the spring of 1998 after successive year on year falls from the most recent peak of 2.9 million in 1993. All the indicators seem to show that during this period average working hours for those with jobs are tending to increase.

In mid 1999, with the unions in Britain and continental Europe preparing protests to the EU authorities that implementation of the 48-hour week Directive needs greater stringency, the Blair Government, with its declared intention to foster full employment, will need to ensure, from the employee's viewpoint, not only that the minimum-wage price is right but that the maximum working-time is right also.

Notes

1. Quoted in Jenkins, C. and Sherman, B. (1979), *White Collar*

Unionism: The Rebellious Salariat, London, Routledge & Kegan Paul, p.151.

2. Wareing, A. (1992), 'Working Arrangements and Patterns of Working Hours in Britain', *Employment Gazette*, March, pp.88–100.
3. Rifkin, J. (1995), *The End of Work: The Decline of the Global Labor Force and the Dawn of the Post-Market Era*, New York, Putnam, p.223.
4. Bienefeld, M.A. (1972), *Working Hours in British Industry: An Economic History*, London, Weidenfeld & Nicolson.
5. Angell, A. (25 September 1996), 'The Signs are Clear', *The Independent*, and 'The Hollow State', BBC2 Documentary (29 September and 6 October 1996).
6. Barratt Brown, M. and Coates, K. (1996), *The Blair Revelation: Deliverance for Whom?*, Nottingham, Spokesman Books, Socialist Renewal Pamphlet Series; see also Mandelson, P. and Liddle, R. (1996), *The Blair Revolution: Can New Labour Deliver?*, London, Faber.
7. *The Western Mail* (19 October 1996).
8. Rifkin, J., *op. cit.* p.222.
9. Russell, A. (1991), *The Growth of Occupational Welfare in Britain*, Aldershot, Gower.
10. Labour Research Department (1994), *Stress at Work: A Trade Union Response*, London, LRD Publications; 'Lecturers Face Intolerable Levels of Work', *The Independent* (7 October 1994).
11. Pakulski, J. and Waters, M. (1996), *The Death of Class*, London, Sage; Gorz, A. (1997), *Farewell to the Working Class*, 2nd edn, London, Pluto Press.
12. 'Brainstorm', BBC2 Documentary (9 April 1997).
13. Commission of the European Communities (1982), *Memorandum on the Reduction and Reorganization of Working Time*, Brussels, p.60.
14. Ceravolo, D. (1983), *Report on the Memorandum from the Commission of the European Communities on the Reduction and Reorganization of Working Time*, Brussels, European Parliament, Commission on Social Affairs and Employment, p.9.
15. A general line of argument in Oliver, N. and Wilkinson, B. (1988), *The Japanization of British Industry*, Oxford, Blackwell; see also 'Siemens to Pour £1.1 bn into 2000 New UK Jobs' and 'UK Drawcards are the Envy of Europeans' in *The Independent* (5 August 1995).

16. Seldon, A. (ed) (1996), *Re-Privatizing Welfare: After the Lost Century*, London, Institute of Economic Affairs.
17. Taylor, R. (1993), *The Trade Union Question in British Politics: Government and Unions since 1945*, Oxford, Blackwell, p.274.
18. Laybourn, K. (1992), *A History of British Trade Unionism c1770–1990,* Stroud, Alan Sutton, p.214; for the view of John Monks, TUC General Secretary, on the future role of the trade unions see Monks, J. (1994), 'The Future of Work', RSA Prince Philip Lecture, *RSA Journal*, December, pp.24–33.
19. Rainnie, A. (1989), *Industrial Relations in Small Firms: Small Isn't Beautiful*, London, Routledge; Storey, D.J. (1992), 'HRM in Action: The Truth is Out at Last', *Personnel Management*, April.
20. Storey, D.J. (1994), *Understanding the Small Business Sector*, London, Routledge.

SELECT BIBLIOGRAPHY

Abrams, M. (May 1960), 'New Roots of Working Class Conservatism', *Encounter*.

(1969), *The Changing Pattern of Consumer Spending*, London, Press Exchange.

Atkinson, J. (1984), *Manning for Uncertainty: Some Emerging UK Work Patterns*, IMS Research Paper, Sussex, Institute of Manpower Studies.

Barratt Brown, M. and Coates, K. (1996), *The Blair Revelation: Deliverance for Whom?*, Nottingham, Spokesman Books.

Beveridge, W.H. (1944), *Full Employment in a Free Society*, London, Allen & Unwin.

Bienefeld, M.A. (1972), *Working Hours in British Industry: An Economic History*, London, Weidenfeld & Nicolson.

Blyton, P. (1985), *Changes in Working Time*, London, Croom Helm.

Board of Trade (1906), *Earnings and Hours Inquiry*, London, HMSO.

(1963) *Staggered Holidays*, Cmnd. 2105, London, HMSO.

Braverman, H. (1974), *Labor and Monopoly Capitalism: The Degradation of Work in the Twentieth Century*, New York, Monthly Review Press.

Brown, W. (1981), *The Changing Contours of Industrial Relations in Britain*, Oxford, Blackwell.

Brown, W. and Walsh, J. (1991), 'Pay Determination in Britain in the 1980s: The Anatomy of Decentralization', *Oxford Review of Economic Policy*, Vol. 7, No. 1, pp.44–58.

Cameron, G.C. (1965), 'The Growth of Holidays with Pay in Britain' in Reid, G.L. and Robertson, D.J. (eds) *Fringe Benefits, Labour Costs and Social Security*, London, Allen & Unwin.

Catering Wages Commission *Staggering of Holidays*, (1945), Report to the Minister of Labour and National Service, Section 2 of the Catering Wages Act 1943, London, HMSO.

Clegg, H. and Narasimhan, P.S. (1963), *Implications for Manage-*

ment of Longer Standard Holidays, BIM Occasional Paper, No. 9, London, British Institute of Management.

Committee on Holidays with Pay (1938), *Report*, Cmd. 5724, and Minutes of Evidence.

Coopey, R. and Woodward, N. (eds) (1996), *Britain in the 1970s: The Troubled Economy*, London, UCL Press.

Desmons, G. and Vidal-Hall, T. (1987), *Annual Hours: A Study of Annual Hours Arrangements in the UK*, London, Industrial Society.

Dorey, P. (1995), *The Conservative Party and the Trade Unions*, London, Routledge.

Edwards, R. (1979), *Contested Terrain: The Transformation of Work in the Twentieth Century*, London, Heinemann.

Edwards, R.S. and Roberts, R.D.V. (1971), *Status, Productivity and Pay, A Major Experiment: A Study of the Electricity Supply Industry's Agreements and their Outcomes, 1961–1971*, Basingstoke, Macmillan.

Evans, A. and Palmer, S. (1985), *Negotiating Shorter Working Hours*, Basingstoke, Macmillan.

Goldthorpe, J.H. *et al.* (1969), *The Affluent Worker in the Class Structure*, Cambridge, University Press.

Gorz, A. (1997), *Farewell to the Working Class*, 2nd edn, London, Pluto Press.

Hakim, C. (1987), 'Trends in the Flexible Workforce', *Employment Gazette*, November, pp.549–99.

Hunter, L. and MacInnes, J. (1992), 'Employers and Labour Flexibility: The Evidence from Case Studies', *Employment Gazette*, June, pp.307–15.

Hunter, L.C. *et al.* (1970), *Labour Problems of Technological Change*, London, Allen & Unwin.

Incomes Data Services (1972), *The Guaranteed Week: Part 1*, Study No. 20, London, IDS.

(1973), *The Guaranteed Week: Part 2*, Study No. 22.

(1974), *Staff Status for Manual Workers: Part 1*, Study No. 73.

(1974), *Staff Status for Manual Workers: Part 2*, Study No. 77.

(1980), *Holidays 1980*, Study No. 225.

(1980), *Staff Status*, Study No. 227.

(1981), *Holidays 1981*, Study No. 251.

(1981), *The Guaranteed Week: Part 3*, Study No. 261.

(1982), *Harmonization of Conditions*, Study No. 273.

(1982), *Holidays 1982*, Study No. 275.

(1983), *Hours and Holidays*, Study No. 300.
(1983), *Flexible Working Hours*, Study No. 301.
(1984), *Craft Flexibility*, Study No. 322.
(1984), *Hours and Holidays*, Study No. 323.
(1991), *Annual Hours*, Study No. 486.
Industrial Relations Review and Report (1979), 'Towards a Shorter Working Week: The Bargaining Record', No. 204, pp.2–4.
(1980), 'Holiday Survey', No. 220, pp.2–10.
(1980), 'The Compressed Working Week: An *IRRR* Study', No. 223, pp.2–6.
(1981), 'Reductions in Working Hours: A Round-Up of National Agreements', No. 242, pp.2–6.
(1981), 'Implementing the Shorter Working Week in the Engineering Industry', No. 262, pp.2–7.
(1982), 'Overtime: Restricting its Level', No. 270, pp.2 –5.
(1982), 'Holidays for Manual Workers', No. 274, pp.12–19.
(1982), 'TUC Proposals for Legislation on Working Time', No. 279, pp.13–15.
(1982), 'Survey of Staff Holidays', No. 283, pp.2–11.
(1984), 'Shorter Working Week: An *IRRR* Review', No. 312, pp.2–5.
(1984), 'Holiday Entitlements 1: Industry Analysis', No. 323, pp.2–6.
(1984), 'Flexible Employment Strategies', No. 325, pp.13–16.
(1984), 'Holiday Entitlements 2: Company Provision', No. 327, pp.2–11.
(1984), 'Shorter Hours in Practice', No. 330, pp.8–11.
(1985), 'Shorter Working Week: An *IRRR* Review', No. 336, pp.2–5.
(1985), 'Holiday Survey 1: Basic and Service Entitlements', No. 347, pp.9–17.
(1987), 'Hours Commitment Schemes Becoming More Popular', No. 385, pp.2–7.
(1988), 'Reductions in Working Time: Running Out of Steam?', No. 407, pp.2–6.
(1989), 'Shorter Hours Drive Slows', No. 433, pp.2–7.
(1989), 'Holiday Survey 2: How Much Leave?', No. 444, pp.6–12.
(1989), 'Shorter Hours in Chemicals: CIA Guidance', No. 449, pp.11–13.
(1989), 'Holiday Survey 3: Absence Rules and Pay', No. 450, pp.10–14.

(1990), 'Engineering Industry Consolidates Moves to 37-Hour Week', No. 461, pp.8–10.
(1990), 'Productivity Offsets for Shorter Hours in Engineering', No. 464, pp.6–10.
(1990), 'After Hours: A Survey of Overtime Working', No. 468, pp.11–14.
(1992), 'Holidays and Hours Survey 2: Recent Changes and Trends', No. 524, pp.4–10.
(1993), 'Decline in Multi-Employer Bargaining Charted', No. 544, pp.7–11.
(1994), 'Whatever Happened to the Shorter Working Week?', No. 572, pp.2–7.
Industrial Society (1963), *The Case for Staggered Holidays*, London, IS.
(1966), *Holidays: Current Practices and Trends*, Information Survey and Report Series, No. 134, London, IS.
(1973), *Security of Earnings and Employment*, Information Survey and Report Series, No. 183, London, IS.
Ineichen, B. (1972), 'Home Ownership and Manual Workers' Life Styles', *Sociological Review*, No. 20, Vol. 3, pp.391–412.
Institute of Administrative Management (1979), *Office Hours, Turnover, and Payment Practice*, Beckenham, IAM.
Institute of Management and Manpower (1994), *Survey of Long Term Employment Strategies*, London, IMM.
Jenkins, C. and Sherman, B. (1979), *White Collar Unionism: The Rebellious Salariat*, London, Routledge & Kegan Paul.
(1979), *The Collapse of Work*, London, Eyre Methuen.
(1981), *The Leisure Shock*, London, Eyre Methuen.
Kirosingh, M. (1989), 'Changed Working Practices', *Employment Gazette*, August, pp.422–9.
Labour Research Department (1994), *Stress at Work: A Trade Union Response*, London, LRD.
Laybourn, K. (1992), *A History of British Trade Unionism c1770–1990*, Stroud, Alan Sutton.
Masuda, Y, (1981), *The Information Society as Post-Industrial Society*, Washington DC, World Future Society.
May, T. (1993), *An Economic and Social History of Britain 1760–1970*, London, Longman.
McGregor, A. and Sproull, A. (1992), 'Employers and the Flexible Workforce', *Employment Gazette*, May, pp.225–34.
McKersie, R. and Hunter, L. (1973), *Pay, Productivity and Collective Bargaining*, Basingstoke, Macmillan.

Millar, R. (1965), *The New Classes*, London, Longman.
Ministry of Labour Gazette (later *Employment Gazette*), monthly, London, HMSO.
Monks, J. (1994), 'The Future of Work', The Prince Philip Lecture, *RSA Journal*, December, pp.24–33.
Murlis, H. (1973), *Employee Benefits Today: A Survey of Attitudes and Company Practice*, Management Survey Report, No. 19, London, British Institute of Management.
NBPI (1970), *Hours of Work, Overtime and Shiftwork*, Report No. 161, Cmnd. 5444, London, HMSO.
NEDO (1986), *Changing Working Patterns: How Companies Achieve Flexibility to Meet New Needs*, London, National Economic Development Office.
Nyland, C. (1989), *Reduced Worktime and the Management of Production*, Cambridge, University Press.
Pakulski, J. and Waters, M. (1996), *The Death of Class*, London, Sage.
Parker, S. (1971), *The Future of Work and Leisure*, London, MacGibbon & Kee.
(1976), *The Sociology of Leisure*, London, Allen & Unwin.
Pelling, H. (1992), *A History of British Trade Unionism*, London, Penguin.
Pickard, J. (1990), 'Engineering Tools Up for Local Bargaining', *Personnel Management*, March, pp.40–3.
(1991), 'Annual Hours: A Year of Living Dangerously', *Personnel Management*, August, pp.28–30.
Pimlott, J.A.R. (1976), *The Englishman's Holiday: A Social History*, 2nd edn, Sussex, Harvester.
Pollard, S. (1992), *The Development of the British Economy 1914–1990*, London, Edward Arnold.
Richardson, R. and Rubin, M. (1992), *The 1989/91 Shorter Working Week Campaign in Engineering: A Pyrrhic Defeat?*, Research Paper, Centre for Economic Performance, London, LSE.
(1994), *The Economic Effects of Reductions in Working Hours: The UK Engineering Industry*, Research Series, Paper No. 34, London, Department of Employment.
Rifkin, J. (1995), *The End of Work: The Decline of the Global Labor Force and the Dawn of the Post Market Era*, New York, Putnam.
Roberts, K. (1970), *Leisure*, London, Allen & Unwin.
Royal Commission on Trade Unions and Employers' Associations (1968), *Report*, Cmnd. 3623.

Russell, A. (1991), *The Growth of Occupational Welfare in Britain*, Aldershot, Gower.

Rybozyhnski, W. (1991), *Waiting for the Weekend*, New York, Viking Penguin.

Skidelsky, R. (1967), *Politicians and the Slump: The Labour Government of 1929–31*, Basingstoke, Macmillan.

(1975), *Oswald Moseley*, Basingstoke, Macmillan.

Sleigh, J. *et al.* (1979), *The Manpower Implications of Microelectronics*, London, HMSO.

Stettner, N. (1969), *Productivity Bargaining and Structural Change*, London, Pergamon.

Storey, D.J. (1994), *Understanding the Small Business Sector*, London, Routledge.

Szyszczak, E.M. (1990), *Partial Unemployment: The Regulation of Short-Time Working in Britain*, London, Mansell.

Taylor, R. (1993), *The Trade Union Question in British Politics: Government and Unions since 1945*, Oxford, Blackwell.

Trades Union Congress (annual), *Report*.

Turner, G. (1963), *The Car Makers*, London, Eyre & Spottiswoode.

Veal, A.J. (1987), *Leisure and the Future*, London, Allen & Unwin.

Walton, J.K. and Walvin, J. (eds) (1983), *Leisure in Britain 1780–1939*, Manchester, University Press.

Wareing, A. (1992), 'Working Arrangements and Patterns of Working Hours in Britain', *Employment Gazette*, March, pp.88–100.

White, M. (1980), *Shorter Working Time*, Report No. 589, London, Policy Studies Institute.

(1982), *Shorter Working Time Through National Agreements*, London, HMSO.

(1987), *Working Hours: Assessing the Potential for Reduction*, Geneva, ILO.

White Paper (1985), *Employment: Challenge for the Nation*, Cmnd. 9474.

(1991), *Industrial Relations in the 1990s*, Cm. 1602.

(1992), *People, Jobs and Opportunity*, Cm. 1810.

Whiteside, N. (1980), 'Industrial Welfare and Labour Regulation in Britain at the time of the First World War', *International Review of Social History*, vol. 25, pp.307–31.

Wood, S. (ed) (1982), *The Degradation of Work? Skill, Deskilling and the Labour Process*, London, Hutchinson.

Zweig, F. (1961), *The Worker in an Affluent Society*, London, Heinemann.

INDEX